Sam Hector

The Last Indian Resident of Mississippi County, Arkansas

By
Sheila McCall

Contents

Acknowledgments

My husband, Tony McCall, whose support has been pivotal in accomplishing this task. He has been my encourager and the one who makes sure I eat when I am involved in serious research.

My son, Tony McCall, who has graciously read, edited, and offered advice and support in the completion of this work, all while working on his PhD.

My children, Charity Lane, who read and edited early chapters of this book; and Chanda Julian, and Jonathan McCall, who have read portions and offered their assistance.

Preface

Sam Hector left an imprint on many in the area of Big Lake, in Mississippi County, Arkansas, including his granddaughter, Hettie Jane Hector, this author's grandmother. I can still remember the twinkle in her eye as she told of old Sam and his fishing ventures at Big Lake and the large fish he would bring home. She told of his Native American heritage and his Cherokee family name. Her fascination with her heritage, in her old age, created a spark in me in my younger years to one day tell his story.

Later, I would find other researchers interested in his story. One of those, my second cousin Cheryl Hector Cummings, and I would pore over every little detail we could find on "Old Sam," as we referred to him, and our heritage. We share a special bond, having never met in person, only online.

In the 1990s, I spoke to Evelyn McMillan, a great-granddaughter of Sam's, when she called the *Blytheville Courier News,* where I worked at the time. In our conversation, she referred to old Sam Hector as "the last full-blooded Indian in the county."

While working on the last chapter, I reread a partially fictional story of old Sam written by Wayne Capooth in his book, *Red Letter Days*. What he wrote about Sam was based in part upon a newspaper article from 1895, when a group of hunters met Sam and told their story in a Memphis newspaper. Those hunters only learned a small portion of Sam and his history, but knew his story was unique and worth retelling.

This author and other researchers can only rely on what is written or remembered from the past to tell Sam's story. Research has led to answers about Sam and his life, but it also has led to more questions, some of which will never be answered. From his early youth in a remote Indian camp, through changes in the land and community, to the dawn of the next century with a promise of new horizons, he led an interesting life.

May Sam's legacy live on.

The narratives at the beginning of Chapters 1-9 are partly based on what Sam said and may have said to Frank L. James on a trip down the St. Francis River in 1872 or 1873 to visit the Miller Mounds in Arkansas.

According to James, Sam told him about killing a buffalo just as an earthquake happened and how the land sank, forming the "Gar Hole," at the foot of Big Lake. Sam explained that his grandmother taught him about the red leaves he was gathering for medicinal purposes.

James and Sam would make more trips down the Little and St. Francis rivers and other places in search of artifacts, some of which would be sent to the Smithsonian. On these trips, Sam most likely told James about events in his life.

The narrative at the beginning of Chapter 10 is partly based on what Sam told a group of hunters from Memphis in 1895.

Chapter 1
The Village

Paddling his way downstream, Sam Hector could make out the red leaves ahead as they caught the sun's light. They shone like fire amidst the other plant life on the banks of the St. Francis River. Today, Sam and his friend Dr. Frank L. James were on their way to the noted Miller Mounds, one of the largest collections of mounds in the area.

Nearing the leaves, Sam paused to take a look. "No, not good enough," he said aloud, lost in thought as he remembered the woman who taught him about the medicinal qualities of the tea made from the leaves.

James watched Sam pass up some leaves hanging nearby as he drove the pirogue to shore to gather leaves that were much harder to reach through the weeds and shrubbery growing along the banks.

Soon, Sam noticed some more of the shrubbery located on the bank and steered his canoe closer to gather the leaves. "These will do," he said as he deposited them in his bait box. James noticed Sam didn't just pick any leaves, but seemed particular about gathering them. Why Sam picked these leaves over the others piqued James' interest, but he knew it was better to wait for Sam to explain. He was familiar with Sam's peculiar ways.

Finally, overcome with the need to know, he asked, "Sam, what are you going to do with those leaves?"

"'Make medicine of them,'" said Sam.

Crawling back in the canoe, the two resumed their journey and Sam continued his recollections. After lighting his cane pipe from James' cigar, he began to tell the story. "Once many years ago, there was an old Indian woman who became sick and unable to assist her husband or take care of her daily work."

"'She had misery in her head and misery in her back, and she couldn't cut wood, nor skin game, nor make baskets.'"

"In the tradition of her people, her husband sent her away and took in a younger woman who could work. The old woman walked alone for many days and finally lay down on the ground on top of the grave of one of the old-time folks."

"She knew her time was near," he said. "'Bimeby, [sic] (by and by) she came to an old-time people grave.'"

"Here she would die, or so she thought. As she lay there thinking of her plight in life, one of the old ones appeared to her and asked her why she was lying on his grave."

"'That is what she said, but I 'speck she dreamed she see him,'" said Sam.

After she told him her story, the old one told her to gather some of the red leaves and make a tea in one of the old folk's pots. In time, she would become strong and able to work and her husband would take her back, he said. Soon, she found a pot sticking out of the ground, lit a fire, and set about making her tea. Not long after drinking it, she became well.

"'Now I know that, because she was my grandmother and I often use the same tea myself, but it ain't no good unless the leaves is gathered offen an old-time folk's grave and made in an old-time folk's pot.'" To prove his point of where the best leaves were, Sam took his canoe ashore and promptly dug down to a burial box of the once industrious race of people that inhabited the area. [1]

When Sam was young he lived in the village of Chilletecaux, [2] in Southeast Missouri with his family. He told James a little about his childhood in the village where he would often help the women with the chores instead of hunting with the men. Usually, the meat from the hunts would be rough cut and transported back to camp where the women would continue to break it down, drying some pemmican for their travels. While the women didn't go out on the hunts, they would often camp nearby where they could assist in tanning hides and other chores. Sam would help with dressing the game and tending the corn. His grandmother would gather herbs from the field and he learned at her knee the mystery of medicines. There, at Chilletecaux, [3] surrounded by family and friends of similar culture, he lived a carefree life.

Until, one day ...

While recalling the good times, Sam's thoughts segued into one of the worst memories he possessed. Even though he was only six in 1831, he vividly recalled the tears and the abject fear of those he loved as they faced an uncertain future brought about by the government's forced relocation of Indian nations. That day, the village was visited by several men who came bearing the news that those living in the village and nearby would have to leave soon by the order of the area's Indian sub-agent, Pierre Menard, [4] and join the majority of their various nations who now lived in Indian Territory on the Kansas River.

"They did not want to go," Sam said out loud.

The village of Chilletecaux was located above Buffalo Island in a highland between swamps in Missouri, near the St. Francis River on what was called Big or Grand Prairie. [5] A remnant of some of the formerly great nations lived there in a village named for their principal chief. This was a place where most would not choose to live. The discounted land was considered uninhabitable and not even worthy of survey after the area became a part of the United States in 1803.

Creeping slowly away from population centers, these few people of Delaware, Shawnee, Creek, and Seneca nations living in and around the main village in 1831 sought refuge from the encroach of those who did not want them as their neighbors. [6]

While most of their people had moved further westward, this small group continued to live peacefully, hunting and trading with those in the area. However, in the last few years, after an influx of settlers, some sought their immediate removal.

Their removal began that year in May when Missouri Gov. John Miller received papers from Gen. N.W. Watkins, [7] of Jackson, Missouri, who had received petitions from residents of New Madrid and Stoddard counties requesting the immediate removal of the Indians living in the swampy areas of New Madrid County, Missouri.

This was not the first mention of their removal. There had been talk as early as 1825[8] about removing the Indians living near the St. Francis River.[9] A letter from Richard Graham, U.S. Indian agent to Pierre Menard, Indian subagent of Kaskaskia, Illinois, in June 1825 [10] related that a letter from Doctor Dawson [11] of New Madrid informed him of runaway slaves living with the Shawnee Indians on the St. Francis River and of their refusal to give them up without "positive instructions." Graham asked Menard to visit on his way to or from the White River Indian settlements and demand the release of the slaves so they could be delivered to the authorized agent. Menard responded in August on his way to White River with a letter from Francois Lesieur and son, of Point Pleasant in New Madrid County saying "Considerable … excitement has been produced for these two or three months past, by a report in circulation that those few dispersed Indians consisting of Shawnees, Delawares, & Moscogees [sic] living on the borders of the river St. Francis are to be forcibly broken up."

The "excitement" was brought about by "designing persons" intent upon their removal following an incident concerning three runaway slaves of Alabama belonging to Chickasaw Chief George Colbert. The slaves had settled among the Indians, against the "good will" of the "village chief," said Lesieur. John R. Walker [12] had been paid $300 by Colbert's son to go to the Indian village and remove the slaves to the New Madrid jail. However, according to Lesieur, Walker did not seize the slaves, although the chief told him he could. Instead, he demanded that the Indians bring the slaves into New Madrid, or the Indians would "be forcibly broken up and drove off from their habitations."

The Indians in that area lived in three villages, between the left and east forks of the St. Francis River, and on an island "as it is, surrounded on all sides by an immense body of watter [sic]," according to Lesieur. [13] At this place, the land was made uninhabitable by its unhealthiness and annual frequent inundations and Lesieur didn't see it improving in the future.

Samuel Goode Hopkins, county court justice of New Madrid County, who had accompanied Walker to the village, described the area in 1825. The east branch [14] of the St. Francis River [15] runs parallel to the Mississippi River for 150 miles. It is "sunk by the earthquakes and filled with timbers which have died and fallen into the water, rendering it unnavigable for every species of boats except canoes." According to Hopkins, the west or lead fork, the main body of the St. Francis River, as it was called, had also suffered damage extending 50 miles beyond its confluence with the east fork, which affected its navigability. One hundred miles above this juncture is a bay or bayou, [16] which connects the two, forming an island, only a small elevation above the level of the water. Capt. McCoy, also in the area with Hopkins, was surveying the effects of the 1811-1812 earthquakes. [17]

"It seems that providence in commiseration of their misfortunes had directed them hither, where white men will not live, and where there is just enough fish, food and game to minister to their subsistence," said Hopkins. Living in the area of Point Pleasant for the past two years, he also noted that the villagers were "inoffensive, useful, and in some degree industrious." He and the community found the trade in furs, peltries and bear oil with the villagers "extremely acceptable."

Hopkins went on to say in his letter that he supposed there was nothing that would change the disposition of the government concerning these Indians "in relation to their ultimate destiny." The Indians, he said, were the only people who would ever inhabit the region between the two forks of the St. Francis River, laid in ruins by the 1811-1812 earthquakes. "To remove them from it would be to inflict a sore calamity upon them, without attaining a single object of government, as regards to either population or revenue."

However, those living there, Lesieur said, appeared to be "by nature happily situated in this section of the country, abounding with all kinds of game." Here, the villagers raise large stocks of horses, cattle, hogs, corn and make "breadstuffs for home consumption."

After the attention gained by the 1825 event, relations remained good with these Indians and most of their local neighbors for a few more years, but by 1831, complaints from those who claimed to be threatened by the existence of these Indians in the area resurfaced. [18] Other residents fought for them to remain. In 1825, Lesieur noted that they "are inoffensive, industrious, and honest." [19] The whole community, Lesieur said, "will unite in a petition to government in favour of those poor Indians." And then again in 1831, Francois Lesieur's son, Godfrey, said that he was personally acquainted with every Indian and "will say that they have at all times conducted themselves honestly."

The May 1831 letter to Watkins, forwarded on to General William Clark, U.S. Superintendent of Indian Affairs, stated that the Indians in the area were becoming numerous and troublesome and "threatening to tomahawk" local inhabitants. They requested that something be done to "exterminate" them. In their complaint, they also noted that the Indians were supplied with liquor and "have now been drunk several weeks and murdering each other in a shocking manner."

Fifty-one people signed the petition in May and 44 in October, which included some of the same men. [20] The first name on the May list was John B. Walker. [21]

Clark must have relayed instructions to Menard to take care of the matter, as he sent William Myers [22] to the village. Following his instructions, Myers visited the village, [23] accompanied by guide and interpreter Toussaint Godair,[24] and read the complaints against them. Godair, in a deposition, told how Myers told them that they must forthwith remove to the Kansas River or they would be without protection. They replied that they could not remove immediately as they had been advanced articles of clothing, ammunition, and food for their families and it would be hard to "injure" the men who had treated them so well. And if allowed to remain through the winter and pay their debts, they would "cheerfully remove" in the spring. But if they did have to go immediately, as Myers stated, they "would do so, though reluctantly." Myers agreed to bring them 14 horses in 25 days to expedite their removal.

While there, Myers was asked to take a census of those willing to move and when they would be able, and to ascertain how much corn they had in their possession. Myers reported to Menard that the villagers expressed surprise that others would create a "falsehood" against them.

Area residents soon came to their defense refuting the petitions of those seeking their removal. Fifty-four men signed a petition in their favor in May,[25] and some took time to comment further on their dealings with these Indians.

Godair said that while at the village they were also visited by Mr. Varner, [26] an acting justice of the peace for the county. Varner, who resided near the village, said that Mr. Robertson, a man "of notorious bad character," started the petition. Robertson, of Arkansas, according to the letter to Watkins, had been employed by "the agent" there to order the Indians to vacate. Varner also said that John B. Walker's objective was to remove the Indians so that he might possess their improvements. He also attested that the majority of the signatures on their petition were forged.

Godair noted that except for the last five or six years, he had traded with these Indians for 30 to 40 years, most likely soon after their move to the area, and they were "good honest people."

Hopkins said hunters and followers of the range, who had recently located on the old Indian village, [27] 25 miles distant, instigated the petition in hopes of seizing assets and stock that could not be removed with the tribes. He further clarified, "many of the Indians have adopted not only the manner and customs, but habits and pursuits of their white neighbors."

Hopkins also took issue with Myers, referring to him as an "incompetent young man" who was "abrupt" in his communications with the Indians and was not capable of conciliation. He couldn't conceal the fact, he said, that "he acted under the lure of interest in the hope of receiving a large compensation for being their conductor for the new abode allotted to them."

Godfrey Lesieur said that he had known the principal chief, Chilletecaux, for at least 25 years and that he had always sustained a good character and was "honest to a proverb." The Indians had been residents since before the Spanish authorities occupied the area and lately attracted the jealousy of "idle and wandering persons in the county of Stoddard."[28] Godfrey Lesieur and Gov. Miller both thought there was a need for a person to reside with the Indians until they could be removed, as they foresaw unending complaints.

Raphael Lesieur said he had lived within four to five miles of the village, traded with them for two years while keeping his goods nearby, and he never knew of misbehavior or dishonesty.

Complaints concerning the Indians included the Indians firing the timber in the fall each year, destroying mast and range timber, killing deer for the skins only, and drinking excessively. If not removed "speedily," the unhappy petitioners were determined to drive them out themselves, they said, as they were "in danger of being massacred by these savages during their drunken follies." Recently, they said, several of the Indians had threatened to kill the whites and threatened two men making an improvement about 10 miles below their camp. [29]

Contrary to this claim, residents would later note how Chief Chilletecaux had helped early settlers in 1830 by enlarging the Indian path to allow their ox carts and packhorses to pass through the rushes, grass, and cane.[30]

Hopkins said he had intended to write more on the Indians' situation and position in the area, but knew "nothing" could "alter or affect the disposition of the government already made in relation to their ultimate destiny." Laid in ruins by the earthquakes, the land upon which the Indians lived was commonly thought of as uninhabitable by anyone else.

Chilletecaux told Myers he would move immediately when he visited in August 1831. However, he must have later decided he did not want to do that. In October, he offered a plea to the governor to stay in his homeland.[31] The chief was well known and respected in the area of New Madrid and had amassed quite a homestead in the prairie. He had planted peach and apple trees.[32] There was a common corn patch.[33] They traded their produce and stock with their neighbors, and traded furs and peltries for their livelihood. The two-room log cypress cabin[34] Chilletecaux lived in was known far and wide as a hospitable place where a traveler, who found himself in the neighborhood, either by "necessity or convenience" [35] could find rest and respite and a buffalo robe to sleep upon.[36]

Progressive, Chilletecaux's cabin had a mortar [37] with attachments for pounding corn to make bread items.

In his memorial to the governor, Chilletecaux pleaded to stay in the area where he was born approximately 50 years earlier. He believed and expressed that he had a just and legal right to citizenship, as his mother was of German descent and had raised a large family in the vicinity. He offered to pay taxes. He also claimed he had no affiliation with any particular tribe and had never been a party to the signing of any treaties. [38]

Chilletecaux told the governor how he had coexisted with the earliest of residents of the area and had never been charged with a crime and always opened his door to any traveler, who may or may not have intentionally found his cabin, with courtesy and kindness and "freely divided his morsel." If he and his band of relatives were classed as citizens, Chilletecaux said, they would abide by all the laws, civil and martial.

However, if they are forced "to abandon their birthplace and the graves of their fathers," then he implored Gov. Miller to be a "lamp and light to direct their benighted steps to some tranquil spot where the wicked will cease from troubling and a panoply of peace will cover the evening of their lives." [39]

Spirits were already low amongst the villagers that year. It had been a rough winter and would be talked about for years as the "winter of the deep snow." The winter weather began around the end of December 1830 and didn't let up until the end of February 1831. The consistently cold winter blew in one storm after another, layering the land with snow and ice. At one time, the snow fell and fell until the ground was covered in large patches, some up to three feet deep, far north to Illinois. [40]

Weather Bureau records were not kept, however, weather accounts were given by people living. William Clark kept weather records at St. Louis, Missouri. After he noted in his diary on February 5, 1831, that it was "cold, cold and continuous cold at 20 degrees below the freezing point for the last two days," the temperature dropped to eight degrees followed by a couple more days of 10-degree weather. His diary did not contain any weather reports after February. [41] N. Prior noted in a letter to General William Clark from Fort Gibson, in Indian Territory, near the end of January 1831, that they were "just now finishing one of the worst winters that has ever afflicted this part of the country. The red people have suffered heavy losses in their horses and cattle." The cold was such that it drove the Osages from "their usual wintering grounds to the cane brakes" on the Neosho River. However, the Creeks had suffered the most, he noted, as they had lost most of their cattle, due to lack of food and water because of the dry season, followed by "one foot of snow that has laid on the ground since last Christmas." [42]

During this time, also called the Great Cold, the village of Chilletecaux lost most of its horses. Because of the "severity of last winter," they had lost the "greatest part of their horses," and would require assistance in removing, they told Myers. [43]

In good times, the village of Chilletecaux was a bustling place where the women made breadstuffs, beaded moccasins and ornaments, and raised a crop of corn. [44] The men hunted, trapped, and brought their bounty of furs and bear oil to trade. Visitors to the village noted the extreme hospitality found therein. During the summertime, the villagers cultivated the land, and in winter, hunted and took care of stock. Besides having plenty of food sources for survival, the women would also gather lead ore, somewhere near the St. Francis River, [45] for their guns and in trading.

In 1831, the various villages in the area, including Chilletecaux's, contained 13 Shawnees, 49 Delawares, and 22 Seneca Indians, with the balance of eight half-breed Shawnees and Creeks, according to Myers. [46] At one time, the main village may have boasted of as many as 300 Indians, as well as two White families.[47]

The villagers would assist in the spring removal of the Delaware and Seneca tribes by providing foodstuffs, gunpowder, and horses. Chilletecaux, himself, would provide 350 pounds of beef at two and a half cents a pound and five bushels of corn at 50 cents a bushel for a total of $11.25 to aid in the Delaware removal. A Jacob Taylor, most likely the same who was an early resident of the area, provided three bushels of corn meal at 50 cents each and one-half bushel of potatoes at 50 cents a bushel for a total of $1.75. [48]

The half-breed Shawnees and Muscogees were not willing to move until the spring and wished to join the Muscogees on the Verdigris, a branch of the Arkansas River, Myers said.

Bushels of corn counted by Myers in August included those belonging to Sesarkoxy, most likely Sarcoxie Anderson, Kechotowais, [49] Joseph Smith, and Moonshine. [50]

In 1830, Sarcoxie Anderson, [51] a member of Delaware Principal Chief William Anderson's family, had received permission to live and hunt on land on the "grand prairie" extending from the "little river St. Francis" to the grand fork of the St. Francis River on Buffalo Island. [52] This land was part of a Spanish Land Grant by Charles Dehault Delasses, Lt. Governor of New Madrid, and dependencies in 1796 to trader and explorer James Clamorgan[53] to establish a Canadian company and raise hemp. In 1809, Clamorgan conveyed the land to fur trader Pierre Chouteau. [54]

Sarcoxie would provide 10 pounds of gunpowder at a dollar a pound for use in their removal to the Kansas River. [55] Those who intended to move would be ready by the first of September, Myers noted, although he would try to restrain them, he did not believe the Delaware under Sarcoxie would be persuaded. The petitioners for the removal of the Indians stated in a letter to Gov. Miller that, although the Delawares had left the area, there were still "about one hundred remaining of different tribes," including Seneca, Shawnees, and Muscogees or Creeks.

A John Brown, [56] who was Seneca, was also living in the swamps below New Madrid at this time. In May 1832, he was paid for two horses to assist in the removal of a band of Senecas to lands southwest of Missouri.

Myers received pay for 128 days at $400 per annum and personal expenses for "aiding and removing" the Delaware. [57]

Moonshine, who was also paid $10 for his part in defraying expenses in the removal of the Delawares in May 1832, [58] was also known as William Hector.[59]

He was Sam's father.

Despite the opinion of many in the area that the Indians should stay and despite the pleading of Chilletecaux, all would leave, but Moonshine and his "Muscogee squaws." [60]

James, who first came to Mississippi County, Arkansas, in late 1870 or early 1871 to join Dr. F.G. McGavock in medical practice at Shawnee Village, didn't put much stock in Sam's story about the requirements in gathering his homemade remedy. He would retell the story years later in a paper on the role played by superstitions in therapeutics, in a lecture to the Alumni Association at the St. Louis College of Pharmacy on November 20, 1894. In January 1895, it was published in the *St. Louis Medical and Surgical Journal*. [61]

Sam, however, knew the benefits of the plant. *Rhus Glabra*, a perennial shrub native to North America fits the description given for the leaves Sam picked for his tea. It is a species of the smooth Sumac family of plants.

Today, it can still be found across the United States and is often seen growing in ditch banks and fence rows in the Mississippi County area, with leaves that are green in the summer and turning orange to red in the fall. Flowers in the spring and red fruit in the fall grow in clusters. The fruit can be used to make a drink similar to lemonade. The Sumac plant was just one of the plants used by Native Americans for medical treatment and was precisely the reason Sam gathered the leaves, carrying on a tradition his grandmother taught him. Sam knew the treatment worked, as did many other gifts of the land, however, he would never know why. Sumac (*Rhus spp.*), with over 250 species worldwide, is used as a spice and medicinal herb in a large portion of the world for its antiviral, antimicrobial, antibacterial, antioxidant, and wound-healing properties. [62]

Through the years James and Sam would make many trips together. [63]

Chapter 2

The Land

Sam and James left for their trip, beginning on the Little River below Sam's home. The goal was to go to the Miller Mounds to look for archeological artifacts. James was also interested in getting a better look from the Little River at some possible areas to search for artifacts and Sam knew just where to direct him. [64]

"I remember when there were still buffalo in the area," he told James as he pointed out a hill a few yards from the banks of the river. "I was standing right there when I took a shot at a buffalo," he said.

"Just as the great animal hit the ground with a thud, the earth rumbled and moved under my feet," Sam told James. "It was a huge buffalo, but before I could get a good look at her, the earthquake almost knocked me down." [65]

While telling his story, Sam was standing at the front of the dugout with a pole to guide him, while James, sitting behind him, was busy casting a line, ensuring they would have something to eat later that day. Before long, he snagged a few pickerels or jackfish, which were a favorite in the area. The waters were filled with different varieties of fish. Some of the most common were varieties of gar and catfish, buffalo, bream, and grindle. [66]

"'I saw the ground rise up,'" he said, still pointing to the hill. "'Yes, and I saw that place,'" he noted, pointing backward, "'that you call the 'Gar hole' now, so deep that you can't find bottom with that long line of yours, I see that sink down and down and the water rise up and fill it.'" [67]

James was familiar with that hole, some 25 acres in extent, with an average depth that ranged from 20 to 50 feet deeper than any other portion of the lake. [68]

"'Why, Sam,'" said James, "When was that?"'

"'Away back yonder, when I was a young man, jis a boy, old like my little gal is now, time of the yeth-quake [sic].'" [69]

Continuing, Sam told James how he, his dad William, his brother Jefferson, and a few others left one of their winter hunting camps near the Little River portage on the St. Francis River in their pirogues, checking traps along Little River as they headed toward another camp, near present-day Etowah. Making landfall on that cold January day, the men followed a blazed trail until they came within sight of the herd of buffalo, some 300 [70] strong, grazing on the wild switchcane. Sharing their strategy, each man picked his target and waited for his opportunity.

"As I got closer, I lowered my body, flat as a lizard on the ground to creep through the cane toward a cow I had been eyeing." He recalled how he was careful not to make any noise as he made his way, slowly, to where the cow and a few others were grazing near a rise in the land, dragging his flintlock rifle [71] alongside his body.

The buffalo was an interesting animal to watch, Sam told James. They moved in large herds and didn't appear to be very smart. At times, one could walk right up to the herd and shoot more than one before they would even think to retreat. [72]

"I was just 18, but had heard stories from my father and the other elders about how strong the buffalo were at one time." By 1843, their herds were dwindling, but this place was one of the last areas for miles and miles that you could still see them.

Where the buffalo roamed, their predators also roamed, and one could make out prairie rings here and there where the buffalo would gather in a circle to protect their young, beating down the grasses and earth that indelibly left its mark on the land.

Having never seen a buffalo, James was interested in learning more about them.

"They were quite a sight to see," Sam explained. Those majestic beasts were so large and tall that their matted hair often got caught up in the hanging branches of trees. [73] On that cold January day, the steam could be seen flowing from their nostrils as they exhaled into the frigid air.

In drier months, the large herds would stir up the dust and obliterate the sun in their haste. This herd was part of those trapped on the island, some say by the great earthquakes that opened up the earth, creating waterways and providing no easy way out of the area.

"If the animal didn't smell you, it was possible to get closer for the easier shots," said Sam. It often took more than one bullet to bring a buffalo down, he told, but they usually stood where they were until they died. The buffalo he shot offered a few tasty meals, had a great winter coat, and would serve him well as a winter robe for sleeping.

Sam told James of how he raised his gun and fired from behind her, aiming for her heart, striking her just behind the shoulder blade. On his feet, he readied to move and stay behind her lest she pivot. However, she soon stiffened her body and Sam saw the blood in her nostrils, a sign of a good shot. It wasn't long until she hit the ground. Sam prepared his gun for another kill, but his plans that day were soon changed by the earthquake.

When the earth rumbled and shook, the rest of the buffalo became frightened and took off. He and the others quickly moved out of the way. Reaching the banks of the river, the herd began milling about, afraid to cross it. [74]

It wasn't long before everyone came to help him with his kill. First, they gutted the animal, removing its insides. Then they skinned it, cut it into rough portions, and transported it back to camp, where they built a large fire for warmth and to keep the predators at bay. The earthquake was the topic of conversations around the fire that night.

He had heard the talk of the elder ones that remembered the great earthquakes of 1811-1812 and how they had changed the earth in this area, and he realized this earthquake was not nearly as large as those, but it still affected the earth's surface.

The land in this area was considered uninhabitable to White men, but it had not always been so. Before the great earthquakes shook the earth, the land was much different in Northeast Arkansas and Southeast Missouri, he had been told.

Following those great earthquakes, the St. Francis River was clogged with trees and other debris, [75] *and the land around it was sunken for miles and miles. Sand was everywhere. The old ones said it had been blown up from the ground during those quakes.* [76] *He and his family made their home on the banks of the Pemiscot Bayou, east of Buffalo Island. The bayou was filled with sand for miles, and trees nearby were buried in sand.* [77] *Here and about, one could see circles of sand from where the sand had made its escape from the earth below. Mixed in with it were bits of charcoal, also thrown up from below. Trees were broken, some were tangled together, and some were still standing in water.* [78]

The southernmost portion of Big Lake, near where Sam lived, just east of Buffalo Island, bore one of the more noticeable marks on the land as he knew it. Here, he witnessed the widening and deepening of the lake, which became known as the Gar Hole.

The trip downriver with James took place in 1872, [79] several years after the 1843 earthquake when Sam shot the buffalo. He was no stranger to the land rocking before that and after, yet he knew this was a more significant shake, one that caused the earth to spew forth water and sand. [80] In the two short minutes it lasted, it also caused the land to rise and sink, leaving its mark once again on the surface of Northeast Arkansas. Situated on the New Madrid fault, the land under Sam's feet was no stranger to the earth's tantrums. The lands hereabouts were called the sunk lands as a result of the way the landscape changed in the great earthquakes of 1811-1812. Sam was not yet born when those earthquakes occurred, but he had heard the old folks talk about the great ones.

The buffalo Sam had just shot was one of the few hundred that still roamed this little haven of high and dry land amidst the swamps that locals called Buffalo Island.

This newly sunk area at the foot of Big Lake, called "Gar Hole," [81] would become known for great fishing and huge gar fish.

Big Lake, once a part of a free-flowing water system, was heavily damaged in the 1811-1812 earthquakes and was changed to a lake/swamp environment. [82] The Little River empties into it in the north and continues on the east side, emerging at the southern end.

But even with all that knowledge, Sam could not begin to understand the extent to which the land where he lived had been formed. Once, a long time ago, the great Mississippi River and its overflows had dominated the area. After settling further east, the river left in its stead a collection of waterways, lakes, and narrow highlands. Later, the largest earthquakes ever known to shake the United States would further change the land.

The action of the water and the earthquakes left a land filled with swamps, sunken lands, and highlands called prairies. Surrounded on all sides by water, the highlands were called islands or donnicks. [83]

Sam also could not know that here on this high land they called Buffalo Island, [84] the great beast would soon take its last stand. Buffalo would last be seen in the area around 1865. [85]

Sam, a Native American, [86] would become one of the last of his kind to inhabit the land, remnants of once powerful nations that streamed into this area on their journey west. [87]

The land here was like no other place on earth. The undulations of the earth may have caused Sam to wonder what lay beneath, but one could not have imagined the full extent of its rich past. The land had undergone many changes. The waters carved and enriched it, and the earthquakes reshaped its surface. Earlier citizens formed great civilizations that virtually disappeared, leaving behind their marks in numerous mounds and artifacts. The enriched land would produce an abundance of trees for the timber industry, and once cleared and drained, would offer prime land for farming, causing Mississippi County, where Sam made his home, to be number one in rain-produced cotton in the world at one time. [88]

In 1843, it was a hunter's haven where almost any kind of wildlife could be found. Panthers, deer, black bears, red wolves, foxes, mink, muskrats, otters, and raccoons were abundant. All manner of fish, including gar, bass, catfish, perch, bream, and crappie, filled the waters. The sky was dark with fowl of all kinds: eagles, geese, osprey, ducks, swans, and cormorants. All of which thrived in the swampy lands, where few dared to tread.

The land, sparsely populated by humans at this time, was once heavily occupied. The evidence was everywhere. One could not travel down the waterways without spotting emerging pots or other artifacts from ancient cultures. These people were the "old folks," as Sam referred to those who once lived here.

Long before rivers, or the "old folks," traversed Mississippi County, it lay beneath the ocean. [89] When the water that would later become the Gulf of Mexico receded from Arkansas, it left behind sand, silt, and clay. The great rivers, the Mississippi and Ohio, and their tributaries, heavy with melting glacial waters from the north, began their meandering courses over the land, carrying away marine deposits as they went and laying down sand, silt, and clay in their stead. The area they created is the Mississippi Alluvial Plain, also called the Delta. In some places, outwash deposits from the rivers and the melting glaciers created terraces, higher than the modern river floodplain.

At one time, the great Mississippi River flowed west of the county, on the other side of a geological oddity, Crowley's Ridge, and the Ohio flowed on the east side, nearer to where the Mississippi River flows today. In their journeys, the rivers would leave this narrow strip of land untouched. This land formation, named for early settler Benjamin Crowley [90] with Delta land on both sides, begins in southeast Missouri, just below Cape Girardeau, and stretches almost 200 miles to Helena, Arkansas. The ridge is composed of tertiary sediments and marine deposits that originally covered all of the delta area. On top of that are sand and gravel deposited by the movement of the rivers. Wind-blown dust or loess, up to 50 feet in places, caps the earlier deposits. Loess, soil created by the grinding down of large rocks by glacial waters and deposited in the delta, accumulated at the ridge when the high-lying area disturbed the wind flow. Highly erodible wash-off waters from rains and streams would cut the loess on the ridge into valleys and ridges. Crowley's Ridge is only about 12 miles wide at its greatest width, and its highest point is only about 400 feet. On average, it is about 250 feet high. [91]

After meandering for thousands of years on the west side of the ridge, the Mississippi River would eventually break through Benton Hills in Missouri at Thebes Gap and head toward Cairo, Illinois, where it joined the Ohio River. The two began to flow as one toward the Gulf of Mexico. From Cairo onward, the river would be known as the Mississippi River. Finally settling somewhat, the Mississippi River would provide the eastern border for what would become Mississippi County.

Some of the tributaries of the river would run in its former beds. The former beds of the Mississippi and Ohio rivers also left large swampy areas. One such area stretched from just below Cape Girardeau into Arkansas and was referred to as the Great Swamp. Not only did the rivers leave swamps in their stead, but the great earthquakes caused the land to sink and crack in areas and fill with water, creating more swampy conditions.

In 1843, the St. Francis River bordered Buffalo Island on the west. The Little River flowed on the east side of the island with its left and right-hand chutes. The Little River has its beginnings in Missouri, where it was called Whitewater, and was historically referred to as the east fork of the St. Francis River in Arkansas. Once free-flowing through the Big Lake area, the Little River is now lost in the waters of the lake. Emerging from the southern end, it flows toward its junction with the St. Francis River.

The St. Francis, Black, Cache, Tyronza, Little, L'Anguille, Whitewater, and Castor rivers, as well as others, were also subject to meandering and overflow, creating watery features in this area of Southeast Missouri and Northeast Arkansas. In their meanderings, they created sloughs, bayous, oxbow lakes, and swamps.

14

The Pemiscot Bayou was described in 1874 as a tortuous channel, making its way from the Mississippi River in Pemiscot County, Missouri. It was wide and deep and had two mouths, one near Gayoso, Missouri, and the other at Cottonwood Point, Missouri. It traveled in a southwesterly direction, traveling through several lakes before emptying at the foot of Big Lake into the Little River. A large amount of the overflow water taken by the Pemiscot Bayou deflected into Walker's, Buford, and Grassy lakes, finding its way back to the Mississippi River via Long Lake and Mill Bayou. [92]

After years and years of flooding and overflows in the area, uprooted trees and vegetation further enriched the land with their layers and layers of decomposition. The rich, alluvial soil left behind from these overflows would be a boon to the agricultural industry in years to come.

Layer upon layer, the land had and would continue to change. Indian trails followed the animal trails set down first by ancient migrating mammoths. These same trails became the pioneer trails into the land, and eventually, they became highways and byways by which many would make their way into the area.

Early foot trails into the area ran along Crowley's Ridge. As swampy areas existed on both sides of the ridge, it became a natural land bridge. The first humans to come to this area were Paleo-Indians, most likely on the trail of large animals, like mastodons. The skeletons of these massive animals have been discovered in Northeast Arkansas and Southeast Missouri.

As early Indian culture in the area progressed, a new style of tool-making known as the Dalton point lent its name to a culture overlapping the Paleo-Indian culture and the beginning of the Archaic years. [93] The Sloan site, west of Crowley's Ridge, where many unbroken Dalton points have been excavated, is the oldest documented cemetery in the Western Hemisphere. Paleo-Indian sites are located east and west of Crowley's Ridge, as well as in other places in Arkansas. [94]

During the Archaic period, tribes of people became more settled, utilizing the same village sites from season to season. They hunted smaller, more accessible game, fished, and began to domesticate some plants. Some ritual or sacred sites were marked with mounds or earthen works. Some occupants were even involved in trade with those in other areas.

Characteristics like crop production, gathering, and less reliance on hunting were indicative of the Woodland period tribes. During this time, when tribes became less nomadic, the production of pottery vessels moved from basic containers into more of a craft, and the bow and arrow also came into use. Their sedentary living centered around a more ritualistic structure with small burial and ceremonial mounds.

Around AD 1000, maize became an important element in the diet of many tribes, ushering in the beginning of the Mississippian period. During this time, the people lived in societies with chiefdoms, led by hereditary leaders.

Their towns and villages were often fortified, and they built earthen, flat-topped mounds, further leaving a mark on the land.

A late Mississippian site in Northeast Arkansas is located at Nodena, on what was the farm of James K. Hampson, near Wilson in Mississippi County, Arkansas. This site is located on a relict channel of the Mississippi River. Its artifacts were well documented by Hampson. People who lived here grew beans, maize, and squash, and gathered hickory nuts, black walnuts, hazelnuts, persimmons, and wild cherries to eat. They hunted deer, bear, raccoon, rabbit, turkey, and waterfowl. They fished for gar, catfish, drum, and mussels. They lived in small houses, 10 to 13 square feet in size. This site is typical of the Nodena phase of the Mississippian period.

Several sites of the Nodena phase are located in Northeast Arkansas and Southeast Missouri. One site in the area is the Eaker site, at the former Eaker Air Force Base, on the Pemiscot Bayou. It is the largest and most intact late Mississippian Nodena phase village site within the Central Mississippi Valley. It is hypothesized that the site may have been occupied by the Quapaw before their move south, where they came into contact with Europeans in the late 17th century. [95]

The Quapaw in the late 17th century populated an area at the confluence of the White and Arkansas rivers in Arkansas.

It was during the latter part of the Mississippian period in the Nodena phase that the lifestyles of these Native Americans were interrupted by Spanish explorer Hernando de Soto in 1541. De Soto's route in Arkansas is unknown for sure; however, many archaeologists believe that the Mississippian site at Parkin is the province of Casqui, which was documented by de Soto. Supporting this possibility is the excavation at Parkin of a Clarksdale bell, lead shot from a Spanish firearm, and a Chevron bead. [96]

Parkin is located on the St. Francis River. Here, Native Americans also grew maize, squash, sunflowers, beans, and tobacco. They harvested local fruits and nuts, such as pecans. A moat-like ditch surrounded the village.

It would be more than 130 years after de Soto's visit before Jacques Marquette, a Jesuit missionary, and Louis Jolliet, a fur trader, would explore the Mississippi River into Arkansas for France and Canada.

In their 1673 visit, Marquette and Jolliet would tell of a people that lived on the shores of a Big Lake called the Michigamea. [97] Possibly a predecessor to the current Big Lake near Sam's home. In their travels, Marquette and Jolliet stopped at a Quapaw village called Kappa near the mouth of the Arkansas River.

French explorer, Rene-Robert Cavelier, Sieur de La Salle, would follow in 1682, claiming the Louisiana Territory, which included present-day Missouri and Arkansas, for King Louis XIV of France. Henri de Tonti, who first accompanied La Salle on his initial visit, would return to Arkansas in 1686 and establish Arkansas Post. De Tonti left six Frenchmen there who carried on trade with the Quapaw near their village, Osotouy, in present-day Arkansas County.

Arkansas Post would be the first European settlement in Arkansas. The Quapaw ceded their Arkansas land by treaty in 1824 and removed to the state of Louisiana. However, they returned to Arkansas, and in 1833, ceded their land in Louisiana, and were removed from Arkansas to Oklahoma.

The Osage, who lived along the Osage and Missouri rivers in Missouri, where French explorers encountered them in 1673, claimed Northern Arkansas as hunting territory. The Osage, who claimed a large portion of Missouri, Kansas, Oklahoma, and Arkansas, ceded most of their Missouri land and the Northern half of Arkansas in 1808.

The Chickasaw, who traveled through Arkansas and crossed to the east side of the Mississippi in prehistory, warred with the Quapaw, and often hunted in Arkansas in the mid-1700s. Some Chickasaw were said to have been in the state during the 1811-1812 earthquakes, losing their lives at Cockle Burr Slough. [98] The Chickasaw would trek back across the state in the 1830s when they were removed to Indian Territory.

In 1762, France ceded the Louisiana territory to Spain. In 1800, Spain transferred the territory back to France, and in 1803 the United States purchased the land.

The Shawnee and Delaware first began to settle in what would become Southeast Missouri as early as 1784. [99] In 1793, the Spanish government authorized Louis Lorimier [100] to establish the Shawnee and Delaware in the area to provide a buffer between the Osage tribe and the settlements and also to strengthen the west bank of the Mississippi River against the Americans. On January 4, 1793, a grant to the Shawnee and Delaware for a 25-square-mile tract of land was signed by Francisco Luis Hector, Baron de Carondelet, Spanish governor of the colonies of Louisiana and West Florida from 1791 to 1797. The land was situated between the St. Come River and Cape Girardeau, bounded on the west by the Whitewater River and east by the Mississippi River.

After the first settlements on the west bank of the Mississippi River, the Shawnee and Delaware moved further west, establishing villages on the Whitewater River, Castor River, at Bloomfield, and Chilletecaux in Missouri.[101] While residing in these places, they traded at St. Genevieve with the firm of Menard and Valle. [102] The account book of this firm lists a "Chi lit cou," [103] which was possibly Chilletecaux, as one of those who had obtained credit.

The Delaware also moved further west, having villages on the White River, near Forsyth, the James Fork in Christian County, and Wilson's Creek in Greene County, all in Missouri. Both the Shawnee and Delaware tribes had villages on the Current, Meramec, and Gasconade rivers in Missouri. Some Shawnees lived further west in Arkansas along the Crooked Creek near present-day Harrison and Yellville.

There were also some Creeks mixed in with the Shawnee in Missouri.[104]

Living on the St. Francis River in 1815 were some Piankeshaw. [105] The main body lived in an area that is now western Indiana and Ohio. A portion of the tribe had moved into Missouri in the 1790s, with the rest ceding their Illinois and Indiana lands and moving in 1805, and to Kansas in 1832.

A tribe of Peorias also lived on the St. Francis River in 1815. [106] The Peorias' ancestors were originally from Missouri, Illinois, Michigan, and Ohio. They migrated into Missouri territory sometime after 1763. In 1832, they ceded lands in Missouri for land in Kansas, near the Osage River, with the majority of the tribe later relocating to what is now Oklahoma. [107]

In November 1825, the Shawnee of Cape Girardeau signed a treaty in St. Louis, Missouri with William Clark relinquishing their land near Cape Girardeau in exchange for a 14-mile tract of land on the Kansas River.

According to the St. Mary's Treaty, signed in 1818 by the main Delaware tribe in St. Marys, Ohio, the Cape Girardeau Delaware had already abandoned this land in 1815. Some had moved to Texas, as had some of the Shawnee. Other members of the Cape Girardeau Delaware settled in Southwest Missouri. The main Delaware tribe, under Chief William Anderson, still residing on the White River in Indiana, signed the St. Mary's Treaty in which they ceded their land. They began their trek to Missouri in September 1821, settling on the Current River and the James Fork of the White River. The Delaware were not happy with this land. On September 24, 1829, in a supplementary article to the St. Mary's Treaty, they traded their land for land beginning on the fork of the Kansas River and the Missouri River. Anderson died in October 1831 in Kansas.

The Cherokee began to settle along the St. Francis River in Arkansas as early as 1796, while the land was under Spanish rule. Later, in 1817, some Cherokee would exchange land east of the Mississippi River for land in Arkansas, north of the Arkansas River, and west of the White River. By 1828, these Old Settlers, or Western Cherokee as they were called, were moved to Indian Territory, present-day Oklahoma. The Treaty of New Echota, which ceded Eastern Cherokee lands for land in Indian Territory, was signed by a minority of the Cherokee tribe in 1835 and amended and ratified by the U.S. Senate in 1836. In March 1837, the first volunteer party of Cherokee began their trek westward at the expense of the U.S. Government, after the signing of the treaty. Other groups followed. In 1838, U.S. troops began to enforce the terms of the New Echota Treaty. The first group of Cherokees forced to leave their homeland left in June. By early 1839, most of the Cherokee had arrived in Oklahoma. They traveled in several parties, and although they took several routes, the various routes as a whole would all be referred to later as the Trail of Tears, because many died as they were forced to travel on foot and in all sorts of weather. Some would cross the Mississippi River near Cape Girardeau as they headed westward.

Many emigrant Indians came to the area before one of the most significant land-altering events occurred in 1811-1812 in the form of the New Madrid Earthquakes.

These were a series of earthquakes, including three large earthquakes registering between magnitudes seven and eight and large aftershocks, along the New Madrid Seismic Zone [108] between December 16, 1811, and February 7, 1812.

Godfrey Lesieur, who lived just south of New Madrid, told of how the first earthquake caused the land to roll in waves with swells bursting and "throwing up large volumes of water, sand, and a species of charcoal."[109] Later, he would observe long fissures running parallel with each other for miles and sunken lands on either side of the Little River and the St. Francis River.

The earthquakes induced large-scale soil liquefaction [110] and destroyed small settlements along the Mississippi River. Minor structural damage occurred as far away as Cincinnati, Ohio, and St. Louis, Missouri. Reelfoot Lake, just across the river from New Madrid in Tennessee, was formed. Big Lake, a free-flowing river system before the earthquakes, changed to a swamp and lake ecosystem.

These were not the first earthquakes in the area. Evidence suggests that major earthquakes occurred in AD 900, plus or minus 100 years, and 1450, plus or minus 150 years. [111]

The largest earthquakes since 1811-1812 were in 1843 and 1895.

The land before those devastating earthquakes was dense and covered with a large growth of timber, including oak, walnut, hickory, and gum, as well as weeping willows, cypress, and catalpa trees. On the highlands, cane brakes were matted and entangled with vines. Lesieur noted immense grape vines twined around the trees, loaded with fruit. [112] The great trees obscured the horizon in places and provided cover and protection for many animals.

The earthquakes left behind a land that was more subject to overflows from the rivers, streams, and the great Mississippi River. Because of these overflows and trees that were uprooted, the land became richer and alluvial.

"Within the memory of living inhabitants," H.M. McVeigh, an attorney in Osceola, said in 1889, "this county was high, dry, and less alluvial than it is now." The caving of the banks of the Mississippi River, the clearing of land around its tributaries above the county, and the earthquakes made the land more subject to inundation. [113]

Some of the Indians left the area following the earthquakes.

Sam was just 12 when he and his family moved deeper into the swamps, to an upheaved land full of wildlife and vegetation in Northeast Arkansas. They were no stranger to the area, long recognized as a hunter's haven.

Chapter 3

Moonshine

Pulling ashore for the night, Sam and James lit a small fire to roast their fish and add some warmth to the night. While watching the open fire, the memories of Sam's youth seeped into his mind, much like the warmth from the blaze enveloped his body. He could almost see the faces of those from his young days peering back at him through the jumping red flames.

When he was just a small boy, he would often sit near the fire where his father and the others gathered at Chilletecaux [114]and listen as they talked and bragged about their great hunting exploits.

"What was it like to live in the village?" James inquired.

Sam told him about the late summer festivities of the Green Corn Ceremony, the holiday that followed a fast, celebrated the ripening of the corn crop. He remembered the sound of the drums when the chief would sit in the middle of a circle and pound on a drum while the men and women danced around him.[115] He recalled stories of the hoopla surrounding competition between the tribes and listened in awe as the men bragged about the times when they and another tribe would race their best horses until they or the other tribe had garnered all the ponies and blankets. [116]

He also told James how he and his family stayed among the Cherokee on the banks of the St. Francis River in Arkansas when he was young. Here, he would often pick up musket balls along the banks of the river. [117]

He recalled the talk about the great earthquakes that had drastically changed the land. Some, including his dad, saw those great earthquakes as a blessing in this countryside, for with one climactic event the land was transformed into a market hunter's paradise, overflowing with fur-bearing game. It was an area that few dared to venture into, making it lucrative for those who did.

"My father was one of those who saw the great earthquakes as a blessing," said Sam.

He told James about his father, a man with his feet in two worlds, that of a White man and that of a despised Indian.

William "Moonshine" Hector had struggled to find his place in life.[118]

He was most happy with his feet in swamp waters, where the wild animals filled the air with the sound of their calls and the skies darkened with fowl.

His father told him about the changing times and how they affected him. "At first," when the Native Americans came to the area they were greatly appreciated. Their very being in the land offered a protection that comforted the settlers, Sam told James, remembering what his father had said. "They were offered land by the Spanish, and a chance for a better life," and his father's people "took that chance," he said.

However, when the country became a part of the United States, the Native Americans became despised yet again as more and more Whites settled near them. The settlers were constantly taking advantage of them and stealing their horses. While they were gone on their winter hunting trips, their homes were often broken into by some of those settlers.

His father, known as Moonshine, found it easier to live among his native family. He first moved further south and west of Cape Girardeau in the Big Swamp [119] near the road to Bloomfield. Some Cape Girardeau Shawnee and Delaware had moved to the Castor River, near Bloomfield, around 1816 because they could not live peacefully with the settlers near their former home on Apple Creek.

By 1830 or 1831, Sam's father had gone further into the swamps, making his home at Chilletecaux, where he was known as Captain Moonshine. For several years after the others moved on from the village, he and his family would stay there, reuniting with their friends when they came down the rivers or overland for the hunting season. He would often visit the remaining Cherokee at their old camp further down on the St. Francis River and meet up with old friends there.

Sam remembered being happy at Chilletecaux. He loved his grandmother dearly, for it was with her that he first learned about many plants and their uses. Because of her, he knew what to gather and dry that would be used in healing salves or teas. [120]

In 1837, Sam's father and his family went even further into the swampy, sunken lands of Arkansas, where settlers and paths were few.

Not long after Louisiana became a United States territory, in the early 1800s, a push began to remove those Native Americans residing on the east side of the river to the west. As early as 1803, Native Americans on the east side of the Mississippi River had been encouraged to become agriculturized or move to the west side. By 1817, land cession treaties offered land exchanges east of the river for land on the west side. The Cherokee were the first to exchange two tracts of land in 1817 for one of equal size in present-day Arkansas. Other such treaties followed.

In early 1825, President James Monroe requested the creation of the Arkansas Territory and Indian Territory and encouraged Indians east of the Mississippi River to move voluntarily west of the Mississippi River. But while the Senate accepted the request, the House did not.

When Andrew Jackson became president in 1829, things began to change as he aggressively pursued plans to remove all Native Americans west of the Mississippi River. The ensuing Indian Removal Act of 1830 did not authorize forced removal. It authorized the negotiation of land exchange treaties and would eventually bring about the greatest relocation of humankind ever in the United States.

The emigrant tribes of the Shawnee and Delaware had been feeling the push westward for several years as more and more settlers moved in and around their lands. Some had already taken it upon themselves to move on. Some Cape Girardeau Shawnee and Delaware had taken refuge in less populated areas near their former home, settling in the swamps. By the 1830s, though, even those who had settled where not many others would live were being pushed out by visionary men who had begun to see more of a future in the possibility of retrieving that land. Expulsion, coupled with government plans in the works for further removal to Indian Territory, would include the last of the Native Americans to inhabit this region.

A group of Shawnee, Delaware, Muscogee, and Seneca Indians settled along the St. Francis River in Missouri and Arkansas and were referred to as the St. Francis Indians. At one time, those in the area also included some Piankeshaw and Cherokee.

By 1831, the St. Francis Indians had dwindled to the few living at and near Chilletecaux. In the mostly inaccessible area, they hoped to be out of the way and live in peace in the land that most had known their whole life.

Chief Chilletecaux was not the first in the area to want to live in peace among his neighbors. A little further north of Chilletecaux's village had been the village of Wapapilethe [121] on the Castor River. He was no stranger to the territory. He and his people first crossed over the Mississippi 30 years before, as part of the Shawnee group granted land on Apple Creek by Spanish authorities. [122]

"We live among the Whites, and our behaviour has been such as that no honest man can have any cause to find fault with us," Wapapilethe told William Clark. In 1815, Clark and other commissioners, along with Missouri Governor Ninian Edwards and Col. Chouteau, were appointed to treat with "Indians of the Mississippi and its waters" at Portage des Sioux, Missouri.

"We have always conducted ourselves honestly and intend to continue so."

He told of how recently his home had been broken into while he was away on his winter hunt and all that he owned was taken. Because of this, he made a move to the Castor River, provided "Gov. Clark would be pleased with my doing so." He and his people had followed the advice of the governor and raised stock and cultivated the land, but they still could not live in peace with the encroaching settlers and hoped to remain at their new settlement, as they did "not care any thing more for our old town." His new town would be referred to as Shawnee Village and was situated near Bloomfield, Missouri.

But even in his new town, Wapapilethe had to deal with the same problems. "Lately, we have been encroached upon by a White family by the name of Jenkins…"

At the same meeting, Wapapilethe's sentiments were reiterated by a fellow Delaware chief. The Delaware would abandon their Cape Girardeau land that same year, leaving behind cultivated fields and improvements, joining others from the east who moved westward. [123]

Their grievances were "well-founded," noted the commissioners at the meeting, who were "well acquainted with the sobriety and general good conduct of those Indians." They also told of the problems the Cherokee in Arkansas were experiencing with White settlers who stole their game and "act in a manner as to produce disorders, discord, and confusion."

Within 22 days of this talk, White intruders were ordered off the land of Shawnee and Delaware; however, this only provided temporary relief. [124]

Wapapilethe was so willing to accommodate his fellow settlers and to live in peace with them that when a member of his tribe committed a crime against a pioneer citizen in August 1820, he ordered the man brought to justice. After the perpetrator was killed, he had his head displayed on a pole.

Shawnee Little George had been persuaded by John Boyce [125] to murder Jane Burns in exchange for 10 dollars and a gallon of whiskey.

By September, the news of the murder had spread far and wide. The September 9, 1820, *Arkansas Gazette* newspaper reported the story of the "horrid murder," noting that "pursuit has been made after the murderer, but he is not yet taken."

Wapapilethe sent two warriors to find Little George, and they did so on the banks of the St. Francis River, on Crowley's Ridge in Arkansas. [126] Little George refused to surrender and began to sing a death song. He was shot and decapitated, and his head was taken back as proof that he had been killed.

Botanist and explorer Edwin James told of seeing this head displayed at Jackson, Missouri, while traveling through the area in October 1820. He said the head was displayed on a pole on the side of the road leading from that town northward to the Indian settlement of Apple Creek, which contained about 400 Shawnee and Delaware at that time. [127]

Wapapilethe did enjoy some peace with early settlers while at the village on the Castor River.

In 1816, Indians living on the Castor River traded at St. Genevieve twice a year, traveling the Indian path, also known as the Shawnee Trail, that led northward and connected with the Vincennes and Natchitoches trail. Southward, this trail traversed a strip of highland and led into what would become Dunklin County, [128] and then into what would become Arkansas. In the spring, they sold their bear and winter deer skins, and in the fall, honey, bear oil cased in deer hides, and summer skins. They traveled single file on ponies.

They were dressed in deerskins, the men wearing leggings, breech clouts, and hunting shirts, with a blanket during cold weather. In the summer, they wore a red blouse trimmed with white and blue beads, a red handkerchief on their head, and moccasins. The women dressed similarly with ornaments in their ears and noses. They were said to be peaceable and orderly and never intoxicated. [129] Near the cabin of Chief Wapapilethe was a lake, hand-dug and fed by a spring where the villagers bathed. Nearby was a Delaware Indian settlement and the two tribes often conducted horse races together. [130]

Native Americans of various tribes, including the Shawnee, camped in other areas at different times before moving out of Southeast Missouri. In 1823, some were camped in the Big Swamp area, south of Cape Girardeau, possibly for hunting pursuits. Among those men was one called Moonshine. He was with a group of five Native Americans and six or seven White men, camped on or near land owned by Jacob Jacobs. [131] Jacobs said in a deposition[132] that "some Indians were settled within a mile of him about the first of March," of that year. Sometime after camping there, Moonshine had a bay gelding horse taken by a Samuel Jones, of Cape Girardeau. Jones was indicted for larceny related to the theft of the horse however, that was not all the Indians accused him of taking. They also claimed he took some pelts. Jacobs, Ezekiel Hill, and Joe Blunt all gave depositions in the case concerning Jones. Hill stated that Jones told him "several times that he was not afraid of being found guilty as an "Indians testimony could not be taken … against a White man."

It appears he was correct, as in August, he was acquitted and discharged. [133]

Jacobs was a brother-in-law of Andrew Ramsey Sr., and there had been Native Americans settled near or on Ramsey's land also in the Big Swamp area in 1815 and before. His will of that year stated that he bequeathed to his daughter Elenor, "all the land lying [by] my plantation and where my daughter Elenor now lives to begin on my westline below some indian camps …" [134]

In 1828, William Hector was still in the Big Swamp settlement when he and others of Cape Girardeau County signed a petition to the Lutheran Tennessee Synod to renew the license of the minister Ephraim R. Conrad for another year so that he could continue in his work in the "desolate wilderness." Conrad worked in the area for the past two years as a Lutheran minister. More than 250 residents of the county signed the petition. [135]

Some of those settled in the Big Swamp area, who were also signers of the petition, would make their way to the area around Chilletecaux at the same time William did in 1830.

It appears that some of those stopped in the area of Wapapilethe's village, on the road to Bloomfield, before moving southward to Chilletecaux village.

Abijah Rice, whose family would become part of William's family in the future, settled two miles northwest of Hornersville in what would probably become the Cotton Plant area. He, Jacob Taylor, and Michael Brannum had settled at Bloomfield before moving on to Dunklin County. [136] Chief Chilletecaux had enlarged the existing trail to allow the settlers' bridle carts to pass through the canes and rushes. Taylor settled near a slough that would bear his name. Brannum settled near Hornersville at what would become Brannum's Point. [137] Abijah's wife, Jaley, also a signer of the Lutheran petition, was part Native American, [138] and their family was often in the Indian camp at Chilletecaux. [139]

Even after the residents of Chilletecaux were told to leave in 1831, some remained until 1835 and most likely until 1837 when William and his family moved to Arkansas. In 1835, the Indian village of which Chilletecaux was still the principal Chief had dwindled to about 50 inhabitants and was encompassed by the newly-formed county of Stoddard. At this time, some Cherokee lived among the Seneca, Shawnee, Delaware, and Muscogee villagers. Cherokees were not among those enumerated in 1831. The villagers subsisted by farming on a small scale, stock raising, hunting, and trading in peltries. [140]

Francis Lesieur of Point Pleasant, Missouri, first began trading with the St. Francis Indians in 1824. He and his son, Francis, were granted a license to trade with the Shawnee and Delaware at the Muscogee town on the St. Francis River by Richard Graham. [141] In addition to the Lesieurs, Hypolite Tirard [142] and Henry Godair [143] assisted in trading. After the death of his father Francois, Godfrey Lesieur continued to trade with these Indians at the designated Muscogee town. In 1827, he was granted a license by Graham. Under the bond of J. B. Valle Jr., [144] Lesieur had Francis Maisonville, [145] Francis Lesieur, Toussant Godair, [146] Hippolite Tirart [sic], and Mark Gamlin [147] assist him.

A list of items purchased from Menard and Valle [148] in St. Genevieve, Missouri, in November of that year and brought to the village, contained items both for comfort and for ornamentation.

It was customary among some tribes for men to wear a turban, adorned with feathers. Silver brooches might be attached to the turbans or articles of clothing. Madras handkerchiefs, shawls, ostrich feathers, vermilion, ear bobs, arm bands, and brooches were among the items for ornamentation.

Items of comfort included three-point and two-point blankets.[149] Fabric included blue calico, light ground, and scarlet cloths. Useful items included nesting brass kettles, inlaid butcher knives, Wilson's butcher knives, trace chains, depth powder, gun flints, gun locks, lead, scissors, saddles, and bridles.

By 1824, laws in Missouri limited trade with the Indians by not allowing anyone to reside in the hunting camps or towns of Indians without a proper license, and no one could induce an Indian to come into the White settlements for trading. However, that law provided that no person incur penalties for trading with those Indians settled on the "Merrimac" [sic] River in Franklin County [150] or the St. Francis River.

According to Francois Lesieur, Adam Rittenhouse, of Ohio, had traded with these Indians since 1820. Lesieur, whose trade with the Indians was injured by Rittenhouse, was concerned that he was operating without a license and distributing liquor to the Indians. He wrote Graham in 1825, asking how to deal with the situation and what court had jurisdiction over the matter. He said that he had been told by Menard that Rittenhouse did not have a license and had relayed that information to him and his traders. He had at least fifty witnesses to back up his accusations. [151]

Graham was familiar with Rittenhouse. N.W. Watkins, of New Madrid, had sent a request to Graham for a license for Rittenhouse to trade with the Indians on the St. Francis River in March 1825. [152] Graham sent a license application to trade with the Indians on the White River to Rittenhouse in April of that year. [153] He also must have approved a license for trade with the St. Francis River Indians in August 1825. [154]

Rittenhouse also had some residents in his court. Hopkins wrote to Graham attesting to the character of Rittenhouse after hearing that the U.S. Attorney had launched an action against him. He believed private interests and fear that Rittenhouse would rival some of those in the area in the trade were the impetus for the accusations against Rittenhouse. [155]

By this time, however, Graham had already taken action and wrote Hopkins telling him it was out of his hands. [156] Hopkins also requested a license from Graham [157] to trade with the St. Francis Indians in January of that year so that he might supply some of his friends in the upper country with peltries and furs difficult for them to procure, he said. In his request, he asked to trade with those Indians on the White River. Hopkins must not have followed through with acquiring a license, although he had received an application for trade with the "St. Francis Muskogee Indians at their village on the St. Francis River." [158]

In 1831, when Hopkins pleaded for the inhabitants of Chilletecaux to be allowed to stay in the area, he noted that he did not have ulterior motives, as he had never gained "a cent" in trade with these or other Indians. [159]

On different sides of the trading business, Moonshine, like the Lesieurs, Hopkins, and Rittenhouse, saw the potential the land offered after the great New Madrid earthquakes. It was worth a little jockeying to be on top in the trading business. The land after the earthquakes had been transformed into lakes and marshes, vastly increasing the trade in fur-bearing animals.

In the year 1845, there were 50,000 raccoon skins, 25,000 muskrats, 12,000 minks, 1000 bears, 1000 otters, 2,500 wildcats, 40 panthers, and 100 wolves taken in the area. The earthquakes were a blessing to the country and helped establish New Madrid in the fur trade. [160]

After Moonshine and his family left Chilletecaux and went to Arkansas, he continued to trade with the Lesieurs, hunting and trapping in the swamps, Crowley's Ridge, and the waterways of the St. Francis River, L'Anguille River, Little River, and Pemiscot Bayou.

Moonshine and his band of hunters would often follow the Little River toward the St. Francis River on hunting excursions. A little south of the confluence of these two rivers, there was a land bridge or portage that would cut off several miles of water travel.

Near this portage stood an oak tree, marked, some would say, in later years, with an "M" to show the way where the distance between the rivers was only about a quarter of a mile. Traveling upstream on the St. Francis River, one could drag their canoe across this land bridge to the Little River, which would soon meet up with the St. Francis River and cut off about eight miles of upstream paddling.

Legend would long associate Moonshine with this marked tree. He and his hunting partners would often use this portage and camp nearby, as had those who had long traveled these water and land routes.

"Far up among the wild tangled vales of the southwest portion of Mississippi County, Arkansas, upon the tree-shaded banks of Little River, lived a wily old Indian chief named Moonshine," reads one account of his adventures. [161]

"The daring of his braves and hunters were unequalled," and he often sent them off to search for game. One day, when he traveled down Little River to welcome home the hunters, he looked across the marsh and saw the St. Francis River nearby and began to portage across the land to the river. On its banks, he "blazed" a mark on a tree and directed the hunters to cross at this spot.

This well-traveled spot between two rivers would one day host a town called Marked Tree and continue to carry the legend of Moonshine.

It appears that William tried to live in both worlds, that of a citizen and that of a Native American, bearing the name sometimes of William Hector, and sometimes of Moonshine.

In 1823, he seemed to embrace his native heritage as Moonshine while he camped in the Big Swamp with other Native Americans.

In 1827, as William Hector, he owed 50 cents on an account to John J. Delashmutt and L.B. Delashmutt of New Madrid, as stated in an inventory of debts for the estate of John J. Delashmutt, deceased. [162]

In 1829, as William Hector, he owed David Hunter, of Winchester, New Madrid County, a debt of $3, which had accrued interest for a past due balance of $6.13 in principal and interest after Hunter died in 1847. [163] Hunter operated a store in Winchester, Missouri at one time. [164]

In February 1830, Hector appeared before Thomas Neal, Justice of the Peace of Castor Township, Cape Girardeau County, for a debt on a note of $35, of which a principal of $2.70 was due. In August, Hector paid $1.35 to Joel Ramsey, a constable in Pike Township, of Cape Girardeau County, in this case. [165]

In April 1830, Hector assaulted Daniel Randall in Byrd Township in Cape Girardeau. Hector, also previously, "of the Township of Byrd," with "force and arms" did "strike to the great damage" of Randall. He and his security, William Long, [166] "both of the county of New Madrid," appeared in circuit court in April 1831, and acknowledged the $200 debt owed for the assault. [167]

He was also enumerated in Cape Girardeau County as William Hector in 1830. [168] William was on a delinquent tax list for New Madrid County, Missouri, in 1833, along with Abijah Rice. [169]

Perhaps his recent appearances in court and unpaid debt are why he made his next home in Chilletecaux as Moonshine and was counted there in August 1831 at the village.

At some point before Elias Hopkins of New Madrid County, Missouri died in 1846, William as "Bill Moonshine (Indian)" incurred a debt with him for $2.50. Hopkins lived at the mouth of Pemiscot Bayou. [170]

In 1837, as William Hector, he was in trouble with the law once again when he was accused of cohabiting outside the bounds of marriage with "Jailey" Ann Rice, [171] the former wife of Abijah, aforementioned. Instead of going to court, [172] they both made their way to Arkansas, where in 1840 he would be living as William Hector in Mississippi County. [173]

Chapter 4

Chickalee

"Not long before we left the village in 1837," Sam told James, "we lost our beloved elder, Chickalee."

Elaborating further, Sam told of how each year since they had been forced to leave the region, some tribe members of the Shawnee, Delaware, and Cherokee [174] would travel back to join in the winter hunt in the swamp lands. Chickalee would be with them. Arriving, they would soon place themselves under the command of Captain Moonshine. He would be their principal chief while they were on their hunting excursion. [175]

From their new home, the returning men would travel down the Missouri River to the Mississippi River to Point Pleasant just below New Madrid. It was here that Moonshine and the others took their furs to trade with the Lesieurs, [176] continuing a tradition that started many years ago. And it was here that his father Moonshine, John East, [177] and Keshotte would sometimes meet up with old friends, Chickalee, Big Knife, [178] and others at the beginning of the season.

"We had been expecting them for days," he told James. "I remember watching the river for the canoes."

Soon after the arrival of the hunters, Chickalee died. His passing would delay the hunt until burial arrangements were made. The wailing would continue for several hours. While the men gathered the supplies for the hunt, the women cleansed Chickalee's body in preparation for burial.

They boiled willow root and wrapped him in clean cloths. They decided to bury him in their village. Their canoes would leave at daylight for the trip home. [179]

"That was also my first year to hunt," Sam told James. Recalling how Point Pleasant looked then, Sam told James about the long row of yellow houses, the thorny locust trees, and the apple trees that captivated his youthful curiosity. He remembered wondering about the thorny trunks of the honey locust trees and how the squirrels could make their way up the tree, yet there they were barking at him. As he, his father, and the other men made their way to one of the storehouses to stock up on supplies, the death of Chickalee hung heavy on their minds.

Sam recalled how he couldn't wait to taste one of those apples or dip his toes in the pond at the edge of the village, and rest on the soft moss under the catalpa tree that stretched its arms toward the center of the pond. [180]

His father dealt then with Godfrey Lesieur, the son of Francois Lesieur. After gathering supplies of cornmeal, salt, and other items, they would make plans for the season. But, first, they mourned and buried their friend and mentor, Chickalee, also known locally as Corn Meal. [181] *The mourning would last a couple of days, during which Chickalee's life would be celebrated.*

Sam told James about the talk around the campfire that evening and how it centered around memories of Chickalee's life. This is when he first heard the story of how Chickalee and Keshotte, [182] *also no longer with them, chased Shawnee Little George into Arkansas, assuring peaceful relations with the settlers.*

Chickalee had been a peacekeeper and was well known for his eloquence in speech. It was he who insisted on keeping peace with the Osage, many years ago, even though they had committed depredations against him.

He also told James of how that year Chickalee had been specifically requested by Godfrey Lesieur to come back to the area so that he might reveal the locality of an ore bog. It was well known that the Indians in the area would gather all the lead they needed for hunting, and Lesieur had hoped that now that they didn't live in the area, Chickalee would point out the spot where he had found ore. [183] *He had been asked more than once by others in the area to reveal the location.* [184]

Sam grinned. "They all knew," he said, "where the bogs were, but they never told."

The Cherokee on the east side of the Mississippi became divided into the upper and lower towns following the American Revolutionary War, with more militant tribesmen locating in the far Southwestern portion of their nation among the Chickasaw and Creeks. [185] The group followed War Chief Dragging Canoe, [186] and supported Great Britain during the war.

The new town on the Chickamauga River would come to be associated with this band referred to as Chickamauga. Five years later, following the destruction of their towns by militia, they would become known as the Lower Cherokee. Their early settlements were Running Water, Nickajack, Long Island, Crow Town, and Lookout Mountain. In time, the towns would spread more south and west.

This group would become known for their attacks on White settlements, and some would come to be allied against the United States. [187] Some of the leaders of the Lower Cherokee included Dragging Canoe, Tolluntuskee, Will Webber, Unacata, and Doublehead. [188]

Most who settled early in Northeast Arkansas and Southeast Missouri were Chickamauga Cherokee of the lower towns.

The first of those Cherokees to settle west of the Mississippi began to do so in 1785, following the Treaty of Hopewell. Some of the Cherokee, unwilling to comply with the treaty, traveled the Tennessee, Ohio, and Mississippi rivers in canoes to the St. Francis River, where they found a spot on its banks and settled. [189] In Northeast Arkansas, close to favored swampy hunting lands, they could live peacefully and be self-sustaining. In the ensuing years, many of their fellow Eastern tribesmen would follow.

This may not have been the earliest crossing of the Mississippi River by the Cherokee. Tradition says that some Cherokee, following the Treaty with South Carolina in 1721, followed the warrior Dangerous Man to the "unknown west," possibly the west side of the Mississippi River. [190]

In 1788, Cherokee Chief Tourquin sought permission from Spanish authorities at L'Anse a la Graisse, later New Madrid, Missouri, to settle in six villages in Louisiana. They were granted their request.

Thirty Cherokees received permission to settle near New Madrid in 1790. [191]

As early as 1755, the Cherokees were most likely hunting on the upper St. Francis River, as at that time they had "compelled" the miners at Mine La Motte near Fredericktown, Missouri, to abandon the mine. [192]

Some Cherokee lived on the St. Francis River in Dunklin County, Missouri as early as 1796, when Albert Tison, a land speculator, lived among them. [193]

In 1796, Connetoo, also known as Kannetoo and John Hill, led 10 Cherokee families and a few single men to Spanish Louisiana from their eastern homelands. Their original intention was to settle on the Arkansas River, but they settled on the St. Francis River in what is now northeast Arkansas. Later, he would be joined by White Man Killer and Webber. John W. Hunt, an Indian trader who had previously traded with Indians at Muscle Shoals, would also settle among them. [194]

Their settlement was about 40 miles west of present-day Memphis, upriver on the St. Francis River. These Cherokee settlers feared reprisal by their people for an incident that happened in June 1794 at Muscle Shoals on the Tennessee River, known as the Muscle Shoals Massacre. Two flatboats were attacked at Muscle Shoals, their belongings stolen and their slaves abducted. The party on the boats consisted of William Scott, of Natchez, and his two nephews, James and John Pettigrew, and 22 slaves. Scott and the Pettigrews were slain. John W. Hunt, deposed by Edwin T. Clark, a justice of the peace of Arkansas, would later state that those who participated in the incident included Connetoo, White Man Killer, Leed, The Terrapin, Webber, and others. [195]

Americans retaliated for that attack, and in September 1794, General James Robertson ordered the lower Cherokee towns destroyed. The Nickajack and Running Water towns were soon eradicated.

In 1800, six years later, six of the slaves captured at Muscle Shoals made their way to Fort Pickering, at Chickasaw Bluff, currently the site of Memphis, Tennessee, where they told Zebulon M. Pike of their capture at Muscle Shoals when their owner, John Pettigrew, was killed. Then they were taken to the village on the St. Francis River, where they were owned by White Man Killer, recently deceased. [196]

Connetoo, a chief of the St. Francis River Cherokee in 1810, wrote to Return J. Meigs, Agent to the Cherokee Nation, telling him that when he had first moved to the area, there was war surrounding them, but now he had "firm pease [sic] and was making good times." In the ensuing years, he wrote of the area becoming crowded as others had followed him and were more inclined to farming and raising stock. He also told of how the women were spinning and weaving. By 1813, however, he was concerned with theft by White men whom he had treated well, "in a stile [sic] to render him comfort." [197]

The great earthquakes of 1811-1812 would cause a lot of damage to the St. Francis River settlements, and many would move on to the White River.

Louis Bringier, of Louisiana, [198] while visiting the Cherokee assembled on the St. Francis River for an annual green corn celebration, reported a speech he witnessed on June 3, 1812, at Crowtown. The speech, by Cherokee prophet Skaquaw, also known as The Swan, was about the earthquakes. [199] Skaquaw had a vision about a month before the first earthquake while viewing the "blazing star," [200] on a night "when everything was silent, and the sky was clear as spring water."

Suddenly, he said, four lightnings departed from four points and then alighted at his feet. Picking it up, he saw two children "come towards me, one from the sunset and the other from sunrise." They told him they were messengers of the "Ever Great Spirit," who foretold a warning that the earth "will soon shake, like a horse who shakes the dust from his back." And he told them to move away from St. Francis River and travel toward the "sun set" until halted by a great river that runs toward the sunrise.

"Stop, plant corn, and hunt in peace until the last sign prepares you for happiness," he continued.

Bringier said there was a total evacuation of the St. Francis River area after this prophecy. They abandoned their farms, their cattle, and other property, he said, some moving to the White River and some to the Arkansas River. [201]

Connetoo, however, must have stayed behind for a while. Tolluntuskee, who had led a group of Cherokees to Arkansas in 1810, wrote in a letter to Return J. Meigs, U.S. Indian Agent to the Cherokee Nation, in March 1813, that the Cherokees had left the earthquake-flooded areas.

"For two years I stood in water with patience. I remained in that situation until my feet got cold." Yet, he noted, "Kan,ne,too [sic] is still standing in the water." [202]

Before the end of 1813, Connetoo, also known as John Hill, lived on the White River, along with several other Cherokee, including Chief Chickalee. Those living there were troubled by the White settlers who stole their horses and complained to Benjamin Howard, governor in and over the Territory of Missouri, in 1813.

"Father we a part of the Cherekees tribe of Indians; have settled on the White River a water of the Mississippi by we presume, the consent of the

Government of the United States," they said in a letter. "We are indeavouring to cultivate the soil for our support & wish to live unintirrupted [sic] by the malicious White people; but the revurse; [sic] there are a few bad men combined together for the purpose of stealing our horses." The men they named who were involved the incident, included Nicholas Trammel, Mote Askins, John Wells, Joseph Carnes, Robert Armstrong Barnett, Peter Tileo, Thomas James, John D. Chisholm, Demis Chisholm, Ignatious Chisholm, Jessey Isaacks, John Williams, Robert Trimble, William Trimble, William Smith, John Lafferty Sr., Ace Musick, ? Pain, and Joseph Pain as perpetrators.[203]

The Cherokees also claimed that at the hands of Trammel and Askins, they had lost as many as 20 horses in the last year. They had also solicited them to take part in their killing, robbing, and burning of houses of the honest and industrious White settlers near them.

"If some measures are not taken we shall in short time be left destitut [sic] of property and thereby prevented from pursuing our farms," the letter said. Also signing the letter were Thomas Graves, Wolollenny Doublehead, James Duvall, George Duvall, John Campbell, Corn Tassell, Teleskeske, Zoalkqua, [204] and others, mostly by making their marks. Other signers included Soanetar, Ayaokisby, Qualoloqui, Bare foot, Oakshellaaner, Zoateltar, Cultakenner, Hannelar, Kewarsulusky, Aremokelar, James Kolson, Warhails, Aarchy, Thomas, Toallemar, Bare Skin, Difan, Aitennoly, Gitup, Samuel, Cotten, Cokokattsky, and Choahar. [205]

This was not the first time Trammel had been accused of horse stealing. He and Mote Askey (Askins) were both indicted for horse theft in Livingston County, Tennessee, in 1809. Askey was Trammel's half-brother. Trammel did not appear for the first hearing in March 1810, but was given a second chance by the judge. By September, he was awaiting trial in the county jail. He was later deemed not guilty. The $1000 bail for skipping out was conditioned to be voided if he behaved well for two years. [206]

Both Trammel and the Cherokee village were situated near each other on White River near present-day Batesville. Nearby was an overland route from St. Louis to Natchitoches that crossed the White River. [207]

Trammel's Trace, a route into Spanish Texas, was named for Nicholas Trammel. It was the second major route into Spanish Texas from the United States and the first from the northern boundaries along the Red River, near what would become Fulton, Arkansas. The trails which became Trammel's Trace were used regularly after 1813 to transport horses and trade goods from the Red River prairies to Nacogdoches, across the Sabine River, and into Louisiana. The trace, along with El Camino Real de los Tejas from the east, was the earliest route into the Nacogdoches district of Spanish Texas from the United States. Because the Spanish crown deemed trade goods from the United States and the removal of mustangs from Texas illegal, smugglers needed a more obscure route. Trammel's Trace became such a route. [208]

The Cherokee in that area and possibly Chickalee had problems with horse stealing in 1816 when John Sullivan wrote to Missouri Territorial Gov. William Clark. [209] However, this time the Cherokees were being accused of the act. Sullivan claimed he had two pack horses stolen while near the Cherokee village located a few miles south of the White River. After going into the White settlement on the White River, [210] Sullivan hired "Mr. Shields," [211] and the aforementioned, Asa Musick [212] to go to the Indian village and try to retrieve his horses. Shields retrieved a horse that Sullivan claimed was his. However, the Cherokee, who gave up the horse willingly, complained to their agent, Major William Lovely, [213] that the horses had been formerly stolen from them. Sullivan claimed that the horses stolen from the Cherokees did not fit the description of those stolen from him and pleaded with Clark for help to resolve the matter. Lovely also told the Indians not to return the other horse Sullivan claimed was his and told Shields to return the one he took, according to the letter.

It is unknown when Chickalee left the area, but he would later be found living south of the Arkansas River, near present-day Dardanelle, at a place that would bear his name to this date. Chickalah [214] is the name bestowed upon a small community, a mountain, and a creek. Later settlers there would say he settled there as early as 1790. Perhaps this is when he first entered Arkansas Territory, or possibly he was one of those who received permission to settle near New Madrid in 1790. It is also possible he came with the later migrations, such as the one under the leadership of Toluntuskee.

However, he lived in Arkansas at least as early as 1813 when he and others sent their letter to Howard.

In 1811, Return J. Meigs, U.S. Indian Agent to the Cherokee, of Tennessee, sent annuities to the Arkansas Cherokee, as directed by the Secretary of War, William Eustis, [215] to be delivered by Samuel Riley, who worked as an interpreter for the agency. Riley took the goods in a flat-bottomed boat in December 1811. [216] Items, which amounted to $750, included various cloths and items to make clothing. [217] Riley turned back after reaching Fort Massac in Illinois territory on the Ohio River because of the New Madrid Earthquakes, leaving his goods at the fort.[218]

Fort Massac was damaged in the earthquakes of 1811-1812, possibly during the December 16, 1811 earthquakes, as the *Natchez Gazette* reported February 13, 1812, that chimneys, daubing, and plaster of houses were shaken down during the December 16 earthquakes in Fort Massac, Illinois. [219]

Damages during the quakes required repairs at the fort. On February 11, 1812, Lt. Samuel Price wrote to the Secretary of War that the earthquakes had damaged buildings at the fort. His successor, Lt. E.A. Allen, requested funds for repairs. [220]

The supplies left by Riley would be picked up by John Ross, as emissary, sent by Meigs to deliver the 1812 annuities to the Western Cherokees. Ross, who would later be Principal Chief (1828-1866) of the nation, left in December 1812 and arrived sometime before the middle of March 1813, where the goods were signed for by Talontiskee, (Tolluntuskee) Kannetoo (Connetoo), Kalahwaskee, Wahachee, and Oolonake. [221]

Annuities brought by Ross also included items for making clothing, as well as items for hunting and fishing, including shotguns, lead, gun powder, butcher knives, beaver traps, fish hooks, hatchets, and flint; items for farming, including hoes, and axes; and food items, as well as items for preparation, such as brown sugar, salt, bacon, coffee, a coffee pot, one skillet, two kettles, and bowls. Tobacco and many other items were also on the list, amounting to $902.[222]

Before returning home, Ross would assist Talontesky (Tolluntuskee) and Kannetoo (Connetoo) in writing the aforementioned letters back to Meigs and Lovely in Tennessee.

William Lewis Lovely, sub-agent of the Cherokee under Meigs, would depart for Arkansas in early April, "satisfied with Ross's description of the country." [223] After Agent Lovely arrived in Arkansas in the summer of 1813, he settled near Dardanelle. He soon called a council to establish temporary land boundaries between the Cherokee and White settlers. [224]

"In order to keep peace and harmony between them and their White brothers," [225] Lovely defined an area between the White and Arkansas rivers in July.

In May 1814, Lovely helped secure a bond with the Cherokees in favor of John D. Chisholm, aforementioned, in value received in the amount of $2,407.85. Chickalee, Tolluntuskee, who was principal chief, and 19 other Cherokees, signed the bond directing the President "if he shall see proper" to pay this out of their annuities in annual payments of $200. The bond was held by Samuel Moseley. [226]

Previously, it appears Chickalee had little trust in Chisholm when he and others made the complaint in early 1813. Maybe influenced by other Cherokees or possibly Major Lovely, he decided to trust Chisholm. Another of the 1813 group who signed the bond was Thomas Graves.

Chisholm told Meigs in 1814 that he had been contracted by the Western Cherokee to represent them in Washington, D.C., to make a legal claim to the Arkansas lands and for the right to establish a nation separate from the Old Nation in the East. [227]

In 1817, a treaty was concluded at the Cherokee Agency with the "chiefs, head men, and warriors," of the Cherokee nation east of the Mississippi, and the Cherokees on the Arkansas River. Ceded were two tracts of land in the East in exchange for a tract in Northwest Arkansas. The treaty defined a partial boundary of the land in Arkansas as beginning on the north side of the Arkansas River at the mouth of Point Remove Creek in a straight line northwardly to Chataunga Mountain, the first hill above Shield's Ferry on the White River, and running up between the said rivers. The Western boundary was not defined.

While in the Eastern part of the nation in 1818, Tolluntuskee and others, visited Brainerd Mission, a Christian mission to the Cherokee. Here, he gained a desire to see such a work established on the Arkansas River. "We opened our ears with great pleasure to your talk; because our children are becoming numerous, and we love our children," he wrote in June to Jeremiah Evarts. At that time, Evarts was treasurer with the American Board of Commissioners for Foreign Missions and editor of the *Panoplist*, a religious magazine. "When the teachers come to Arkansas they will find themselves at home," he said. [228]

The board assigned the Rev. Cephas Washburn and the Rev. Albert Finney, and assistants Jacob Hitchcock and James Orr to establish the mission.[229]

However, before they arrived, ministers from another mission arrived in June 1819. Chickalee was among the Arkansas chiefs named in a letter from Meigs introducing the Rev. Job C. Vinal and the Rev. Epaphras Chapman, from the United Foreign Missions Society of Utica, New York, seeking to work among them. [230]

However, as these were not from the mission Tolluntuskee had requested to come to Arkansas, the ministers traveled up the river, establishing a mission among the Osage. [231] Washburn arrived in July 1820, and Dwight Presbyterian Mission was founded in August 1820, on the banks of the Illinois Bayou near present-day Russellville, Arkansas.

Tolluntuskee did not live, however, to see the mission established, as he died sometime before the first missionaries arrived. [232]

In November 1820, Richard Searcy, secretary for the Arkansas territorial legislature at this time, [233] was requested by Miller to meet with the Cherokee on the White River. From the contents of the letter, this was presumably to discuss Osage prisoners. [234] At the White River, he discovered the Cherokee were gone. He traveled to Davidsonville to find they had crossed the Black River and gone to the Delawares on the St. Francis River, 10 days before his arrival. Hoping to overtake them, he traveled to the Shawnee on Apple Creek, near Cape Girardeau, Missouri. However, they had not been there. There was one prisoner there, and Searcy was informed that the others were 80 miles distant. He waited for the Cherokee, but when they did not arrive, he traveled on to meet with Col. Menard at Kaskaskia, and finally met up with him in St. Genevieve, Missouri. Menard told him the Indians were all out hunting, and the prisoners were with the Shawnee, except for one prisoner at Apple Creek. Searcy deduced that the Cherokee had not traveled any further than the Delawares on the St. Francis River, [235] and he returned home. [236]

In June 1823, a council meeting, commonly referred to as the Treaty of Council Oaks, was held at the home of Cherokee Agent David Brearley on the Arkansas River. At this council, some of the Cherokee were told that they were living illegally south of the Arkansas River, on land given to the Choctaw in 1820. He also told them he had the authority to have them removed, to which they replied that the Choctaw did not care if they lived there. That was true up until December 1824, when the Choctaw agreed to a treaty redrawing boundaries and doing away with the tract in Arkansas Territory. [237]

It is unknown if Chickalee ever moved north of the Arkansas River again since he had left the White River settlement.

A little further south of Chickalah lived another well-known Cherokee chief and his people. Tachee or Dutch, [238] as he was known, lived near present-day Danville for a time. A creek and a township in that area still bear the name of Dutch.

The Cherokee in this area cleared patches of land for cultivation, designating each plot with cornerstones. They were said to be peaceable and not engaged in war with anyone, except when "they were called upon to resist the assaults of the Osages." [239]

Chickalee would become known as a great speaker when he was chosen by several warriors to speak on his and their behalf concerning continuing warfare with the Osage tribe during a council in the fall of 1823.[240] His words were "a torrent of eloquence, and under its thundering power and melting pathos, the stubborn" Takatoka [241] gave way to an agreement of peace, noted the Rev. Washburn. [242]

It is unknown what Chickalee said to encourage peace, but it is interesting considering his earlier brush with the Osage. Possibly, the incident was his incentive for promoting peace.

Chief Chickalee and his party of hunters were injured by the Osage Indians sometime before 1822 at a "time when the contracting parties were under a positive agreement to keep the peace, and not to injure each other." Representatives from both tribes gathered at Belle Point, including Cherokees, Waterminnow, Young Glass, and Wat Webber, and the Osage, Claremore, and Mad Buffalo, as well as others from both tribes in July 1822 to work out a strategy to resolve disputes and establish ground rules for living nearby. One of the items this treaty stipulated was that the Osage were to pay Chickalee and his party $300 for "an injury" during a time of peace. The treaty was just between the tribes and was not ratified by the U.S. Government.[243]

The incident in which Chickalee was "injured" was possibly in February 1820, when a party of Cherokee hunters was attacked on the Poteau River. Three Cherokees were killed and their furs stolen. The war party was under the leadership of Osage Mad Buffalo. [244]

On February 10, a Cherokee meeting in council at Webber's prepared a letter demanding restitution in the form of payment for the furs and surrender of as many men as they had lost. "Brothers, we have received a blow from the Osages with whom we have supposed ourselves on terms of peace," wrote ten Cherokee chiefs, including Takatoka, John Jolley, and Black Fox, to Reuben Lewis, their agent, and William Bradford, commanding officer at Fort Smith. "We let you know our distresses - our men have not all come in & we cannot say at this time how many we have lost," continuing to say they had lost at least three men and 14 horses. They also requested that the Osage "would let as many of the offenders who killed our people suffer death as we shall have lost by them." The letter ends with their request to be paid for their losses. [245]

Conflicts would continue between the Osage and Cherokee for many years. In 1828, as part of the Treaty with the Western Cherokee, the Cherokee would surrender their lands in Arkansas and move to their new reservation in present-day Oklahoma.

Throughout the years, Chickalee continued to hunt in the swamplands, long after moving out of the area, and kept his associations with those living there. Many local legends in Northeast Arkansas and Southeast Missouri would attest to his strong presence in the area in the 1820s and 1830s.

Chapter 5

Hunting Trails

"It was with a heavy heart," Sam said, *"that the hunting began that year."*

Following Chickalee's burial, Sam, his dad Moonshine, Big Knife, some of the visiting hunters, and a few of the women headed into Arkansas along an old trail, traversed by many before them. Their destination was an old Indian camp that some called home before going west. Leaving Chilletecaux, followed by a few of their dogs, they traveled north along the old Shawnee Trail, [246] *taking a left where the road forked. They crossed several swampy areas with the water coming up as far as the top of the horse's legs in places. Further down the trail, they came to an old pine tree,* [247] *which served as a marker where the trail headed northwest toward the highland and a place to cross the St. Francis River. His dad knew this way well, even though it was just a path. Once they reached the island near the river, they camped for the night to get an early start in the morning.*

At the St. Francis River, the horses were ferried across behind the canoes. [248] *A couple of canoes were hidden in the brush along the banks, further upstream from where they would cross. The men directed the canoes across the river, pulling the swimming horses behind. The dogs, Old Blue, Sis, and Cane, hitched a ride in the canoes.*

"In Arkansas, we would hit Crowley's Ridge and follow an old trail," he said. *From there, they could travel northeast toward another crossing of the river at Chalk Bluff or southeast down the ridge. Sam remembered how the well-traveled road had piqued his interest concerning who and what had made the deep marks upon the land.*

The land on the ridge was much different than what he was used to in the swamps. It was high, dry, and forested with lots of pine trees. The Sassafras trees were huge.

"I am always watching the land," he told James, *"for plants that could be useful."* His grandmother had taught him what to gather at what time of the year. There were plenty of items to collect for medicinal purposes.

Sam told of how that night they camped at the old abandoned Shawnee village on Crowley's Ridge, where the men had spent a few hunting seasons and where he would experience his first bear hunt. They were also planning to gather some lead for the hunting season. With the arrival of the extra hunters, they could use as much as possible.

The old Shawnee village and the nearby Delaware village were occupied not too many years before they camped there. Roads and trails went out in several different directions from there and the old Delaware village. Nearby was a fresh spring where they gathered their water. It was a delightful place, Sam recalled. Not swampy, but hilly with a clear creek running nearby. He could understand why there had been villages there in the past.

"Chickalee had also spent a lot of time in this area," Sam told James. Locally, he was known as Corn Meal. He and Big Knife, Buckeye, and Keshotte had traveled up and down the ridge in their earlier years. The early settlers in this area hunted and traveled along the trails with them. Corn Meal and Big Knife were often employed to help one of the greatest cattlemen on this side of the river round up his stock in the spring.

While the women tended to duties at the village, the men, joined by a few settlers in the area, made several three to four day-long trips to former camps as they pursued bear, elk, and deer. They would head back to the main camp to cache their furs and leave the game for the women to dress before heading out again.

"While we hunted, the women would busy themselves with work around the camp," he said. They would make the bear meat into bacon and dry the venison for later use. They would also render the fat into bear oil and store it away in skins to be used later in trade. In between food preparation and taking care of the hides, they would often head out in search of the gifts of the land - wild plant foods, honey, sassafras root, spicewood, [249] chestnuts, hickory nuts, acorns, persimmons, and poke salat. [250]

Sam told James how the skins were processed.

Soaking them overnight in water helped them scrape the hair off the hide the next day. After that, they would mix the brains with an equal amount of water in a pot, place them in a coarse linen bag, and boil for an hour. When it cooled, they would rub the skins through the bag until the water took on a milky color. Adding the skins to the pot, the mixture was kneaded into them by hand. Then the skins were pulled across a board until dry, white, and soft.

To keep the hides from becoming hard again, they would be smoked. This process involved sewing two of the hides together. Next, a fire was built in a hole dug into the ground. When the fire had a bright glow, old and rotten wood would be added to the coals to make a thick smoke. The skins were placed over the smoke until they turned brown on the outside. Finally, the skins were turned inside out, and the process was repeated. [251]

In camp, a mortar was often made for their corn using the stump of an old tree with a hole cut in it. In this hole, they would pound the maize and use it to make breadstuffs.

"We stayed a few weeks that year at the village and then traveled south toward an old river crossing." The crossing was at Old Town. [252] Here, the river was narrow and an easy place to cross over to Buffalo Island.

"At Old Town, we met up with some other hunters," he said. Those hunters took a land route from Chilletecaux, south down the old Shawnee Trail on the Grand Prairie. Then they took a path across Buffalo Creek and toward Horse Island. They continued southward along the river down Old Town Ridge, where several mounds existed, [253] crossing the river at Old Town.

Although travel through the wetlands was troublesome and hard, time and experience had taught them where and when they could cross the sloughs from highland to highland, during dry times.

"We had lots of hunting stories to tell," he recalled. There were many bear encounters, deer and elk, and the elusive panthers. The men who traveled overland had met up with their old friend Wiley Clarkston along the way.

"The elk, like the buffalo, are long gone now," said Sam.

Together, the hunters traveled to Maumelle Prairie near Deep Landing on the river, where they met up with some more hunters who had come down the St. Francis River.

Those hunters had left the village of Chilletecaux headed westward, entering the spreads of the river in their home away from home – their canoes. They were loaded with their huts, foodstuffs, buffalo robes, guns, and ammunition. Near the village, a section of the river known as Varner's River[254] led them toward the main river.

"It was more of a wilderness then," said Sam. The deeper they went into the area, the more wildlife they saw. Snakes shimmied along the banks, turtles sunned atop old logs, and the muskrats made their way across the water. Around the bends, they often spotted a large cat lounging on a tree limb, seemingly unaware of their approach. Many times, these cats would slink off into the brush rather than encounter them.

A few miles downstream, there was a camping spot where they spent several days setting their traps and checking them. [255] After securing their bounty in their canoes, which contained all they needed for comfort in the wilderness, the group headed toward the main river, camping at Gum Slough Island and Indian Hill Island. There was a mound at Indian Hill, once home to the "old ones." Near here was another good place to ferry across the St. Francis River. On the other side of the river, there was another island. From there, they could make their way toward the ridge following the higher lands. Once on the ridge, the men followed paths to the old Shawnee and Delaware villages in Arkansas.

"We got supplies after meeting up with a trader that year," he noted. Trader John Nicholas [256] had stopped at Maumelle [257] Prairie. He had loaded his canoe with food items, guns and supplies, blankets, cloth, bridles and stirrups, nesting kettles, cups, spoons, tobacco, pipes, coffee, steel traps, and other items to offer the local Indians. Besides bear oil, honey, furs, and skins, the men had to offer; the women had made some deerskin moccasins to trade with him. [258]

Leaving Maumelle Prairie, the men hunted nearby for a few weeks before making their way down to the marked tree area where they planned to meet up with the rest of the hunters. Here, they would again meet up with Nicholas and all the hunters who placed themselves under Moonshine's command, including the hunters who had traveled south down Chilletecaux River toward the Little River and into Big Lake. Following the left bank of the *swampy lake, the Little River emerged from its southern end. A little way from here, they passed an area where the Pemiscot Bayou empties into the river, not far from where Sam lived on a low ridge. Following the Little River, the visiting hunters reached the marked tree area, uniting all four groups of hunters that had left the village of Chilletecaux.*

This area offered them great access to the Little River, the St. Francis River, the Mississippi River, the sunk lands, and Crowley's Ridge. Not far from this hunting spot, on the ridge, they would often travel to where their old friend Judge Hall lived, to trade for supplies of corn meal and salt used in preserving their meat.

"My early years of hunting were great," Sam related. Through those years, Sam listened to the many stories his dad had to tell about the former residents. He had made his way all through these lands and waters encompassed by Southeast Missouri and Northeast Arkansas, and further, pursuing the bounty the land had to offer in the heat of the summer, the cold of the winter, and in the company of his father, brother, and others of like mind and spirit.

Much of Southeast Missouri and Northeast Arkansas near the St. Francis River in those early years was swampy and low or sunken, resulting from consistent flooding and the somersaults of the earth. Waterways offered the best access to the area, as roads, which were mere footpaths, were often impassable during high water. The land paths frequently followed high elevations such as Buffalo Island, Crowley's Ridge, or the prairie near Chilletecaux. Those paths offered a huge challenge. They were easily overgrown and often filled with fallen debris. It was nearly impossible to take an oxcart down any one of the paths. Only the well-trodden prairie paths, such as the old Shawnee trail in Dunklin County along what was called Grand Prairie, were dry year-round.

Wandering animals in search of sustenance first laid down the land paths, followed by hunters searching for the same game. Later, paths by Native Americans would follow a route between one tribe and another, a portage between waterways, a course next to a river, or a route used for trading. Trails in the area were followed first by the "old ones," later the resident tribes, and after that, the emigrant tribes to which Sam and Moonshine belonged, then hunters, and finally more permanent settlers of the land. Near these well-traveled spots and springs, where the animals first walked and watered, camps and villages would spring up, followed by permanent settlements.

From Chilletecaux village, one could travel north or south along the old Shawnee Trail. North to Crowley's Ridge, one could travel southwest into Arkansas along an older trail near the Chalk Bluff, or northeast at this junction toward Bloomfield.

Southward from the village of Chilletecaux, along the Grand Prairie, the Shawnee Trail led to Arkansas and to Buffalo Island. Before reaching Arkansas, one could take the old Shawnee Trail a few miles and then turn west during low water times, following a mere path that would cross Buffalo Creek and then southwest to a St. Francis River crossing. [259]

Below Chilletecaux in Dunklin County, Missouri, large north-to-south fissures, which aboriginal inhabitants said were caused by the great earthquakes, filled with water and fractured the land. These ran parallel to creeks or sloughs, some of which carry the names of Indians or Indian camping spots. [260]

Seneca Slough was named for the Seneca Indians who lived there before removal. During high water, Seneca Slough joined with Buffalo Creek, and an island was formed, called Seneca Island. These Indians were possibly those who were enumerated at Chilletecaux in 1831. John Brown, a Seneca, previously mentioned in Chapter 1, lived in the swamps below New Madrid before 1832. [261]

Indian Camp Slough, in the eastern part of Holcomb Township in Missouri, was said to be the spot of several Indian camps. [262] Kinamore Slough, an old slough or swamp in the southwest part of the county, was named for Chief Kinamore, who is mentioned in local histories. The slough continued into Arkansas. [263]

John Ease Camp, most likely named for Moonshine's long-time friend John East, was a hunting camp used by East long after White settlements were in the area. [264]

Wiley Clarkston and James Baker settled at Horse Island, in Southwest Dunklin County, currently Senath, in 1833. Clarkston's son, Riley, told of crossing the river opposite Bowlin [265] Island when he needed to go to Gainesville, Arkansas, for a physician. He would cross in a canoe with his horse swimming behind him. [266] Gainesville was the Greene County, Arkansas seat of justice as early as 1840. [267] There was a post office at Gainesville as early as 1842.[268]

Young Clarkston killed as many as 50 to 75 bears before Christmas each season in those days. He was associated with the Indians in the area when they still lived there, and his wife told of how she was taught how to pound her bread and coffee in a mortar by an Indian woman. This was before there were any horse mills and before they could afford a steel hand mill. [269] Wiley, along with James Baker, hunted and killed some of the last bison in the area in the 1840s. [270]

W.H. Horner was also an early settler on Little River in 1832. Later, the place where he settled was called Hornersville, but earlier it was called Hornerstown. It was a trading post where Indians and hunters would trade furs for traps and ammunition. [271] The Shawnee trail wound southward through this area on its way into Arkansas.

A lot of hunting travel went through the swampy waterways at that time. It was easier to go from highland to highland or island to island by water, except along the prairie, where it was dry. Westward from the village, one could reach the St. Francis River through Varner's River, named for an early settler in the area. Eastward, this same river, called Chilletecaux, would lead to Little River, except during dry times.

Traveling on the St. Francis River northward from where Varner's River joined it was difficult at that time because the river spread out from the main channel and split into several smaller ones. The junction of Chilletecaux River and Varner's River was clogged with downed trees and cypress knees, rising almost to the surface, impeding navigation. The spreads went on for miles and merged into a cypress swamp before moving to the main channel. From there, northward for many miles, it was not navigable due to large rafts, which consisted of uprooted or downed trees, affixed to the bottom of the river with branches that collected floating debris.

Southward toward the state line between Missouri and Arkansas, the St. Francis River alternated between well-defined channels and a thick cypress swamp with low water levels. Toward Maumelle Prairie, the river was better defined and less swampy but spread out into a lake that reached toward Crowley's Ridge.

Continuing southward, the water that spread out into the sunken lands was obstructed with logs and tree stumps as it traveled toward its confluence with the mouth of the Little River. [272]

From this spot, in what would become Marked Tree and where the hunters often camped, the St. Francis River flowed freely toward the Mississippi River.

The group of hunters that Sam was part of entered what would become Greene County, Arkansas, after crossing the St. Francis River on their trek to the former Indian villages.

Deputy Surveyor William Clarkson noted the two villages near each other when he surveyed Township 16 North, Range 5 East in 1823. One was a Shawnee village, and one was a Delaware village. The deserted villages, along Village Creek, were intersected by several trails. [273]

Northward from the village area, one could travel toward Chalk Bluff, not far from the town of St. Francis. Near here, War Chief Chetana-Lenon, also known as Strong Man, once lived, according to Godfrey Lesieur. This war chief, Lesieur noted, treated him with "marked hospitality," not long after returning from Osage country, along with 100 warriors, and 40 Osage scalps.[274] This appears to be a large battle. The Battle of Claremore Mound or Massacre, between the Osage and the Western Cherokee, took place in October 1817, and many Osage were killed. The Cherokee were joined in their fight by allies of the Shawnee, Delaware, and others.

A trail, connected to a trail that led from the mouth of the St. Francis River, traveled through the Delaware village and on to Davidsonville. [275]

The road northwest from the Delaware village led toward Benjamin Crowley's home. [276] This was the first settlement on Crowley's Ridge, and in 1820, the first road east of the National Road built in Lawrence County was cut from Old Davidsonville to Crowley's home. [277]

Crowley was associated with the Indians and was also interested in where they obtained their lead. A story is told in the history of Craighead County of how Ben Crowley, who was on friendly terms with the Indians in the area, was visited on a cold, wintry day by Corn Meal, Buckeye, and another Indian. They had intentions, it was said, of telling where the lead was located, but were insulted because Crowley did not invite them into his home, and therefore they did not tell him their secret. [278]

On a bluff, north of the village, there was a place where Indians met in council, according to James Hanover, who was a slave in the Crowley home. "Old Jim," as he was called, told of how the Indians met there once a month in large numbers and would go away for a few days, returning with lead. His story added to the legend of lead in the area. Hanover believed they obtained the lead from Poplar Creek. [279]

A lump of lead and a lead bullet were two items recovered at the Delaware village site in recent years, noted Dan F. Morse and Phyllis A. Morse in their *Archaeology of the Central Mississippi Valley*. [280]

A settlement near the former Delaware village was known as Delaware Hill, where a post office was established in 1844. [281] The settlement, south of the former village, was called Greensborough on December 12, 1850, and later Greensboro. [282] Continuing southward, one could travel to Bolivar and Greenfield, where Richmond Hall was the postmaster in 1837. [283] From there, one could go to Farm Hill, Walnut Camp, [284] and what would become Wittsburg, [285] at least as early as 1848 when a post office existed there. [286] The area near here was long occupied by Native Americans, with the Cherokee occupying the area before moving to Western Arkansas.

A trail from the former Delaware village headed southeast and led to the St. Francis River at Old Town, now Lake City. There, one could cross the river onto Buffalo Island. Southward from Old Town, one could travel to Maumelle Prairie near Deep Landing on the St. Francis River, and down beside the river to its mouth, near Helena, on the Mississippi River, founded in 1833. Springs along a trail several miles west and south of Greensboro, on the west side of the ridge, included Wood Springs and Martin Spring, where Daniel Martin settled in 1829. This area would become part of the city of Jonesboro in Craighead County. At the time, this area was Greenfield Township in Poinsett County. There was, at one time, a Native American village at this site, and in the ensuing years, Indians would continue to camp at this spot. Martin was one of their hunting companions. Martin kept mail at his house in 1835, and it was considered the first post office in what would be Craighead County. Martin may have lived in Old Davidsonville, an early settlement in Randolph County, as early as 1820. [287]

A map constructed from a manuscript map attached to the 1860 census of Craighead County shows some early roads in the area. From Crowley's, one could travel south to Greensboro, William Puryear's [288] home, westerly through Jonesboro, and south toward Martin Spring and McDaniel's [289] before heading eastward and south toward Bolivar [290] in Poinsett County. A different route led south from Crowley's toward Big Creek settlement, [291] Broadway, [292] Matt Love's, [293] and Grinder, [294] before heading to Jacksonport [295] in Jackson County. A road led from there to Bolivar. Another route led from Davidsonville. [296] The route crossed both southward roads from Crowley's, crossing an area near where the Delaware Indian village was, but not designated on this map. From there, it went southeast to Lester Landing, [297] and Old Town (Lake City), [298] where it crossed the river and headed onto Buffalo Island to Stottsville, [299] Old Town Ridge, north of Stottsville, and on toward Big Lake. At Old Town, the road also went south to Maumelle Prairie and further southward. Northward from Lester Landing, the road went to Gainesville. Indian villages are shown at Old Town, north of Martin Spring, south of Puryear's, on the L'Anguille River, Southwest of Old Town Ridge, Maumelle Prairie, southwest of Stottsville, [300] and west of Maumelle Prairie. [301]

At Oak Ridge, near present-day Bono, [302] some Delaware lived at one time. Along a trail that went from north to south, there was an early post office in what became Craighead County. [303]

In the spring, following the hunting season, Big Knife and Corn Meal often assisted Joe Radford in gathering his cattle. He was called "the great cattle man" by early Greene County settler Henry Holcomb. [304] They helped Radford locate, mark, and brand his cattle. After the frost killed the vegetation on the ridge, planters and stockmen in the area often drove their livestock into the bottom lands for the winter, where they came out in the spring "beef fat," according to State Representative James M. Livesay, in the 1868 Survey of Arkansas Counties by the State Land Commissioner J.M. Lewis. The soil of the bottomlands, a rich black and sandy mix, was covered with a winter grass that resembled wheat fields, offering an everlasting range for the livestock. There were thousands of acres covered in cane, he said. [305] Livestock usually roamed free at that time and often strayed far away in the winter months. [306]

Radford, who appears to have moved around, lived on the west side of the ridge in what was Greene County at the time, when Corn Meal and Big Knife helped gather his cattle. [307] Joe Raotiford [sic] was enumerated in Greenfield Township in the 1840 Poinsett County census. [308] Joe Ratchford (Joseph Radford), along with James Ratchford (Radford), were on the Greene County tax records in 1834-1836 and 1837-1840. [309] Radford and his brother James were at different times referred to as Ratchford, Raditsford, Radisford, or Ratsford.

Joseph Radford operated a store at the site of Old Bolivar in 1839. Noted as Ratchford, he settled in 1844 near an area that became the Grinder

Settlement in Craighead County, near Jonesboro. Here, he raised horses and cattle. Many of the horses were never bridled, and when he died, the horses became wild and wandered into the Cache River bottoms in the "wide savannas of an island where the grass was luxuriant." This highland in the Cache River spreads between Bono and Egypt, became known as Horse Island. [310]

Other early settlers also befriended the local Indians, joining them in camp and on hunts.

Rufus Snoddy came to the area in 1830, settling near what would become downtown Jonesboro. Southwest of Snoddy's farm, Indians lived or camped in the woods, as well as a couple of miles east on Whiteman's Creek, on the east side of where the current city of Jonesboro is now. He would often hunt and camp with the Indians in the area and be away from home for long periods. [311] Snoddy's hunting partner, Daniel O'Guinn, settled in the area in 1836. His son, William, told of spending his youth hunting in the woods with the Indians and his 20 hunting dogs. [312]

Maumelle Prairie had been home to Native Americans in the area, and the trader Nicholas spent many years offering his goods to the local Indians still in the area in the late 1830s and early 1840s.

The first attempt to settle in that area was when Mr. and Mrs. Rittenhouse left Chilletecaux village in 1815 with a group of people who planned to look for places to live. The Rittenhouse family decided the adjacent prairie to the river landing would be a good place to raise a crop. Others in their party went downstream to look for other places to live. Not finding what they were looking for, they returned to Chilletecaux. Not long afterward, a dog that had been with the Rittenhouse family returned to the village, looking starved and whining. This alarmed those at Chilletecaux, who armed themselves and set out for Maumelle Prairie, where they found Mr. Rittenhouse dead near a cabin he had been building. Mrs. Rittenhouse was never found. Another version says Mrs. Rittenhouse was decapitated. [313]

Indians were settled on the prairie, but were considered friendly and not to blame for this tragedy. Mrs. Rittenhouse was the sister of Nicholas. [314] Nicholas met his wife, Amanda Snoddy, at Maumelle Prairie during his 1837 trading venture. The daughter of Rufus Snoddy, she was visiting with her uncle, Alanson Snoddy, who had made his home at Deep Landing in the late 1830s. The Snoddy brothers first lived in Poinsett County as early as 1823. Rufus bought land in what would become Jonesboro in 1830. [315]

Others who offered staples to the nomadic travelers included Richmond Hall, who settled in Poinsett County in 1828 when it was a "wilderness of woods and canebrake," according to local history. [316] He held the positions of county and probate judge as well as sheriff at one time, and in 1844 served in the state legislature.

"A noted Indian Moonshine with two of his trusty partners, corn meal and butcher knife, made their annual visit back to spend the fall and winter hunting and trapping," noted Thomas Stone in his recollections of his early life in Poinsett County. They would come into the area near Old Bolivar and go to the home of Judge Hall, who lived near Newman Springs, east of Harrisburg.

"They made it to their base," said Stone, "after getting a supply of cornmeal, salt, and other items. They would proceed on to their camping ground, which was at or near where Marked Tree is now located." [317]

Friendships were forged and memories were made with the early settlers and the Indians, who shared their knowledge of survival in the swamps and the ridge, which helped build a way of life for the early settlers.

The younger Lesieur, Godfrey's son F.V., recalled Chief Chetana-Lenon personally bidding him farewell and presenting him with a tomahawk when he left from Point Pleasant, Missouri, when Lesieur was a small child.

"Letle captain," he said, as he laid his hand upon his head, "Maybe sometime maybe Ingun and Big Knife make heap war, you be Big Knife captain, you talk French; Ingun no hurt you – good bye, Letle Captain." [318]

Many left the area during the 1830s, most never to return. A few remained behind, secreting themselves in the swampy land.

They were all remembered. [319]

Chapter 6
The Blessing

Today, wildlife was plentiful in the river, on the banks, in the trees, and the sky, as they paddled along. They shared the space with ducks, geese, and otters, and watched the deer come in for a drink. Once, rounding a bend, they spotted a panther slapping at a fish, but she quickly ran off. She and the coyotes, wolves, and bears were a bit more elusive, but they were there.

Sam still hunted bears and wolves, but it was his first bear hunt that he chose to tell James about. It was the first year he hunted, and they were camped at the old Shawnee village on the ridge. The sound of the hounds was almost deafening as they hit upon a bear while he and a few of the men were walking through the woods on their way to gather water.

"Some of the others and I were on our way to gather some fresh water from a spring when the dogs hit upon a bear," he recalled. "The hounds made an awful racket," as they started toward the bear.

"Yip, yip, ahwooo," and off they flew, as if they had wings instead of legs. The men sprang into action. "I was unsure of what to do, but I followed them." Slashing and cutting briars and cane, the men found their way through the brush.

Following the sound of the dogs, they came upon one that lay dying with a huge slash across her back. "That scared me and sent a chill up my spine, but the others trudged on with little fear, so I followed."

Catching up with the animal, the dogs flew toward its sides in an attempt to bring it down. The large black bear swiped at the hounds, daring them to come closer. The sound of the approaching men sent the bear scurrying up a tree. Moments later, a couple of shots rang out. His dad's long-time companion, John Big Knife, [320] had called the bear his and shot it. The bear fell, hitting the earth with a thud and shaking the ground like an earthquake. The dogs pounced as the men attempted to call them off. Injured but not dead, the bear jumped up and attempted to flee as Big Knife felled him with another shot to the head. The bruin let out a loud cry as he lay dying.

Retelling that story brought a gleam to his eye, and a smile crept across his face. "I wasn't one bit ready." That encounter in his first year to hunt is how he learned; through fresh and raw encounters, smack in the middle of the harsh realities of life. Sam was a real trouper and gained the respect of the seasoned hunters.

"We never went back to the village of Chilletecaux to live that year, after my first hunt," Sam told James. The wild environs of the Pemiscot Bayou, in what would become Mississippi County, Arkansas, became their haven following the hunt of 1837-1838.

For years, the villagers at Chilletecaux had faced the threat of leaving their beloved home as more and more of the native peoples were pushed westward. Only a few short years ago, some of their friends from the area had been moved west.

The hardships of those traveling west and those who had left before did not escape their ears. "We heard some of the stories of those traveling through the area on their way west," Sam told James.

"Some of those stories still send chills down my spine," he said. The stories of removal only got worse as the years passed. Stories were told of how the people were driven from their homes like cattle; how they suffered and died while others took their belongings; and how they were left to freeze just on the other side of the river, not too far from there. The tears did not belong only to those travellers; they filled the eyes of those who knew, as well.

"We shed many tears, too," he said.

While many native peoples had traveled westward over the preceding years, it was the travels of the Cherokee that worried them then, and the fear that all would soon be forced to leave their homelands.

"We were all afraid," Sam said, "Some of us were Cherokee."

The plight of the Cherokee was not the only factor that influenced them to leave their beloved village. Indians were just not wanted in the state of Missouri. They knew it was only a matter of time before they would be evicted.

Deeper into the swamps, where watery footsteps were not noticeable, became an ideal place for them. Pemiscot Bayou had been a favored camping spot for them for years. The higher land here had always proven to withstand the flooding from the rising water of the bayou and had been the home of earlier peoples in the area, Sam had been told.

"This area became a safe place for us," Sam said. Besides, it was also a hunter's paradise, where all kinds of wildlife existed, providing a way of life, not unknown to the region but sustaining to the new settlers. His family continued to live through the pursuit of hunting, as did many generations before them.

They were happy with their move to the area, he told James, as it has been a blessing in hunting and trapping. He and his dad had traveled all over the area, and up and down the rivers in pursuit of wildlife to trade. It was a good living.

While James listened, he did not understand very well, having spent most of his early life not worrying about where he was going to live or what he was going to eat. He had never been forced from his home. Growing up, his father, gone now, was an architect in Mobile, Alabama, [321] and in 1860 held five slaves. [322] Just a little more than 30 years old, James had traveled quite a bit and had studied abroad before the war. He was accustomed to a fine lifestyle, traveling aboard steamboats, visiting Memphis and other places, going to the opera, and eating at fine establishments. He was well-read and *kept up with the world news, subscribing to several publications and books, as well as the Memphis Appeal.* [323]

Sam, not yet 50, was used to a simpler lifestyle, walking or canoeing to where he wanted to go, and killing what he ate. He was content living off the land.

Their differences didn't stop at lifestyles. Sam looked like his ancestors with long, dark hair and copper-colored skin. He was a small and wiry man. [324] *James looked dignified with freshly trimmed hair and fine clothing. He was stout and rather portly.* [325]

They were quite the incongruous pair.

The Cherokee had been moving westward since the late 1700s. In 1817, some of those who had moved westward lived on a reservation in western Arkansas. Following a treaty with them in 1828, Western Cherokee moved to Indian Territory in Oklahoma. More voluntary groups of Eastern Cherokee moved to the territory not long after traveling down the Tennessee, Ohio, Mississippi, and Arkansas rivers.

The Indian Removal Act, signed into law by President Andrew Jackson in 1830, authorized the president to negotiate with southern Native American tribes for removal west of the Mississippi River in exchange for their land. While this act negotiated with several tribes, it paved the way for the forced expulsion of the Cherokee.

The Cherokee who came the closest to the area where Sam lived included the Benge Detachment of Cherokees, who traveled north of them. The Benge Detachment, conducted by John Benge, crossed the Mississippi River at Iron Banks, now Columbus, Kentucky, in November 1838. After crossing the St. Francis River, the group headed southwest, crossing the Current River in Arkansas. [326]

In Arkansas, a part of the group went into the town of Batesville to have their carriages repaired and horses shod, while the rest of the party continued toward Izard County. One account in December from the *Batesville News* in the *Arkansas Gazette* noted the travelers were "destitute of shoes and other necessary articles of clothing," and had suffered the loss of 50 members of their party since leaving Alabama. [327]

After receiving repairs, the party rejoined the others in Izard County and crossed the White River at Talbert's Ferry. A young man, W.B. Flippen, assisting the ferryman, said that while some of the party were well dressed and riding good horses, most were "poorly clad. Some of the women had only blankets wrapped around them." Some carried infants, wrapped inside a blanket or cloth, attached to their mother's backs.

"Instead of their stopping to make terms to cross on the ferryboat, they never pretended to halt but waded across the river, women and men, all except the few who had horses and carriages. They did not pretend to let the women who had papooses ride. It reminded me of a drove of cattle crossing a stream," he said.

Southward, the closest a Cherokee route came to Sam and his family was one that crossed the Mississippi River and traveled on the Military Road from Memphis to Little Rock, across the Mississippi River bottom lands. A detachment under the leadership of Lieutenant Edward Deas, U.S. Army, traveled through the area following their departure from Ross's Landing in Tennessee in October 1838. On this route, they would cross the St. Francis River at William Strong's home. [328] Strong, an early settler of St. Francis County, was a postmaster there in 1827. [329]

The Cherokee were not the only ones to suffer in this mass expulsion. During the years following the Indian Removal Act, an estimated 60,000 Indians, their slaves, White spouses, and Christian missionaries traveled through Arkansas on their way to Indian Territory. The removal included an estimated 21,000 Creek, 16,000 Cherokee, 12,500 Choctaw, 6,000 Chickasaw, 4,200 Florida Indians, and an unknown number from various smaller tribes.[330]

The Military Road was authorized in 1824 by a U.S. Congress act for a road opposite Memphis, Tennessee, through the swamps of Eastern Arkansas. The easternmost section of the road proved difficult to construct because of overflows and sickness of contractors. It was completed in 1834.

When the Creeks emigrated, some of them took the Military Road after crossing the Mississippi River at Memphis, while others continued on a water route. Some of these would stay behind in the Mississippi swamps to hunt. One group of Creek Indians, emigrating under the direction of Lieutenant J.T. Sprague in the fall of 1836, was left to hunt for bears in the swamps and later had to be rescued by Lt. Deas. The starving Creeks, consisting of 300-400, were rescued by Deas near Strong's. [331]

The road across from Memphis proved to be quite impassable for some of those travelers in 1836, and many lagged behind. An exploratory group led by Sprague showed the road to be good for the first 15 miles, but soon after, wet and "impossible to pass through with loaded wagons." Another five miles and it was almost "impassable on horseback. [332]

Some of the Chickasaw and the Choctaw also used this road. Some of the Chickasaw struggled through the swamps east of Strong's. Capt. John Millard arrived at Strong's with 700-800 of his party still in the swamp, "and will not reach here for some days owing to the desperate condition of the road," wrote a correspondent to the *Arkansas Gazette* on December 11, 1837. Millard estimated that no less than 70-80 ponies were bogged down and left for dead in the mud. [333]

Emigrating Indians would also travel down the Mississippi River, bordering Mississippi County on the east. Early in 1837, a group of Creeks, under the leadership of Lt. Deas, traveled down the Mississippi River from the Ohio River toward Montgomery's Point, where they entered the White River. On their way down the Mississippi River, they stopped at New Madrid to procure some corn, and as they passed Memphis, it was intimated that some of the group intended to leave the party to visit the Chickasaw country. [334]

While no known routes went through the swampy area Sam and his family called home, it was likely that they were well aware of the travels and the struggles of the emigrants. It is possible they, like others in the area, witnessed the journeys or met or assisted some of those who left the trail.

The story of the Cherokee stranded in the cold winter of 1838-1839, between the ice-clogged Mississippi and Ohio rivers, probably reached them. Here, many died.

"It is distressing to reflect on the situation of the Nation. One detachment stopped at the Ohio River, two at the Mississippi, one four miles this side, one sixteen miles this side, one 18 miles, and one 3 miles behind us. In all these detachments, comprising about 8,000 souls, there is now a vast amount of sickness and many deaths," wrote Daniel S. Butrick, a Christian missionary who accompanied Richard Taylor's detachment of Cherokee to the Indian Territory that winter. He described them as houseless and homeless in a strange land, exposed to a cold to which they were not accustomed. At times, the weather was "piercing" and "excessively cold." Because of floating ice on the Mississippi River, only half of the detachment crossed, and the others held up for three weeks on the other side. During this time, in their detachment, five had died, making it 26 who had passed away since crossing the Tennessee River, he noted. [335]

While mass removal was going on all around them, Missouri was also moving out any stray Indian groups in the southwestern part of the state. Referred to as the Osage War, the state militia was ordered out by Governor Lilbourn Boggs in September 1837 to remove any hunting parties of not just Osage, but Shawnee and Delaware, into Kansas and Arkansas. This followed complaints by settlers who were uncomfortable with their presence in the southwest counties. [336]

During the early removal years, some went west and turned around to go back; some left the trail, never making it to Indian Territory; and some never left where they lived. However they came to be at Chilletecaux village, Cherokee lived there in 1835.

When the Indians of Chilletecaux and the area were enumerated in 1831, the Cherokee were not counted among them. By 1835, they were mentioned in an article about Stoddard County, which at that time encompassed the area that would later be Dunklin County.

The approximately 50 residents subsisted by farming, stock raising, hunting, and trade in peltries. Furs, ranging from $20,000 to $30,000, had been taken from the swamps in the county in the last few years and sold at New Madrid and other places.

"Chilitican [sic] [337] is the principal chief and exercises a species of patriarchal government over them," reads the article about Stoddert [sic] County. "There is still one Indian village situated on the edge of the swamp between West and Grand prairies," the article reads. The village was composed of fragments of tribes of Senecas, Shawnees, Muscogees, Delawares, and Cherokees. [338]

The Cherokee were not new to this particular area, though, and had lived in the area at least as early as 1796 when Albert Tison lived among them on the St. Francis River. [339]

John East was one of those Cherokee living in or near the village in 1835. He had a son born in 1837 in the village. [340]

Chief Chilletecaux, concerned with removal and his desire to become a citizen, requested assistance from Thomas Moseley Jr. in 1835. Moseley wrote William Clark on July 4, informing him of their situation. While they were willing to remove, they lacked the means as they were "poor and destitute." They had been threatened by the citizens of Stoddard County, to which the future Dunklin County belonged, to be driven off in an "uncouth and unfriendly manner." At that time, those in the area consisted of 35-40 Delaware, Shawnee, Seneca, Cherokee, and Piankeshaw.

Chief Chilletecaux was unsure as to which tribe he belonged to. His father was Muscogee, his mother White, and his wife Delaware. He had lived in the area for approximately 50 years, and he and his wife had raised a large family.[341]

Clark referred the letter on August 5 to Gen. George Gibson, Commissary General of Subsistence in Washington, D.C. [342]

Sometime during the removal process, Thomas Varner, a physician, moved to Missouri. He was employed by the government in the Indian removal from Georgia. [343] After stopping at Chilletecaux, he discontinued his work, married a local woman, and began a second family. In 1844, he left the village on a tributary of the St. Francis River, at one time called Chilletecaux River, and later Varner River. Reaching the St. Francis River, they continued their travels to the Arkansas frontier.

Here they lived for a year. Afterward, in their travels, they would stop for a while at Clement's Donic, [344] [345] before moving down to Young's Landing on Upper Poplar Ridge, near the present-day Monette, Arkansas. Traveling further south, he came to the clearing that was Edward Mattix's land and purchased it.[346] The 1848 original survey plat map of Section 6, Township 13 North, Range 7 East, shows a plot of land with Dr. Varner's name. [347]

Mattix, who had formerly lived in Lawrence County, settled on the island near present-day Mangrum to hunt and trap. Here, Mattix also raised a patch of corn and hunted with the Indians. [348]

Varner may have come to Missouri in 1832 or before, as a daughter was born in Missouri in approximately 1832, according to census records. Another was born around 1834. [349] He remarried in 1839 to Susan Moore, the daughter of Howard Moore. [350] Moore had bought Chilletecaux's cabin and an old mortar the chief had made. [351]

Varner and Mattix both hunted with the local Indians. Varner, with previous medical training, also learned some methods of treating disease from the Indians. His son, Francis, would later tell of how his association with the Indians helped him be proficient in forest life and plants. [352]

On one of these hunting trips, Varner and those with him killed two buffalo and captured a young female buffalo, which Varner tried to corral with his calves. The calves were no match for the buffalo, which soon escaped after being separated from the calves. [353]

Buffalo Island, where Varner lived, was sparsely settled then, having only three to four settlers on the whole island area even as late as 1850. [354] There was only one neighbor between Varner and William Hector on the 1850 census.[355] That didn't necessarily mean that they lived close to each other, but were on the route traveled by the census taker. Hector, near Big Lake, would have been approximately 25 miles away from Varner on current roads.

For all the early settlers, living on the land was difficult, but it was also a blessing; one that Moonshine and his predecessors had enjoyed for a long time. Here, one could sustain life with the land's bounty and have plenty to trade as those before them had done.

This rough and wild environment wasn't tamed by a mild and meek group of men and women. These were men who might attack a bear with just a knife, subsist on bare necessities, if any, for long periods when needed; wade through swamp and muck; sleep in the hollow of a tree, in the snow, or canoe – all in the quest for a better life.

A trapper told Sir Charles Lyell, as he hunted on the Little River, about the abundance of wildlife in the area. In 1844, he noted, a herd of buffalo lived on Buffalo Island that was 300-400 strong. Harvested game in 1846 included 50,000 raccoon skins; 25,000 muskrats for making caps and hats; 12,000 minks for trim on dresses; 1000 bears, 1000 otters; 2,500 wild cats, 40 panthers, and 100 wolves. [356]

The rivers in the area had long been major highways for trade.

After La Salle's claim on the area for France in 1682, more explorers traveled into the region, offering the Indians trade goods, and in turn, they were offered pelts. By 1712, the French had learned of the value of bear oil and how abundant bears were in Arkansas. They, along with the Quapaw, hunted and traded for bear oil, tallow, buffalo meat, and fur skins. Many were Coureurs des bois, who lived and traded with the Indians.

The hunters were drawn to the St. Francis River area because the bottomland forests and canebrakes provided a good habitat for game such as bison and bears. The hunters supplied a large portion of buffalo tallow, bear oil, and skins.

At one time, hunters from Canada and the lower Mississippi River would rendezvous yearly at the mouth of the St. Francis River for the winter hunt. At the end of the season, they would begin rendering bear oil and processing meat for shipment to New Orleans. [357]

Many of the Frenchmen traversing the waters of the Mississippi, St. Francis, and Arkansas rivers, as well as other rivers, were Canadian, such as the Lesieurs.

It was in pursuit of the trade in the area that two young brothers, Francois and Joseph Lesieur, left their home in Canada, arriving in Pain Court, Missouri, later St. Louis, in 1778. The two found employment with fur trader Gabriel Cerre, the father-in-law of Auguste Chouteau, also a fur trader.

Cerre sent the young men down the Mississippi River to find a suitable place for a trading house. The two stopped at a Delaware village in an area that is now New Madrid, Missouri. Nearby, on the margins of the Lewis and Big Prairies, were several other Indian villages. The two named this place Lagraisse, translated as The Grease, due to the large quantity of furs and bear's oil in deer skin sacks ready to be transported to Kaskaskia to be marketed.

Although they explored further downriver and up the White River, this was the spot that they reported to Cerre as a suitable place for a trading venture. In 1780, they returned to Lagraisse and built a stockade and houses to do business. By 1781, after transporting Indian goods to Lagraisse, they were ready for business.

Francois's son, Godfrey, carried on the family business, reporting some years later that as an agent for Pierre Chouteau Jr. and Company, of St. Louis, he averaged 60 or 70 thousand dollars a year. [358]

Following the tradition of those before him, Moonshine also continued to trade with Lesieur, as evidenced by a notation presumably written by Lesieur on the backside of a description of a strip of land in Arkansas and Missouri that appears to be Buffalo Island, but is not named as such. The strip of land is east of the St. Francis River swamps and west of the Little River and Castor River swamps.

The notation, amidst various figures, is a list under the heading of Moonshine. Herein are listed 49 and 21 coons; 32 minks; 12 av…; three bears; 14 "D" skins, which are probably deer skins; and a note that appears to say "Hectors raws;" for a total of 119 skins. [359]

Chouteau authorized Leseiur to add 10 cents "if you think it is a good policy," on the raccoon and mink skins for that year. Prices for raccoon skins were 50 to 52 cents for number one skins, 25 to 30 cents for number two skins, and 10 to 12 cents for number three skins. Mink skins were 50 to 55 cents for number one skins, 28 to 32 cents for number two skins, and 12 to 15 cents for number three skins. The rest of the skins and furs would remain as previously given. [360]

Top prices for number one furs included wild cats at 33 1/3 cents; grey foxes at 30 cents; otters at $3.50 and cubs at 50 cents; muskrats at 11 cents and kittens at 2 cents; badgers at 30 cents; opossums at 10 cents, and if cased 12 cents; bears at no more than $2 for the best, with cubs at 75 cents; shaved deer skins at 25 cents with well-stretched red skins at the same price, and grey skins at 17 cents.[361]

One request Chouteau had of Lesieur in 1849 was to help fulfill an order for bear oil. "We have made this day a contract with an Englishman for 300 gallons of bear's oil to be delivered here by the 20th of next month," he wrote. He suggested that Leseiur obtain the commodity at a price as low as possible to ensure a good profit. "We have always understood that it comes in abundance in your market." [362]

A major commodity, bear oil, which had flowed up and down area rivers for generations, was considered finer than butter or lard and preferred in cooking as it did not become rancid as fast as butter.

An area on the White River took on the name of the containers used to render bear lard, which were then transported down the river by early hunters, according to stories associated with the area. [363] Oil Trough was referred to by that name as early as 1838 when German hunter Frederick Gerstaecker traveled through the Oiltrove Bottoms. [364]

A couple of unusual requests made to the hunters included copal buds,[365] requested by a Mr. Sarpy, [366] "who has not enjoyed a very good health." Chouteau said that he had been informed that it was in abundance in the area, and this was the time of the year, early spring, to obtain it. [367]

Another request was for panther skins, in particular those with tails, because they were wanted by upper Indian traders for use in "some fancy dresses." [368]

Area settlers often joined the local Indians in hunting. James A. Davis, who lived in the Big Lake area, told of being in camp with Moonshine and John East. "I have been camped with him," said Davis, speaking of East, "many different times when he and William Moonshine, his Indian companion, were hunting and trapping." Davis settled there in 1846. [369]

Some early residents who didn't join the Indians in hunting excursions were still aware of them hunting in the area. Sterling Hood came to Poinsett County in 1840 when there were but five or six families living on the Tyronza River [370] within 50 miles, and the road to Memphis was but a trail. When he moved there, many of the men made their living trapping. At that time, Indians still "roamed the woods." The chiefs, "Moonshine and Cornmeal, came with their tribes and hunted during the winter, but went west in the summer." [371]

Little did he know, but Corn Meal went west while Moonshine lived up the river, assimilating, in a way, into the culture of those around him.

As William Hector, he was taxed in Mississippi County from 1840 to 1856. Besides land, he was taxed for horses and cattle, owning up to four horses in 1854 and 50 cattle in 1852. [372]

Chapter 7
Great Waters

The lilies at the water's edge still offered a few blooms on this trip. As they neared the end of their blooming season, they were changing colors – some to a golden yellow. Their pads lay down a carpet of green and yellow and looked as if you could walk across them to dry land as they floated on the surface.

Nearby, rising higher than the lilies, were water lotus, "yancopin," as Sam called them. They were long past blooming, and now the only evidence of them was the dried seed pods. Sam watched as a red-winged blackbird landed on one of them, and he drove the pirogue into the patch to grab a few pods to use later. The seeds could be ground and used as flour, and the tubers below in the mud could be cooked like a potato. Sam didn't take the time to harvest those today. At another time, he might gather them and some of the "duck potatoes" from the Arrowhead plant, which was now past its blooming season.

In places, along the banks of the river, were canebrakes, so tall you could not see over them and so thick you could not penetrate them. Thickets of shrubbery, including pondberry, [373] with its little red berries, flourished. The bald cypress trees, looming tall, had taken on their fall colors of cinnamon and fiery orange and were losing their needle-like leaves. Sycamore, Sassafras, Osage Orange, Sweet Gum, and oak trees could be seen on land.

Standing in the canoe with his long pole guiding him, Sam saw huge gar floating near the surface. He watched as some of the large fish would hit the surface with a quick motion, agitating the waters, then sink below, leaving a radiating circle in their wake.

"Cast that way," Sam advised James as he pointed to his right, where he saw circles in the water.

The water was teeming with all sorts of fish, some large, such as the Long-nosed Gar Pike and the Short-nosed Gar. The Long-noses were very common in the area. The less common Short-nosed could be found more than 10 feet long. Channel catfish was a favorite food in the area. It, along with goggle eye, large-mouth black bass, and stone cat, was abundant. There were also bream and crappie.

In shallow areas of the water, one could see the minnows jump. When frightened, some of them would jump out of the water and land for a moment on the vegetation before darting back into the water. [374] Some of these were gathered and placed in the bait box.

When the waters were high in the spring, large fish would get trapped in the shallow bayous or on land. Locals gathered them, or they were eaten by the hogs. Often, large fish such as buffalo perished for lack of water because there was no outlet. [375]

Dr. James was enjoying the solitude on the river. While he often took a steamboat down the Mississippi River to enjoy fine dining in Memphis, he found the meal on the side of the river to be quite pleasant.

After leaving the Little River, which was swifter, the difference in the water of the St. Francis River was more noticeable. The water of the St. Francis River was calm and clear today as they neared the mounds, unlike early spring when the water was high and muddy, when the rains set life in motion in the waterways. Flooding in areas was common then.

The sound of the rushing water could be deafening. Its movement, swift and furious, altered all that stood in the way. The grasses shimmied and swayed. The trees, huge and strong, standing on the banks of the waterways, trembled at its passing. Sandy foundations of the Mississippi River would be cut away at a pace of 40 feet in as many hours. [376] All manner of life had to seek higher ground.

Sam had seen the water come in flashes, wiping out all in its path, even life. He had seen the water rise more slowly as the river, bayous, and streams in the area overflowed, congested from the many rains and the melting of the snow way up north. The waters traveled down the Mississippi River, spilling over into the area's waterways and coursing through the swamps.

As county surveyor, [377] James was always recording how the water behaved, and where it went when it was raging. His forte was the lay of the land and the behavior of the elements influencing it. Traveling down the river was no exception. While Sam guided the dugout, James took notes. [378]

Freshets occurred often along the streams and bayous in the spring. Sometimes the overflows were treacherous and deadly, such as the flood of 1844. That year, the high waters left the Mississippi and spilled down through the swamplands and waterways near where Sam and his family lived.

The hunter's paradise became hazardous for their family and other settlers. Some settlers he knew lost several cattle that year, and some left the area for good. Afterward, sickness and death followed the onslaught of mud and muck. They hunted on the higher land of the ridge and camped on Martin Spring for a while after the 1844 flood, and the subsequent one in 1848.

From the ridge, they could follow an old Indian trail toward Black Fork Bayou and then to Bayou De View. On the prairie, the buffalo left their mark in huge wallows. [379] From the bayou, one might go down toward the Cache River, where there was once an Indian village. Sometimes, while on the west side of the ridge, they would go on toward the "Langee" [380] bottoms and other places to hunt.

The flood of 1844 was the beginning of dramatic changes in the lay of the land as they knew it. It would not be the last of great waters, however, that Sam would witness flowing across the land. Nor was it the first time the waters overwhelmed the land.

Once it began to rain in May 1844 near Wyandotte, Kansas, it didn't stop. Days of rain became six weeks. By June, the waters were very high along the Missouri River. [381]

Communities near St. Louis, then known as Illinois Town and Brooklyn, now East St. Louis, were nearly submerged, with occupants taking refuge in the upper floors of homes as the Illinois, Missouri, and Mississippi all rose to flood stages. The surface of the Mississippi River was nearly filled with floating debris. All lowlands along the Missouri River were flooded. Houses, barns, stock, and property were destroyed. Some survivors were rescued by passing boats as they clung to driftwood or floating dwellings. [382]

Western Missouri counties along the upper Missouri River reported huge losses of crops and some loss of life. In Carroll County, the river was said to reach from bluff to bluff and up to 12 miles wide in places. "Houses, barns, horses, mules, hogs, cattle, and the gathered crops were swept away." At least one citizen lost his life. [383]

In Boone County, the entire town of Nashville was completely submerged and swept away. The town of Rocheport had up to six feet of water inside a local hotel. Four citizens of Columbia, who tried to travel through the water to help those in Nashville, were stranded in trees all night. The next day, after resuming their trip, they found their horses succumbing to the disaster. Three sought refuge in trees and a floating log, and one lost his life.[384]

Many similar stories existed in other counties along the Missouri. "There was not a dry acre in the river bottoms from Kansas City to the mouth of the river," at St. Louis.

The American Bottoms, a geographical region extending from Alton, Illinois, to Kaskaskia, a floodplain of the Mississippi, was submerged. Many had to be rescued from their homes and farms.

Following the flood, sickness abounded. "Chills and fever prevailed in their most malignant form, followed in the winter by spinal meningitis." [385]

The group that suffered the most from sickness after this flood was the Wyandot Indians, who had recently moved to Kansas. They lost up to 100 of their tribe in the following months. The 1844 flood would become known as the biggest flood ever recorded on the Missouri River and Upper Mississippi River in terms of discharge and the highest recorded for the Mississippi River at St. Louis. [386]

The natural course of the flooding rivers would have sent the waters down the Mississippi toward the Gulf of Mexico, passing Mississippi County on the east. That year, the high waters didn't reach New Madrid, downstream from St. Louis, noted Francis Valle Lesieur, in his early history of New Madrid. They passed off "through the swamps south of Cape Girardeau" and spread "over the sunken lands of Southeast Missouri and North Arkansas." [387]

Unlike St. Louis and some areas on the Missouri and Mississippi rivers, the swamplands were not heavily populated during the 1844 flood.

Overflows of the waterways were common in the Northeast Arkansas area and deluged any low-lying areas. Higher areas or ridges between these areas were where animal life and others took refuge as the waters encroached. Cattle would often be driven to these areas when flooding began. [388]

During the 1844 flood, Ed Mattix of Maumelle Prairie lost a great number of cattle. [389] Mattix had a cabin on Buffalo Island near present-day Mangrum. He sold his claim that same year to Thomas Varner, [390] moving to higher lands, south of present-day Jonesboro, Arkansas. [391]

Overflows of the Mississippi and other waterways were a regular occurrence before 1844 and would be for many years to come. Descriptions of the high waters from the backwaters of the St. Francis and Mississippi rivers during those times would include an almost solid sheet of water from the edge of Crowley's Ridge in Craighead County to the Mississippi River, except on higher ridges. [392]

A large Mississippi River flood prior to 1844 occurred in 1785, south of Cape Girardeau and north of the Big Swamp. Set down in history as L'anne des Grandes Eaux or the Year of the Great Waters. The waters went from bluff to bluff in the upper Mississippi Valley, presenting a sight not to be soon forgotten. [393] Equally disastrous floods occurred in 1811, 1823, and 1826. [394]

A flood in 1828 inundated the St. Francis River bottoms, which at that time were entirely unprotected by levees. [395]

The 1844 flood, however, excelled these floods, entering the lower lands through Big Swamp. When the waters of the Mississippi, Ohio, and Missouri converged, disasters followed, as the water inundated more populated areas, such as those in 1815, 1826, 1848, 1849, 1862, 1867, 1882, 1884, and 1886. [396]

The St. Francis River bottom was deeply flooded in 1850. In 1858, a flood washed away miles of insignificant levees along the St. Francis Riverfront and poured rapidly into the bottom lands. For miles above the mouth of the St. Francis River, waters returning to the Mississippi River washed over the banks, carrying the remains of the levees with them. Stone (Chapter 5) tells in his recollections of his early life in Poinsett County how his father, who owned a cattle ranch on the St. Francis River, lost most of his cattle by drowning. [397]

In 1859, the bottom overflowed again, but it wasn't as severe as the year before. During the Civil War period, the levees were not kept in repair. Floods in 1862 and 1865 caused widespread damage to levee lines, and the waters overflowed in wide areas. In the 1865 flood, a wide crevasse occurred at Sans Souci on the McGavock plantation. Three others occurred, one at Morgan's Point near Wilson, which was 440 feet wide and five feet deep.

The floods of 1867 and 1874 damaged the levee lines even more. Between 1874 and 1882, only 1881 brought serious flooding, and the levees, except those in the St Francis River basin, were repaired. [398]

The 1882 flood began in February with intense rainstorms, resulting in a rapid rise of the Ohio River that caused flooding from Cincinnati, Ohio, to St. Louis. In the lower Mississippi Valley, the effects were even more disastrous. In Arkansas, an estimated 20,000 people became homeless. [399]

North of Mississippi County in Dunklin County, Missouri, the waters that year were the most destructive that had occurred. Considerable amounts of livestock and produce were destroyed. Low places north and south of Hornersville were inundated. "The waters flowed with as much swiftness as a mountain creek after a heavy rain," wrote author M.F. Smyth-Davis in her *History of Dunklin County, Mo.*

This caused great concern among the residents. James A. Mizelle, who lived in a small log house south of town in a low area on the banks of the Little River, told how he and his neighbors built a scaffold for his corn crop and moved his belongings into the upper floor of his house. He then left the area with his family and livestock. Returning in a canoe, he found the scaffold down and his corn floating "in every direction." His furniture was found floating near the top of the house inside his home. The St. Francis River also overflowed in places. Fortunately, the waters soon receded. [400]

No doubt, the few residents of Mississippi County, south of Hornersville, not far from Sam's home, endured rising waters as well.

The growing population and the infant levee system made each flood more disastrous, with the 1882 flood being a good example of this effect. Rail traffic between Memphis and Little Rock was curtailed as early as January. By mid-February, business in Memphis slowed as many river landings were underwater. There was a 400-foot break in the levee below Helena that flooded thousands of acres. A railroad trestle at Marianna was underwater. Continuing rains threatened Helena when waves washed over the levee around the town during high winds. Levee breaks occurred, with the counties of Crittenden, Lee, and Phillips being hit the hardest. Hopefield was completely underwater, as was Arkansas City. By February 23, it had been reported in the *New York Times* that there were only 12 points of land visible between Cairo, Illinois, and Memphis. The St. Francis and White river valleys also had deep water. Many drownings and disasters were reported. An Arkansas refugee who made his way to safety in a dugout reported that the Black Oak Ridge area was underwater for the first time in history. The refugee estimated that more than 10,000 cattle had been lost in that area. Pemiscot County, Missouri, was submerged. Starved and isolated people, including those in Osceola, were desperately awaiting relief from the Corps of Engineers. [401]

While the waters were receding by the end of March, the public pleas for flood control were rising. The River and Harbor Act of August 2, 1882, gave the Mississippi River Commission its first funds for improving the lower Mississippi. A stipulation stated that funds should not be used to build protective levees, leaving the traditional position that levee building was a private and state responsibility. Snag removal and channel lights became a focus. A troublesome area on the river was around Osceola in the bend known as Plum Point. In this stretch, the river was wide, the banks were low, and the sediment was loose, with the snags being thick. Osceola was at the apex of the bend, known as an area of "constant menace and a graveyard of sunken or beached steamboats." Time and money were expended to make the area open to navigation in the belief that if this problem could be solved, then so could other areas. By 1884, however, the first of the projects was abandoned because of failure. [402]

The waters in 1884 were two inches above those in 1882 in places and extended from the hills in Tennessee westward to Crowley's Ridge, 60 or 70 miles wide, with a depth averaging seven feet. In places over the sunken lands, depths of 50 and 60 feet could be found. [403]

In Mississippi County, the floods of 1882-1884 hindered growth and prosperity in the area for a while. Many farms were temporarily abandoned, and some left the fields they had cleared on public lands. [404]

Until the late 1880s or early 1890s, an overflow was expected just about any spring, with the waters covering a large area, and in some places several feet in depth. [405]

Travel out of the Big Lake area was often in a dugout. During the week of late February and early March 1879, several Big Lake residents visited Osceola. "Of course, they traveled in dugouts," noted *The Osceola Times.* [406]

Some high-water stories were later told by Francis Varner, son of Thomas Varner. He was affectionately referred to as "Uncle France."

On the higher ridges were older settlements, where wildlife gathered during floods. One of those was about a mile east of Monette called Cow Pens. This area was seldom, if ever, inundated by high waters.

However, sometimes a rise would occur suddenly, leaving other plans to be made. On one of these occasions, Francis sent some of his workers to construct a raft of logs and place the work oxen on the raft, tying it to a nearby building. The plan was for the raft to rise with the rising water and provide a safe spot for the oxen. Unfortunately, the workers did not tie the raft to the building. As the water rose, the raft drifted away, resulting in the loss of the cattle.

In 1867, an overflow sent Francis to check on some cattle that may have taken refuge at the Cow Pens. Near his destination, he encountered a panther searching the waters for a meal. It was not unusual to see a panther, and France was slightly amused by the sight until the cat jumped into a nearby tree, intending to attack. Grabbing his gun quickly and firing just as the cat leaped, he was able to fell his adversary. [407]

Mosquitoes by the millions filled the swampy areas, but the extra water of flooding created more breeding grounds for the insects, which carried diseases such as malaria.

Those traveling in the swampy areas of the county had to fight them off aggressively. "I had, at times, to carry burning punk close to my face or a hand full of vigorously waved bushes to fight the mosquitoes away from my nostrils so that I could breathe," told S.E. Simonson of his visits to the swamps after coming to Mississippi County in 1902.

"Notable floods occurred in 1897-98," wrote Simonson, in an *Arkansas Historical Quarterly* article in 1947. Those floods reached 37.66 and 37.22 on the Memphis gauge, with serious levee breaches resulting in damage to buildings and livestock. In 1903, there was notable flooding around Random Shot and Holly Bush in Mississippi County. Random Shot was a landing near Pecan Point. This occurred not long after Simonson came to Arkansas. "I was tremendously impressed with the might and magnitude of a major Mississippi River flood," he said.

While most took an interest in the levee system, which was immature and constantly being improved then, there was an element that thought the land should be left to nature. There were also those "from the river side of the levee," and islands, as well as those in the overflowed lands of Tennessee, who were "hostile" concerning improvements and made attempts to cut the levee. "Armed guards constantly patrolled the levee during high waters with orders to shoot anyone making such an attempt," he said. [408]

Simonson came to the area from central Illinois and helped reclaim a great area of rich, wetlands there through drainage canals. "I saw the possibilities that lay in the swamp lands in Mississippi County and eastern Arkansas," he wrote in another *Arkansas Historical Quarterly* article. There was about five percent of the land in cultivation, with five percent susceptible to cultivation, but "about 90 percent was regarded as a hopeless permanent mosquito and malaria-infested swamp," he noted. [409]

Hunting trips on Crowley's Ridge and the west side of the ridge may have been common during times of high water. Martin Springs, on the west side of the ridge, where there was once an Indian village, was likely a camping spot used by Moonshine in the late 1840s or early 1850s. Bill Irwin of Jonesboro would tell historian Harry Lee Williams about three Indians camping at Martin Springs when he was eight years old, which was approximately 1849. [410]

More than once, (old) "Billy" Moonshine, Old Buckeye, and John Big Knife stopped at W.W. Nisbett's mercantile business to purchase corn meal, W.W.'s widow, Mary Nisbett, recalled in her later years. Nisbett initially settled in Greene County. He settled in Craighead County in 1853, purchasing land in Jonesboro. [411]

Those who left the land for a while during high waters would go back.

Men of vision saw the land, beneath the waters, as a treasure, in its rich, dark soil and huge trees, much like the hunters saw the area as a paradise in its wildlife. One day, it would be a boon in the timber industry and an agricultural giant in cotton, if only the land could be reclaimed.

James B. Bowlin, U.S. Representative from Missouri, a member of a Select Committee, reviewed the memorials of the legislatures of Missouri and

Arkansas, as well as the memorials of citizens of the two states concerning reclaiming swamp or submerged lands. He reported how some or most of the "swamp" lands in Southeast Missouri and Northeast Arkansas were neither "sobby lands," as found in a swamp, nor submerged lands that would be dry and then wet due to overflows, but were underwater year-round.

These lands, except for the cypress swamps, were the way they were due to the actions of the 1811-1812 earthquakes, he said. This land, in its natural formation, is elevated enough to be dry, and if the causes were removed, it would be sufficient for agricultural purposes. It was impossible to determine what areas were swamps until the great sheets of water over the land could be removed. Obstructions from the upheaval of the river beds, landslides into the rivers, and fallen timber that formed rafts choked the rivers. This forced overflow onto the lands. Removing these obstacles would restore the "face of the country in its original beauty," he said.

The committee believed this could be accomplished by removing the river rafts and adding canals for drainage and levees. A bill conceding the lands to the states upon condition of reclamation should be passed. [412]

On the heels of the great flood of 1844 and a subsequent one in 1848, Congress introduced the first series of acts to reclaim swamp lands in 1849. In late 1850, Congress passed a second act to enable Arkansas and other states to identify and sell lands described as unfit for cultivation. The proceeds could finance improvements, such as levees and drainage ditches.

The Act of 1850 was of immediate benefit to Arkansas, allowing the state to address citizen concerns for improvement. Between 1851 and 1860, land sales raised more than $2,500,000, used to build more than 13,165,000 cubic yards of levee. [413]

From 1850 to the Civil War, the state tried to use the grant as described, intending to use funds from the sale of lands to fund levees and drains. After the war, less direct methods of using the land for reclamation were tried. Later, levee boards were the main agencies administering swamp lands.

An act in January 1851 placed the swamp lands under the control of a three-man board appointed by the governor for two-year terms, known as the Board of Swamp Land Commissioners. In 1851, the commissioners met, established an office, and divided the state into three districts under one commissioner and staff. Mississippi County was under District One. Despite claims of fraud, the commissioners reported progress in their October 1852 report. In Mississippi County, 16 miles of levee had been built. Also, in the county, 746,160 acres of swamp land had been located that conformed to the requirements of the Surveyor General.

The report was not satisfactory to Governor John S. Roane. He felt that the swamp land legislation should not be changed, but could be modified and made to work. However, he soon left office, and Elias N. Conway became governor. Not long after assuming duties, he sent a message to the House and Senate suggesting a complete overhaul of the "swamp land laws."

The Swamp Land Act of January 12, 1853, brought the land sales under State Land Agents from five offices: Dardanelle, Jacksonport, Washington, Pine Bluff, and Helena. The sale of state-owned swamp and overflowed lands fell under a public auction system. The act also provided for a Board of Swamp Land Commissioners. The commissioners were to divide the state into five districts to serve the offices of land agents.

While an improvement over the former act, it continued to be fraught with problems. There was friction between the state land agents and the board of commissioners, creating uncertainty about who had the right to sell the land, resulting in confusion of legal titles.

Governor Conway noted in early 1854 that he did not know what was happening with the swamp land administration. Unable to find out, he suggested new laws. He also suggested looking to the future and investing a portion of the lands to perpetuate a swamp land fund. Many legislators and citizens believed Conway wanted to invest swamp land funds in railroad stock.

Because this caused more confusion, the activities of the board of Swamp Land Commissioners were suspended by a legislative resolution on January 16, 1854. A second resolution in December called for a legislative investigation of all swamp land affairs. Newspapers were filled with editorials concerning the swamp land situation.

Following this, efforts were made to re-establish the commission more favorably. An editorial in the *Arkansas Gazette* noted that they thought a "'new leaf' has been turned in Swamp Land matters and the prospect of making something of the grant is better than it has been for the last two years."

The report of the board in September 1856 was unusually complete. Appended to the report were reports from swamp land engineers. Davis Thompson reported for the Eastern Division. He said that the levee in the Eastern District was good and secure except for 10 miles, two of which were in Mississippi County, needing additional dirt. There were gaps in the levee and the district. Concerning the system of drainage by ditches, nothing had been done that was "worth noticing," he said. The greater part of the work was motivated by "selfish design." Individual lands had been drained, "without regard to the quantity of swamp lands reclaimed."

An act of the state legislature in December 1856 abolished the office of Swamp Land Commissioners, except the office of land agent. The five districts were abolished, and seven were created. Land offices were set up at Fayetteville, Batesville, Clarksville, Helena, Champagnolle, Washington, and Little Rock. The duties of the land commissioners were assigned to the governor. The act was amended in January 1857, and allowed for a Swamp Land Secretary. [414]

For Sam and his dad, the Swamp Land acts meant a chance to own the land where they lived. As a result, Swamp Land patents were issued. This would transfer the title of federally owned swamp lands to private ownership. In Arkansas, the act put over 7.6 million acres of swamp or overflowed lands, which may be or are unfit for cultivation into private hands at little or sometimes no cost under the condition that the lands were drained and put back into productive use.

On May 9, 1855, Sam received a patent to 160 acres in the southeast section of Section 12, Township 14 North, Range 9 East, near what is now Dell, Arkansas, through the act.

His dad, William, would acquire many more acres in three townships in the county. In Township 14 North, Range 9 East, he acquired the east half of Section 1, 401.56 acres in Section 14, and the southwest section of Section 12, adjacent to Sam's land. In Township 12 North, Range 8 East, he acquired the west half of Section 22, the southeast section of Section 14, the east half of the southwest section of Section 14, the southwest section of the southwest section of Section 14, the southeast quarter of Section 20, the northwest quarter of the southwest quarter of Section 14, and the west half of the northwest quarter of Section 14. In Township 13 North, Range 8 East, he acquired the southwest half of the northeast section of Section 25, the southeast half of the southeast half of Section 28, the west half of the Northeast section of Section 28, the Northeast section of the Northeast section of Section 28, the southeast section of the northwest section of Section 28, the north one half of the south one half of Section 21, and the southeast section of the southeast section of Section 21. This land totaled 2,243.26 acres. [415]

During the Civil War, the drainage program and levee systems were almost completely abandoned. Levees during that time were cut by the armies and damaged by floods. The levee system was in worse shape in 1869 than it was in 1858.

In 1868, the office of Commissioner of State Lands was created. The creation of the office brought about a new way to handle land management and reclamation. Two acts in 1869 established a new system for repairing and building public levees.

By 1879, the Mississippi River Commission was established. Arkansas and other states bordering the Mississippi River enacted legislation creating levee districts. Working directly with the commission and the U.S. Engineers, the modern flood control program began in the alluvial valley of the Mississippi River.

Mississippi County fell under the direction of the St. Francis Levee District, created on March 21, 1893. The sale of the remaining swamp and overflowed acreage from the original grant was used to fund the districts at first. Later, they would receive "handsome" grants of tax-forfeited lands. A lot of the land was sold to lumber companies and large plantations in the delta area. [416]

Without funds for the levee system through the Swamp Land Act, progress in the levee building would have been delayed. The funds provided for levee construction in the St. Francis River Basin in 1851-1858, when small, three-foot levees were built on an intermittent line on the west bank of the

Mississippi River from Commerce Hills to near the mouth of the St. Francis River. However, the flood of 1859 virtually wiped the levees out. Nevertheless, the system was at the highest stage of lower Mississippi River levee development and demonstrated how effective a better levee system would be. [417]

The St. Francis Levee District of Arkansas and Missouri encompasses the lower St. Francis River Basin. In Arkansas, it included all of Mississippi and Crittenden counties, and part of Craighead, Poinsett, Cross, Lee, St. Francis, and Phillips counties.

In Missouri, it includes all of Pemiscot County and part of Dunklin and New Madrid counties. Without levees, this area would be subjected to overflows either directly or indirectly by the Mississippi River. In Arkansas, the extent of the land includes 2,500 square miles. [418]

The first levees in Arkansas Territory along the Mississippi River were constructed by private landowners. They were usually small, three to four feet high, and made with earth from borrow pits. While trees were cut down, the stumps were left in the levee. As they were extended and made larger and more secure, they were free of stumps or other materials that might harm the construction. [419]

The first actual railroad in Arkansas was built from the Mississippi River, opposite Memphis, to Little Rock, following an act in 1853 granting a charter to a company to build a railway. The first section of the road from Hopefield to the St. Francis River at Madison was completed, and trains began running regularly in early 1858. The company, The Memphis and Little Rock Railroad Company, advertised that the railway was open between De Vall's Bluff and Brownsville in January 1862, and trains were running between De Vall's Bluff and Little Rock in February. The fare from Memphis to Little Rock was $10. [420]

The St. Francis River levee had not been built at this time, and flooding of the Mississippi River would extend 40 miles westward with moving water that ranged from a depth of two to eight feet. Crossties and rails were wired and chained to the embankments and fastened to trees on the upstream side of the track.

A large portion of the track, between Hopefield and Madison, was built on pile trestle bridges as it was impossible to build a stable embankment. Between Cache and Eden, the track was laid entirely on the form of underpinning.

The company claimed 150,000 acres that the state had claimed under the Swamp Land Act of 1850, which helped them to advance their line. [421]

In 1879, James made a map of Mississippi County for the Mississippi River Commission, accompanied by a memoir detailing the topographical features of the map. In the memoir, he told of how he took notes during the flood of 1874, as he "traveled over almost every portion of the region during that overflow," as a basis of reference for statements and conclusions in his map. He also used data from authentic sources such as the field notes of the U.S. surveys of 1848 and 1849 of the area, "modified and corrected by surveys made by myself and others" from 1874, 1875, 1877, and 1878.

As an agent for large landowners in various portions of the county, who were considering making improvements through levees and drainage, James "paid particular attention to the depth of the overflow, direction of currents," while he "accumulated a mass of information not to be obtained in any other manner."

The commission printed the memoir in 1881, but did not print the map, because of its size. [422]

In June 1879, *The Osceola Times* mentioned the map, calling it a "choice specimen of rare skill, and for beauty and design of execution can hardly be surpassed."

The map was four feet square and was on a scale of one inch to one mile. From the map, it was concluded that the riverfront of the Mississippi River in the county was 81 miles, considering the meanderings, with an average width of 18 miles. The Little River from Big Lake to where it exits the county was 41 ½ miles. There were 22 lakes in the county, averaging four miles wide. Buffalo Creek was the only perpetually running stream in the county. [423]

James described another phenomenon that changed the water level on the land in this memoir.

Besides the earthquakes (1811-1812), James said the Devil's Elbow Cut-off affected the general appearance of the land in the southern part of the county, more than any other event in "recent years."

The event happened in 1876 when the Mississippi River cut its way through a narrow neck of land and "plunged at one leap down the descent which it had formerly crawled 25 miles to make."

The action from this event lowered the water level on the river at Osceola by 22 inches in a few hours.

It drained Golden Lake and the bottoms between it and Frenchman's Bayou. James was at Shawnee Village, 10 to 12 miles away, when the event happened, but "distinctly felt the shock and heard the roar of the mighty mass of water" cut through the land. [424]

Sam's lifetime would be filled with times of uncontrolled great waters. Sam did not live to see them, but larger, disastrous floods were on the horizon.[425] Sam also did not live to see the full transformation of the land from a hopeless, malaria-ridden swamp, cleared and groomed, to a great agricultural area.

Levee work and drainage would change the value of the somewhat worthless swamp land. After some of the lands, which brought a price of around $2.50 an acre just before the turn of the century, were drained, they brought a price from $8 to $15 an acre in 1902, said J.A. Fox, of Osceola, assistant engineer of the St. Francis Levee District, in a turn-of-the-century publication about Mississippi County. [426]

Chapter 8

War at Home

"The last time the water was pretty high," Sam told James, "was just after the war."

He recalled how he and his wife Belona laid in a crop of corn, full of hope for the future. Sam pushed the plow, and she guided the mules. As they dropped seeds into the earth, Sam remembered how they talked about the new life that would spring forth and their hope and dreams now that the war was over.

"The war took its toll," Sam told James. "Some things will never be the same." His family had sacrificed and done without, as everyone had.

Sam told James how two members of his close family fought for the Confederacy. His brother-in-law, James, served as a Lieutenant.

His younger brother, William, became well known in the area for his part in a battle in Missouri early in the war.

"He was with the Swamp Fox," Sam told him, "when they captured the Big River Bridge and caused the surrender of the Dutch there." William, Sam said, "loved to tell about his part in the burning of the bridge" over the railway and how it delayed the Union troops.

Dr. James also saw some action during the war.

"I was right in the thick of it," James told Sam, sharing his part in the making of torpedoes, some of which were used by the Confederacy at Mobile Bay to destroy federal gunboats. He was referred to as Captain by those in the area who knew him, [427] and he still kept his Navy Colt close by. [428]

James told Sam about how he was in Paris, France, at the beginning of the war. He had just finished school when he decided to go home to be with his family and support the Southern cause.

Getting across federal lines since a blockade had already been established would be a challenge upon his return to the States, he explained. However, his knowledge of the German language and his physique aided him in finding a way with the help of his friends.

"Speaking fluent German, I simply donned the guise of a military officer and traveled to Havre, [429] where my friends helped me gain a passport."

With a sidewise glance at Sam and a half-smile, he told of how, after arriving in New York, he pretended to be a German interested in the war between the states. Under these pretenses, he visited Washington and Alexandria, where he was the guest of federal officers. [430]

While he told Sam this story, he still held back some of what happened during that time and what he really did. It was too soon after the war, and possibly there would be repercussions as reconstruction was still underway in the county and times were precarious. Racial unrest was currently brewing in the county and had recently erupted into a deadly conflict that would become known as the Black Hawk War.

While all that was fresh on their minds, today, it was also a thousand miles away for Sam and James. On the river, they were on even ground despite their cultural differences, despite their education, or how far they had traveled.

In 1850, Sam lived near his father with his wife, Belona Elizabeth, and young daughter Matilda, who was three. He was a hunter, making his living in the way he and his father had for years. His father, William, was still hunting but also doing some farming. William was with Belona Elizabeth's mother, Jaley Brown Rice Hector. [431] Jaley and her first husband, Abijah Rice, Belona's father (Chapter 3), settled near Hornersville in 1830.

William and Jaley were living with James Alfred, 13, her son with John East, [432] and William Hector, 7, Jaley and William's son. [433] Others in William's household were Sam's brother, Jefferson, 23, who was also a hunter; George Clemens, 19, [434] and Jaley's daughter, Susan, with her young daughter, Saluda.

That year, the United States House Committee on the Post Office and Post Roads was instructed to inquire into the "expediency" of establishing a postal route from Mill Bayou in the southern part of Mississippi County connecting Chickasawba, to William's house, to Big Lake, to Grand Prairie in Arkansas, and on to Chilletecaux in Missouri. [435]

Most likely in 1850, at least part of this route, if ever undertaken, would be by water – from Chickasawba to William's house, both on the Pemiscot Bayou, and to Big Lake. A road or trail did exist from Grand Prairie to Osceola. Near Big Lake, the road crossed the lower end of Big Lake, and crossed some of William's land, where it intersected a path to the Pemiscot Bayou before going on toward Osceola. [436] The path leading to the bayou was near where Sam and William lived. [437]

A post office existed at Chillitecaux as early as 1846. [438]

Mill Bayou had a postmaster in May 1841. Elliott Fletcher was the first postmaster. It was discontinued on April 1, 1847, and re-established on May 24, 1847. It was discontinued again on October 31, 1857. [439]

The economy was good in Arkansas during the last few years of the 1850s, in part due to cotton farming and rising prices, which in turn caused the growth of slavery in the state. While cotton farming was mostly in southern and eastern counties, including Mississippi County, the boom affected the whole state.

With the election of President Abraham Lincoln, whose platform was to halt the growth of slavery, Arkansas was pulled into the national debate on the subject. By the first of February 1861, following the November election, seven states had passed ordinances of secession. That month, those states formed the Confederate States of America.

A secession convention was held in March in Arkansas. Secession was defeated, but another public referendum was set for August. The convention agreed that any attempt to coerce the seceded states back into the Union would be grounds for Arkansas to secede.

In April, Confederate forces fired upon Fort Sumter in South Carolina. As a result, the President called on Arkansas for volunteers to suppress the rebellion. Arkansas had to decide whose side it would take. The Secession Convention reconvened, and on May 6, they voted to secede, overwhelmingly. The vote was 69 to 1. [440]

William, the younger, and Belona's half-brother, James (James Alfred East Hector), both raised in the William Hector household, joined the fray. Both enlisted in the Confederate service. William would receive local notoriety for his involvement in the battle of Big River Bridge in Missouri.

William joined first, becoming a member of the Missouri State Guard. He began his service in Dunklin County when a regiment was formed there in 1861. [441]

William's service was for six months and 13 days, as a private under J.E. Dooley as captain, [442] in Company E of the 1st Regiment, Missouri Infantry State Guard (1st Division). Dooley's service record shows him on a roster commencing on June 21, 1861, and ending on January 4, 1862. [443]

William's service likely began around the same time as Dooley's, as the burning of the Big River Bridge, which he was involved in, was part of the Battle of Fredericktown, Missouri, in October 1861, under the direction of Brig. General M. Jeff Thompson.

Earlier in the year, Thompson assumed the command of the First Military District that encompassed Southeast Missouri, following the resignation of N.W. Watkins, who had been appointed by the Governor of Missouri, Claiborne Fox Jackson. The State Guards were organized by the Missouri legislature in May 1861.

"Leave your plow in the furrow, your ox to the yoke, and rush like a tornado upon our invaders and foes to sweep them from the face of the earth," rallied Thompson as he encouraged the people to join the effort at the Bloomfield, Missouri headquarters on August 1, 1861. "We will strike our foes like a Southern thunderbolt."

Following their organization at Clarkton, the Dunklin County recruits spent their time drilling in preparation for fighting. Soon they joined Thompson's force and were in the fight at Fredericktown. [444]

While his infantry headed to Fredericktown, Thompson, known as the "Swamp Fox" for commanding the First Military District of swampy Southeast Missouri, led 500 dragoons from Piketon in Stoddard County to Blackwell Station in early October. His intentions were to destroy the Big

River Bridge at the station in Jefferson County. The three-span bridge was part of the Iron Mountain Railroad system and was heavily used by Union troops.

The dragoons, anxious to fight, arrived ahead of the scheduled time. "My men being more anxious to fight than I anticipated, traveled so fast that I reached the Big River Bridge, near Blackwell Station, two days ahead of my appointed time," Thompson wrote to Gen. Albert Sidney Johnston.

Arriving at daybreak on October 15, Thompson sent some troops around to attack a stone redoubt that the Union soldiers had built on the north side of the bridge, and another portion advanced on the railroad from the south. Just after daybreak, the first group of soldiers "charged upon the redoubt and carried it by storm," wrote Thompson, and when the group coming in from the south dashed over the bridge and fired upon the Union soldiers, they surrendered. After securing their property on the other side of the bridge, Thompson instructed it to be burned down.

After moving the plunder and property to Blackwell Station to be distributed, they were attacked, "and then occurred one of those bushwhacking fights which proved the mettle of my men," wrote Thompson to Johnston. Altogether, six of his men were killed and several were wounded, and they took 55 prisoners. [445]

"It was Capt. Moonshine's son, Billy Moonshine who Jeff Thompson transmigrated into a thousand Indians, at the battle of the Big River Bridge in Missouri, thereby causing a surrender of the Dutch stationed there," wrote Lesieur in his New Madrid history. [446]

Could William be one of the "Indians" Thompson referred to following this incident? "The Mississippians with me acted splendidly, and my Indians with great propriety?"

A news article in *The Morning Democrat* in Davenport, Iowa, about the Big River Bridge battle noted that "Several Indians are said to have been in the ranks of the rebels." [447]

William may have spent time at home following his six-month service and before enrolling, along with James (James Alfred East Hector), into Captain Andrew F. Jones' company on August 30, 1862, in Dunklin County, Missouri, for three years. In this company, a part of Clark's Recruits, Missouri Volunteers, James would serve as Sergeant, while William continued to serve as a private. [448]

This company would become Company H of the Seventh Missouri Cavalry in Stoddard County, Missouri, as part of the Confederate States Army, under the leadership of Col. Solomon George Kitchen.

William and James, as members of the District of Northern Arkansas, were surrendered to Maj. Gen. G.M. Dodge by Brig. General Jeff Thompson on May 11, 1865, at Wittsburg. They were paroled on May 25 and allowed to return home. James was 28 years old and described as five feet eight inches tall with black hair, black eyes, and a dark complexion. William was 22 years old and described as five feet five inches tall with dark hair and a dark complexion. [449]

While many were somewhere else fighting, the effects of war did not escape Mississippi County.

A naval battle on the Mississippi River, just south of Osceola, occurred on May 10, 1862. The Engagement of Plum Point Bend was not long after Confederate forces fell at Island Number 10 near New Madrid on April 8, 1862. This defeat opened the river for the U.S. Mississippi Flotilla to proceed downriver. Near Osceola, they were attacked by the Confederate River Defense Fleet as the flotilla was shelling Fort Pillow, across the river. The battle was considered a Confederate victory as two Union gunboats were sunk. However, the two forces met again in Memphis on June 6, 1862, where the Confederate fleet was destroyed and the Union gained control of the Mississippi River north of Vicksburg, Mississippi. [450]

While this took place on the water, it appears there were troops prepared for a land engagement if needed. A correspondence from the Mississippi Flotilla near Fort Pillow on April 19, 1862, in the *Chicago Tribune,* reprinted from the *Cincinnati Gazette,* tells of "'strong intrenchments' [sic] at Fort Oceola [sic] that many show a 'stubborn resistance.'" The story continues, telling of two deserters who came within Union lines, reporting that batteries in "Fort Osceola" were manned by five regiments and talked of "fighting desperately." The "fort," said the article, was "probably a battery of a few guns." [451]

A map showing rebel fortifications on the Mississippi River, printed in *Frank Leslie's Illustrated Newspaper* on May 10, 1862, shows Fort Osceola at Osceola, Arkansas. [452]

The war was a time of turmoil for everyone. There were roaming bands of bushwhackers and guerrillas on both sides of the conflict. A Confederate guerrilla band under the leadership of "Nate" Bolin operated out of nearby Greene County, Arkansas. He was joined by the notorious bushwhacker, Sam Hildebrand. They frequently raided Union units in Southeast Missouri. [453] Hildebrand wrote his autobiography, which tells of his exploits.[454]

On at least three occasions, federal forces entered Mississippi County searching for guerrilla bands.

The Big Lake Expedition began when Col. John B. Rogers of the Second Missouri State Militia Cavalry ordered Frederick E. Poole to lead 200 troops and one artillery piece into Mississippi County in September 1863. Before leaving Camp Lowry in Missouri and heading toward Northeast Arkansas, the troops received additional troops of 50 from the Second Missouri State Militia Cavalry, 100 from the Sixth Missouri State Militia Cavalry, and 50 from the Eighth Provisional Enrolled Missouri Militia Cavalry, plus another artillery piece. Arriving in Osceola, he was joined by members of the Twenty-Fifth Missouri Infantry, under Colonel Chester Harding, stationed at New Madrid.

The troops proceeded toward Big Lake, per orders to return to camp through Pemiscot County, Missouri.

Poole noted his disappointment in his report that they did not "meet the rebel force said to be in that vicinity." However, on the expedition they killed 13 "noted guerrillas" who "fought with desperation," captured 26-30 others, plus several horses, mules, and guns. He reported that only four of his men suffered wounds, "none dangerously."

Overall, he felt the people of the county were loyal to the Union. "The people of Arkansas I found to be much more loyal than those residing in Missouri, and it is my firm and decided belief that the people residing in the neighborhood of the river ... only require a show of protection to establish their loyalty and fidelity to our government." [455]

As a result of hearing of the federal troops in his area at this time, Cpl. James Bunch, of Company H, surrendered to federal authorities on September 13, 1863, at Hornersville, Missouri. He had been advised to do so by a Captain Priest under whom he took the oath of allegiance in March 1863 at Hornersville. Captain Priest "told me to do so when ever [sic] I would hear that there were federal troops in my area."

In November 1863, Bunch, 34 years old, was a farmer and most likely did not want to be a part of the war, but was conflicted in his loyalties. He was "conscripted" into Confederate service in July 1862 by Maj. Dooley for three years. He said he stayed with his company for about four days before deserting and going home. Armed only with a butcher knife, Bunch said he had "been in the woods for about two months last winter to avoid the rebel army." That would have been the winter of 1862-1863.

He said that he was not a Southern sympathizer and was a "loyal man," however, he was "not willing to take up arms for the federal government. I would rather go South." [456]

The Confederate Conscription Act was passed on April 16, 1862, and called for all healthy White men between the ages of 18 and 35, not in restricted war-related occupations, to join the military for three years. Conscription was unpopular and some fled Arkansas to avoid it. [457]

For most, the war was an unavoidable circumstance in one way or another, despite their feelings or opinions. Regardless of what Bunch thought would happen because of his surrender, he was sent to Gratiot Street Military Prison in St. Louis, Missouri. After an examination in November, it was recommended that he be exchanged as a prisoner. That did not happen, as he would be transferred to the hospital there in February 1864, where he died of inflammation of the lung on February 7. He left a wife and two children at home in Dunklin County, Missouri. [458] He is buried at Jefferson Barracks National Cemetery in St. Louis, Missouri. [459]

The Hector family and the Bunch family were closely allied. William would later marry James Bunch's sister, Lucinda, and Sam's daughter, Melissa, would later marry James' brother, Sam.[460]

In April 1864, Major John W. Rabb of the Second Missouri Light Artillery reported that in the few weeks prior, guerrillas had committed "numerous depredations" upon those living in Dunklin, Pemiscot, and New Madrid counties in Missouri, and Mississippi County in Arkansas. However, he noted, the area was "nearly all strong secession sympathizers" and often wouldn't report robberies right away. Most of the guerrilla bands in the area consisted of deserters from the Confederate Army. Having learned where some of the camps of guerrilla bands in the area were, Rabb said he was determined to "make a vigorous effort to break them up."

On April 5, he ordered Capt. Valentine Pruiett to move into the area with his available force in the First Missouri Cavalry.

Taking the steamboat *Silver Moon* from New Madrid, Rabb, and companies H, I, and K, consisting of approximately 200 men, headed to Mississippi County. At Barfield Point, he ordered Company H, under Capt. W.C.F. Montgomery, Second Missouri Artillery, to disembark with about 100 men and march to the Chickasawba settlement on the Pemiscot Bayou, currently part of Blytheville. Rabb and the remainder of the artillery disembarked at Osceola, some 20 miles below where Montgomery landed. Upon arrival, he learned that the town had just been robbed.

The company began a march toward Pemiscot Bayou, planning to reach a point approximately 10 miles below the point where Montgomery would reach the bayou. During this march, he said they killed five or six mounted guerrillas on the road.

After marching 12 miles on the road that led into swampy country, filled with hard timber and thick cane, with water one to three feet deep, the men finally reached a house after dark and made camp. The home was occupied by Mark Walker. He informed them he was a "rebel," and his son was in one of the guerrilla bands nearby.

From Walker's comments, Rabb determined he would be attacked and posted pickets around the house. Rabb settled in with some of Lt. L. J. Phillips' men as a continuous rain fell, rendering the area "very dark." Awakening at 3 a.m., and after speaking with Phillips, Rabb returned to sleep. Shortly after, he heard someone within a few feet of him command him to surrender. The attackers were "thoroughly acquainted with every part of the ground, and it was so dark, and the rain falling in such torrents that they could neither be seen or heard," Rabb said.

A fight between them and approximately 100 guerrillas ensued. It was a short fight, only about five minutes, before the guerrillas retreated. Rabb's men then fell back toward the house. "I felt that as it was impossible to see five feet it would be folly for me to pursue them in the woods," Rabb noted. Phillips was killed in the attack and Sgt. Handy was mortally wounded. Rabb left Handy in the care of the women of the house, who promised to bury him. "The ground was covered with blood," he said, describing the scene the next morning. He believed the attackers were under the command of Col. Clark of the Confederate Seventh Missouri Cavalry. [461]

In the 1850 census, Mark Walker lived in Big Lake Township with his wife Temperance, one son, William, and two daughters. [462]

By 1860, he lived with his son William, 23, and his young family, still in Big Lake Township. [463] William was most likely the guerrilla Mark mentioned. Mark would die in Big Lake Township a few years later, in February 1870, of pneumonia. Mark, a widower, was 60 then. [464]

In 1855, Mark acquired 140 acres in a patent for swamp land in Mississippi County, in Section 28, Township 15 North, Range 9 East. [465]

Leaving there, Rabb and his men traveled on through a "very bad swamp" for about six miles with their wounded in tow on litters. On April 7, he met up with Captain Montgomery and his men who said they had killed six or seven guerrillas, but lost no men. Rabb lost one officer and two men and had one officer and six men wounded.

The men continued toward Barfield, where they boarded the steamer, *Darling*, and traveled back to New Madrid.

Captain Pruiett reported after marching 45 miles on April 6 that he and his men came upon two known guerrillas who were part of Bulge Powell's gang. Pursuing them, they killed "the famous Luke Bussell."

The next morning, they crossed a swamp and the Little River. Just after noon, they came upon another group of 25 guerrillas. Charging them, they killed 12 and took five prisoners. The rest, some wounded, escaped into the swamps. The next night, they camped five miles outside of Hornersville before heading back to camp, by way of Clarkton. Of Pruett's men, only three were wounded.

Rabb reported that papers on one of the guerrillas, a man named Williams, showed that various bands in the area may have as many as 1000 men. One order in the papers was dated from Blue Cane in Greene County, Arkansas. "This is a dense canebrake, in the center of which is one of the rebel camps. They have a store supplied with stolen goods, a distillery, several houses, and a large amount of stock." [466]

William, and or James, were possibly involved in some of these incidents.

Confederate companies raised in the county included "Fletcher's Rifles," the "Osceola Hornets," and the "Tyronza Rebels."

The "Tyronza Rebels" were organized in the county on June 3, 1861, with Robert L. Harding as captain. The volunteer soldiers became Company I of the First Regiment, Arkansas Troops. Later, it would become part of the Fifteenth Arkansas Infantry Regiment (Josey's). [467]

Funded by Elliott Fletcher Sr., of Mill Bayou, [468] "Fletcher's Rifles" had its inception following the recruitment of men in June 1861. After gathering at least 45 men, a vote was scheduled to elect officers. Elliott Fletcher Jr. was voted First Lieutenant. This company disbanded, but

Fletcher's men said they would re-form the company if he would be their leader. Fletcher agreed and, at 21 years old, became captain of the company. His younger brother, Thomas, 15, would serve as his sergeant. A few days later, the company received orders to be in Memphis with 68 men ready to serve. [469]

Spirits were high then, early in the war. "The men are in glorious spirits, wrote Fletcher to his family back home on July 19, 1861. [470] Fletcher's company was attached to the Third Confederate Regiment, under Col. John S. Marmaduke, in Hindman's Legion, commanded by Maj. Gen. Thomas C. Hindman. Less than a year later, both Fletchers would die at the Battle of Shiloh in April 1862. [471]

Charles Bowen was serving as sheriff of Mississippi County when he organized the "Osceola Hornets" in Osceola. [472] They mustered into service on August 10, 1861, for 12 months at first and were assigned as Company G, Second Confederate Infantry. Later, they would be transferred to Company I (new) of the Ninth Arkansas Infantry in May 1862. Like most troops raised in the early part of the war, the Ninth would serve its time east of the Mississippi. They would participate in several campaigns and battles, including Shiloh, the Siege of Corinth, the Iuka/Corinth Campaign, and the Battle of Coffeeville, Mississippi. [473]

Bowen said his company was at the Battle of Shiloh and Baker's Creek,[474] also known as the Battle of Champion Hill near Vicksburg. On April 11, 1862, just a few days after Shiloh, Bowen sought a 10-day leave to return to Osceola to gather recruits. His company was down to nine "effective men having been badly cut to pieces in the recent Battle of Shiloh," he wrote. [475]

"I lost twenty-one men Sunday and Monday at Shiloh, the 6th and 7th of April, 1862. We fought there all day," said Bowen in his memoir. [476]

Belona's brother, Paschal Rice, would serve in the Ninth Arkansas Infantry under Bowen, joining in August 1861. He was 43 years old. This company was also known as the 25th Regiment, Mississippi Infantry. [477] John East, James' biological father, also joined at the same time for three years. Serving as a private, he was 49 years old. [478]

Bowen resigned on November 2, 1863, because his company had dwindled to only two lieutenants and 12 enlisted men. In addition, he had been re-elected sheriff of Mississippi County.

However, after retiring and returning home, Bowen did not "retire."

When Lt. Col. J. T. Burris of the Tenth Kansas Volunteers, in command of 500 troops, made a sweep through Mississippi County in August 1864, they encountered Captain Bowen and a rebel force on August 2, outside Osceola, after following a picket toward the camp. The force fled and "a running fight ensued," reported Burris, in which Bowen, their commander, and 25 others were captured and seven killed. [479]

Bowen, with McVeigh, had been recruiting men for Confederate service. Also captured was Col. Elliott Fletcher, father of Elliott and Thomas.

Captain H.M. McVeigh and about 70 men pursued them into Missouri. [480]

Bowen was taken to Gratiot Prison in St. Louis, where he was tried and found not guilty and released on September 8, 1864. [481] Following his release, he returned to the county, gathered his men, and continued to operate. [482]

McVeigh had previously been in the Missouri State Guard, and after their disbandment, he was authorized to recruit men for service. Captured in Northwest Missouri, he was held for a year and exchanged. He re-entered service as a Confederate and served in the Trans Mississippi Department from the winter of 1862 until its surrender. At that time, he was serving as the enrolling officer of Mississippi County. [483]

Burris was joined by a battalion of the Second Missouri State Militia Cavalry under Lt. Col. Hiram Hiller; detachments of the Second and Third, under Major James Wilson; and the First and Sixth Missouri Cavalry Volunteers, under Capt. Valentine Pruiett. Previously searching for guerrilla activity in the county, Pruiett had telegraphed Col. J.B. Rogers in Cape Girardeau that Kitchen and 800 men were in Osceola. He passed this information on to Brig. General Thomas Ewing Jr. on June 10. Ewing commanded the St. Louis District for the U.S. Army. He sent a letter to Burris passing on information from Lt. O. P. Steele, acting provost marshal, New Madrid, and asked him to investigate. "'Kitchen, with 400 men infests that vicinity, stealing, murdering, cutting the wires,'" Steele wrote, "'the condition is horrible.'" Burris replied that he would move with troops that could be spared into Pemiscot County, "and perhaps into Arkansas," which he did.

Before wading through 20 miles of swamp to reach Osceola, Burris and his men had traveled through Hornersville, Missouri, and then on to Big Lake, marching through swamps and along the lake in a southerly direction. During the day, they surprised "bushwhackers and thieves," capturing their arms, horses, and "negroes," which had been "previously stolen by these marauders." They also burned five houses in the area.

Leaving Osceola, they traveled toward Chickasawba, crossed the Pemiscot Bayou, and camped at Cowskin Settlement [484] in Pemiscot County.[485]

During the 17 days in Arkansas, Burris noted the "brisk fight" in Osceola with Bowen's and McVeigh's companies. They captured their camps, killed seven, and took two prisoners, including Bowen. Burris and his men lived off the "enemy," he boasted in his report during these operations in the area. "Having started out without transportation of any kind, and almost without subsistence, both men and animals subsisted off the enemy." [486]

Federal troops from Fort Pillow, across the Mississippi River and south of Osceola, would come into the county at Osceola at times. On one occasion, they took wood from abandoned homes to use in building barracks. [487] Originally, Fort Pillow was built as a Confederate fort, and one of the first places the Fletcher brothers went after joining the service. While Fort Pillow was a Confederate fort, thousands of federal soldiers landed at Osceola in preparation for an attack on the fort. This attack never materialized. [488]

After Fort Pillow came under federal control, Gen. Pope used the plantation Sans Souci, in the southern part of the county and across the river from Fort Pillow, as a field hospital and headquarters. Sans Souci was the home of Georgia and John Harding McGavock. John died in 1861, and during the war, his widow returned to her family's home in Columbus, Mississippi, later returning to Sans Souci, living with her daughter, Sue Grider. [489]

Dr. F.G. McGavock (Felix Grundy), [490] whose family first came to South Mississippi County in the late 1830s, later settled in an area called Shawnee Village, where there was a settlement of Shawnee in the past. [491] During the war, those in that area organized themselves into a group called the Shawnee Legal Association and sought protection from the guerrillas and outlaws operating at that time. McGavock headed up the organization and received the endorsement of Gen. Stephen A. Hulbert, 16th Army Corps of Memphis, and Confederate Gen. Sterling Price. When an offense was committed, the perpetrator or perpetrators were secured and turned over to either the Federal or Confederate authorities, depending on the offense. For offenses deemed petty, a horsewhipping and an order to leave the county were sufficient. [492]

In November 1864, Dr. McGavock requested of Hulbert that his plantation be declared within the lines of the United States in order to ship his crop, raised "entirely by free labor." McGavock told Hulbert that he had been to Washington and was told his only relief was with Gen. Canby and requested Hulbert speak on his behalf. Hulbert noted that McGavock had been "very efficient" in giving notice of guerrilla bands in the area in the last two years.

McGavock made the Union army aware of guerrilla bands, but it also appears he helped Confederate troops.

C.H. Hurst, who may have been some of McGavock's "free labor," said that in exchange for his work, McGavock would keep him out of the "rebel army." McGavock told him that "the rebel army would not trouble any of his men, and they did not." He continued that the doctor always helped the "rebel" troops, providing flour, sugar, coffee, clothing, or "anything he had."

Hurst, who claimed not to be a member of the "rebel army," was captured along with some other Confederate soldiers in Crittenden County on November 30, 1864. These men and Hurst testified in late November while in custody of the provost marshal in Memphis.

E.H. Holmes, of Col. G. Lyles' company, told of how he and his company had been to McGavock's seeking supplies and obtaining them, "if he had them." In November 1864, he noted that they had spent the night there recently.

Wilson Hay, an orderly sergeant in Lyles' command, further related how McGavock helped them with supplies, including "clothing, provisions, or ammunition." Once, McGavock gave the rangers four bales of cotton to pay for supplies from Memphis. Other items included heavy cloth, used to make blankets and shoes.

On November 28, 1864, Hay, along with two captains and one private, attended a dance "with the girls" at McGavock's house. Also, there were two deserters from the Union army, John Blocker and John Wilson, now in the Confederate army.

Once, when Hay and some men were moving 520 muskets and 25,000 rounds of ammunition across the Mississippi from Tennessee, they were almost discovered when a gunboat passed nearby, "but we lay on our oars and she passed without hailing," he said. [493]

It is unknown what Sam and some of the other family members did during the Civil War years, especially during times when guerrillas or federal troops were in the area. His father, William, was in Poinsett County at this time, moving there before 1860. [494] It is known that some residents in southern states left during the war years, becoming refugees. Possibly, they, like James Bunch, hid in the woods at times to avoid conflict.

Dr. James, however, saw action at Mobile Bay where he participated in the making and planting of the first torpedoes used in the battle, according to one of his obituaries.[495] Another obituary said he was a member of the Nitre and Mining Bureau.[496] This was a civilian government bureau that provided the Confederate States of America with materials, including saltpeter, copper, iron, lead, and sulfur, as well as other materials.[497]

James was in Germany before the beginning of the war in the U.S., studying under the famed Baron Justus von Liebig. [498] After leaving Liebig's laboratory, he went to Paris, where, at the start of the war, he was encouraged to go home. James received a degree from the Ludwig Maximilian University of Medicine in Munich, Bavaria, in 1861. [499]

His family home was in Mobile, Alabama. Before leaving, however, he received dispatches from Confederate Commissioner to France John Slidell and James Murray Mason, Confederate Commissioner to Great Britain and France, to deliver to Confederate President Jefferson Davis. Getting there took some ingenuity on James' part, as he pretended to be a "'German interested in the war between the States'" upon arrival in New York. He then made his way to Washington, D.C., and Alexandria, Virginia, as a guest of federal officers, all the while with the dispatches concealed in the holsters of his pistols. After crossing Confederate lines and making his way to deliver the correspondence, he met with Davis, who was impressed with James' "youthful daring and discretion" and appointed him to the Secret Service. [500]

Even though the war was over, the adjustment period would take a little longer. States that had seceded had to begin a process to be readmitted to the Union. Presidential reconstruction began during the war when federal forces occupied the Confederate states. After Little Rock fell to Union forces in 1863, steps began to establish a state government loyal to Washington, D.C. Isaac Murphey was selected to serve as governor after a constitutional convention in early 1864; however, the government did not expand past federal lines. When the two senators, William Fishback and Elisha Baker, were selected to represent the state in Washington, D.C., they were not allowed to serve.

When the war ended, the Arkansas General Assembly voted in April 1865 to ratify the 13th Amendment which abolished slavery. Congressional elections were held in October, but only voters who had taken an oath that they had not supported the Confederacy were allowed to vote. [501]

The Reconstruction Acts of 1867 created five military districts for the 10 Confederate states, except for Tennessee, which had already been admitted back into the Union. Arkansas and Mississippi became the Fourth Military District. Major General Edward Ord, with headquarters in Vicksburg, Mississippi, served as the first commander, and artillery and two companies of infantry were stationed in Little Rock. Other towns also hosted troops, the closest to Mississippi County being Batesville in Independence County and Madison in St. Francis County. The troops were to enforce laws and protect freedmen.

In September 1867, Ord called for an election for November. Legal voters were registered across the state. [502] In Mississippi County, on the first list, there would be 491 legal voters in September 1867. In the Big Lake precinct were Sam, James, and William A. Hector, as well as J. D. Daugherty, Sam's son-in-law, married to Matilda. Also, on this list is Mark Walker, aforementioned. This list would have 19 registrants in Big Lake. Isaac Daugherty was listed in the Chickasawba precinct. [503]

Names were added to the county's list in March 1868 by Eli H. Mix, president of the board of registration for the county. The second list, which didn't have anyone from Big Lake, included the color of the registrants. All are White. [504] Mix, the superintendent and agent for the Freedman's Bureau, was stationed in Osceola. He served from April 1866 to October 1868. [505]

The Freedman's Bureau was established on March 2, 1865, by a congressional act to provide food, clothing, medical services, and land to displaced Southerners, including newly freed African Americans. It was to operate for the last year of the war and a year afterward. It established schools, supervised contracts between employers and employees, and managed confiscated and abandoned lands. The Freedman's Bureau Act of 1866 became law in July of that year and extended the work for two more years.

While Mix was stationed in Osceola, he would report in October 1866 on the treatment of area Blacks in the county. "I have released three colored persons from slavery, one of whom was a woman having been held for the last year without any pay or agreement for pay," he reported to the Little Rock office. "She was badly beaten and horse whipped several times." He went on to say the other two were a husband and wife who were threatened with their lives if they left the plantation where they were under contract for 15 cents a day. [506]

In January 1868, 70 delegates gathered in Little Rock to draft a new state constitution. The new constitution gave Black males the right to vote; recognized the right of all persons to equality before the law; and forbade depriving a citizen of their rights due to race, color, or previous servitude. Free public education was also established.

Following the state's ratification of the 14th Amendment to the U.S. Constitution, the state was readmitted to the Union on June 22, 1868. [507]

Powell Clayton, formerly a Union officer, was elected governor after readmission. Clayton immediately began to exercise the newly expanded powers of the office, using his position to appoint Union veterans and other Republicans to many offices at the county level.

Many of those who had supported the Confederacy were frustrated with the expansion of Republican power. The Ku Klux Klan, founded in Tennessee in 1866 as a secret fraternal organization, began to take hold in the state in 1868. Murders of both Whites and Blacks took place across the state. In August of 1868, Clayton began to organize a state militia. With violence continuing across the state, Clayton declared voter registration impossible in several counties. In the November election, Republicans held the state, and Democrats claimed the election would have been different if voting had been allowed or not thrown out in 14 counties.

Clayton declared martial law in 10 counties the day after the election. Later, four more counties were included. Mississippi County was among the first 10 counties placed under martial law. The militia moved into these counties without arms, uniforms, or other supplies, forcing them to gather food when available from the local population. Receipts were issued for the supplies, but were not honored by the state government. Martial law was lifted for all counties by March 1869. [508]

Not long after Charles B. Fitzpatrick was appointed registrar for the county, political and racial violence erupted and came to be known as the "Black Hawk War." Fitzpatrick came to Arkansas in 1869 and was known as a "striker," or one who introduced bills in the state legislature with the idea of being bought off. [509]

"I was not a resident of that county when appointed to the office, but had been sent over by Powell Clayton," testified Fitzpatrick in the L.C. Gause versus Asa Hodges case, "to try and carry the county in the interest of the Republican party." Fitzpatrick was one of those who were deposed when L.C. Gause challenged the election of Asa Hodges in the First Congressional District in 1873. [510]

In late August 1872, Fitzpatrick alleged in a speech in the county that the sheriff, J.B. Murray, as a tax collector, embezzled school taxes. Later, when the two met, the sheriff reportedly punched Fitzpatrick, and he, in turn, shot Murray, fatally wounding him.

Fitzpatrick surrendered but requested a guard of African Americans. He had gathered a group of 75-100 guards and posted bail. In the afternoon during the trial, several armed White men with Capt. Charles Bowen paraded through Osceola. Fearing trouble, Osceola Judge Palmer, filling in for the regular judge, adjourned court that day and the next when no witnesses or jurors showed up. Palmer attempted to disperse the groups gathered, but was not successful. Shots were soon exchanged, and one of Fitzpatrick's men was killed. [511]

Bowen tells of gathering men, some from Clear Lake, and waiting for some from Big Lake. "So, we got together about 65 of them," he noted in his memoirs, following Fitzpatrick and his men into the swamps. The next day, they overtook them in the "bend of 35 and at Cottonwood Point," and Shawnee Village. "A heap of them are lying there yet, I reckon," he said. They brought back 18 men with them. [512]

A Memphis paper would report in November that a couple more bodies of Blacks were found floating in the river, near "Somers," making a total of seven, who were mysteriously slain recently.

Fitzpatrick never went to trial in the death of the sheriff. [513]

In the November 5 election that year, 13 residents of Big Lake voted, all for the same candidates. For governor, they voted for Joseph Brooks, who ran against Elisha Baxter. Brooks carried the county. Baxter won in the state, but that election was contested by Brooks. Controversy surrounding that election would result in the Brooks-Baxter War, an armed conflict in Little Rock in 1874.

The polling place for the Big Lake precinct was held in the home of Sam Hector, who served as judge as early as 1878 when a new voting precinct was established at "Sam Hector's house in Big Lake Township." [514] In the 1880 election, Sam was listed as a judge, as were John Perry and John Peterson.[515] In 1888, Jim (Sam's son) Hector served as one of the clerks for East Big Lake for the July 7 primary, with Sam as one of the judges.[516]

In 1870, Sam was appointed superintendent of public roads in Big Lake Township following the war. [517]

Sam did not join the war efforts, although family members did. Possibly, he had a disability that kept him from being conscripted, or he was a guardian for elderly family members. Possibly, as well, he had a deeper understanding of the struggles of non-white humanity.

James or Alf (James Alfred East Hector), as he was often called, suffered no wounds from his service, but William's parole papers described him as having yellow eyes, which may have been an indication of sickness. Twice as many soldiers died of chronic disease during the war as in combat. Diseases soldiers acquired included malaria, typhoid fever, measles, dysentery, yellow fever, and syphilis, with gastrointestinal disorders being the most common. [518]

William died young in 1875, leaving his wife, the former Lucinda "Cinda" Bunch, and two children, James Alfred and Mary Elizabeth Hector, in Dunklin County, Missouri. [519] Lucinda was the sister of Sam Bunch, who married Melissa Hector, Sam Hector's youngest daughter, in 1878. [520]

James, however, lived a long life. He married Mary Daugherty, and they had four children between 1859 and 1877.

The benefits of a good economy before the war may be represented in some of James' shopping trips to Wittsburg in the late 1850s. Some of his purchases in 1857 at a Cross County store included a saddle for $13.50, stirrups, a saddle blanket, a riding whip, coats, a linen bosom shirt, pants, a vest, a cravat, and pocket knives. Most likely, for Mary, he purchased needles, hairpins, shoes, corset laces, and a silk mantilla for $10. [521]

It is possible that the Navy six-gun he used to kill a couple of deer on his way to Osceola in 1873 was his service pistol. "Our friend, Alf Hector (James Alfred East Hector) was again in town and during the week and on his way in succeeded in killing two nice fat deer, with his navy six," wrote the editor. "He did not forget, but brought us a ham, for which he positively refused to receive a cent." [522] The Colt Model 1861 Navy was a six-shot percussion revolver used by soldiers during the Civil War. [523]

In 1891, Arkansas began granting pensions to indigent Confederate veterans. James applied for a pension based on his age and incapacity for manual labor. He was granted $100 annually in July 1913. He was 76 years old. The doctor examining him noted that he had no wounds, but he did have chronic rheumatism of the forearm and malformation of some of his fingers.[524]

Sam's dad, William "Moonshine" Hector, a legend in his time, died in 1865. [525] He lived in Poinsett County, later Cross County, in 1860 with Louiza Hector and children, James, John, and Joseph Hector. He was 67. His daughter, Martha Ann, was born in 1861. [526]

Chapter 9

Mounds

Knowing Dr. James' interest in artifacts, Sam told him of how every time he dipped the steel blade of his plow into the earth and overturned the rich, black soil, up popped pieces of pottery, some with little zigzag marks on their surface, and occasionally a little color. He marveled at the design and then recalled what he had once been told about this piece of land from Chickalee.

"The land has many stories," he told James. He knew that even though it was his home now, it had been a home many generations earlier. The signs were everywhere.

He remembers standing in the field with Corn Meal [527] (Chickalee) when he was a child, and Corn Meal telling him about the land's past. "This was an Indian village," he said. Sam's field, where he planted corn, was rich with relics from the past. Corn Meal also told him about several other places along the Little River where villages once prospered, partly evidenced by the apple and peach trees growing near the banks. All along the river and on his property on the Pemiscot Bayou were the signs of occupation left behind in pottery, brick, arrowheads, and other items. Often, he'd find an arrowhead, sometimes a pipe, and when he was lucky, an old folks' pot might be unearthed.

The land had stood the test of time: earthquakes, flooding, and the recent war. It was rich and full of promise.

"Sam," James said, "tell me more about the old-time folks who built the mounds."

James knew it was best to let Sam talk, for if he asked him too many questions, he might not get an answer, but if he just left him be, Sam would tell him more. So, he waited.

Sam had tromped all over the mound near his home. He often wondered why and how the mounds came to be. While he knew a lot about the lay of the land and the medicinal properties of plants, he didn't know much about those who built the mounds in the area.

He knew one thing, though: those who built the mounds "loved to work," he told James.

"'You, a big doctor,'" said Sam, "'and you know a heap of things; but we Injuns know something too. You think Injuns built them mounds, but they didn't.'"

Sam went on to explain that neither his father nor his father's father knew who built those mounds. They were there long before the Indians occupied the area. [528]

James determined that he would find out as much as he could about the "old-time folks," while he lived in the area. As Mississippi County

Surveyor, he had an opportunity to learn about the land and locate prehistoric sites.

Sam was paying more attention to where he was at the moment. He knew that it wouldn't be long before they reached their destination. He had passed the mounds many times before, even stopping there a few times. Before his father died, he would take this route to visit with him after he moved downriver, out of Mississippi County, to Poinsett County. Then, as now, his dugout would be outfitted to be a home away from home. He never left without his trusted rifle and ammunition, knife, bait box, blankets, an extra guide pole, canteens, a pole for fishing, and something to eat, whether it was bread, dried meat, or nuts and seeds. On this trip, a couple of spades were also brought along for digging.

"We are getting near," Sam told James. "Just around this curve to our right, we will see the first mound soon."

Before long, they were stepping onto shore onto a very rich, black dirt, no doubt from generations of overflows. The woods here grew oak, hackberry, pecan, gum, hickory, and cottonwood trees. A smattering of cane also came into view. [529]

The mounds, though, were what the trip was all about.

The Miller Mounds [530] *were a group of 12 mounds located on the west bank of the St. Francis River, not far from Marked Tree.*

Both Sam and Dr. James approached the mounds with excitement.

A man of "rare intellect," James had an interesting life and career. His "facility in the acquirement of languages was little short of marvelous," noted his obituary in an American Microscopical Society publication. [531]

Reading at the age of three, he began the study of Latin and Greek early. By the age of 12, he composed a play in French, which was presented to his classmates during commencement. At 16, he studied civil engineering in Germany. Following this, he studied chemistry and later studied medicine in Paris, France. He received a PhD from the University of Munich. [532]

Before coming to Mississippi County, James was associate editor of the *Memphis Appeal* in the early 1870s and was noted for his reconstruction histories. [533] Even after coming to Arkansas, he would still write an article occasionally for the *Appeal.* [534]

After assisting Dr. McGavock at Shawnee Village and practicing medicine at Frenchman's Bayou, [535] James was the Mississippi County Surveyor from 1872 to 1874. [536] He was assigned the duties of Deputy to County Court Clerk James Best. Later, Best would join him in a partnership as Real Estate Agents and Conveyancers. [537] In April 1874, he opened a physician's office in Osceola with attention to diseases of the eyes, skin, and ears. A couple of years later, he began to keep a journal, commencing in September 1877 and ending in April 1878, in which he revealed his thoughts on the citizens of the area and his treatments of their ailments, as well as his disappointments, judgments, interests, the weather, and other happenings in the county.

"A 'harder' lot of human beings do not exist under the blue canopy of heaven," he wrote, noting that he had two applications for abortion in a week in the fall of 1877. And that from "strict church members." [538]

During that fall, "business was dull," he wrote a couple of times, which may have given him time for other pursuits. In November, he acted as "arbitrator" for John Matthews with former riverboat Captain Dan Matthews and "Semmes" [539] against "Ike Doherty" (Isaac Daugherty). After examining papers, they decided to "'saw off' even," he said, with John paying the court costs. This agreement was "very advantageous" for John, he said, as he believed had it gone to a hearing, Daugherty would have received $485.[540]

Daugherty married Mary Ellen Johnson, a niece of Sam's wife, Belona. Isaac's brother, James Daugherty, was married to Sam's daughter, Matilda. He died in 1868. [541]

December brought even "duller" business. "I have not made twenty dollars this month," James lamented. Later that week, he was busy but made "very little," as most of it was charity work.

James would often begin his diary entries with a thermometer reading of daily temperatures and comments on the weather. On December 23, 1877, it was "raining like the devil," he noted as he went to sleep on board the *Osceola Belle*, at the beginning of his trip to Memphis.

James' interests were varied. He was interested in astronomy, calling attention to the reaction of the citizens of Osceola when an occultation of Venus by the moon occurred on December 8, 1877. The town was "agog" at the sight, he said. An occultation occurs when one object is hidden behind another object as it passes between them and the observer. In this case, the moon obscured the view of Venus. "I rarely ever looked upon a more brilliant and beautiful sight," said James. [542]

Archaeology also piqued his interest, and the region between Big Lake, Miller Mounds, Little River, and beyond was exactly what James was interested in on this and subsequent trips he and Sam would make.

On these trips, James gathered many artifacts which he later shipped to the Smithsonian and other scientific institutions in this country and Europe. "You cannot dig away the alluvial soil without coming upon man's handiwork," he wrote in his 1895 paper, "in the shape of fragments of burned clay, pottery, arrow heads, spear heads, etc." [543]

During these excursions, Frank gained knowledge of the former inhabitants of the area. He was told that while digging a grave at Carson Lake, a "cement floor" was found, and further investigation revealed a "barrel-shaped vault" that contained the skeleton of a woman in a seated position with a child in her arms. He planned to investigate further after being told there were hundreds of these tombs in the area. [544]

Other evidence of early inhabitants included a buttress of a bridge built of burned brick on Little River. Remnants of which could still be seen in the 1870s, James said in his 1895 paper. [545]

In the area, beginning just south of Big Lake, lay one big graveyard, James told, evidence of a once vast occupation. "In the delta of Little River, immediately after its exit from Big Lake, may be found evidence of an immense settlement, extending 15 or 20 miles down the stream," he said. In that area, hundreds of wagonloads of artifacts could be unearthed, including burial crypts, pots, vases, pottery, stone implements, and ornaments, some of which showed "beautiful workmanship." Some of these items were sent to the Smithsonian. [546]

Joseph Henry of the Smithsonian Institution contracted with James to open mounds in the area and send specimens to Washington in 1877-1878. James sent a collection to the Smithsonian in December 1877. "I packed a box of vases, etc. to send the Smithsonian this evening," wrote James on December 22. Upon receipt of some items from James, Henry said that the items were "full of interest, the pipes representing an extremely ancient and unusual form of earthen ware. The hoes are among the most perfect that we have ever seen." He said the "vases with two openings" are of "exceptional interest." [547]

Items in the Smithsonian attributed to James include celts, vases, vessels, knives, a chunkey stone, a rubbing stone, hoes, arrow points, cups, bowls, an earthenware image of a tortoise, pipes, and pots. Some of the items, which include items from the Big Lake Mound, may be viewed on the Smithsonian's online website. [548]

Spencer F. Baird, Secretary of the Smithsonian Institution, wrote in his annual report about items received from James in 1878. The collections are of "great beauty and variety," he said. [549]

In his correspondence with the Smithsonian, James described vases with an "orifice on the side of the neck" and showed evidence on the bottom of the vessel of having been "moulded upon a gourd which was subsequently burned out." [550]

These artifacts are the first documented collections from the Mississippi County area. [551]

James D. Middleton, with the Bureau of Ethnology, explored and collected items from the 12 Miller Mounds in 1884. The report was printed in the Annual Report of the U.S. Bureau of Ethnology, 1890-1891. [552] Artifacts from the mounds, collected by Middleton, can be viewed on the Smithsonian website.[553]

The report noted that mound 1, under cultivation at that time, may be, in part, a natural formation. The rest were in the adjoining woods. While mounds 1, 2, and 3 remained above ground during the overflows, the rest were submerged to a depth of three to four feet or more. "Quantities of potsherds, broken stone implements, burned clay, and arrowheads are plowed up every season and scattered" across the mounds and fields.

Mound 1 was the largest. At its greatest length, it was 900 feet and 225 feet wide. It was long, flat-topped, and not level. Its height varied from four feet to 12 feet. Since houses were present, permission to dig was not granted.

Mound 2 was 110 feet in diameter and 18 feet high, conical, and symmetrical. Mound 3 was oval and flat on top. Mound 4 was three feet high and circular. Several human bones were found in this small mound, as well as whole earthen vessels. Mound 5 was 20 feet in diameter and two feet high. Mound 6 was 40 feet in diameter and three feet high. Several whole earthen vessels, including water bottles, pots, bowls, and pottery fragments, were found.

Mound 7, five feet high and 60 feet in diameter, was on low, wet ground with water all around it. Eight pots were found, with two beside an adult skeleton. Mound 8 was 20 feet in diameter and two feet high. Nothing was found. Mound 9 was circular and flat, with a large pecan tree on top. It was 30 feet in diameter and four feet high. Several artifacts and skeletons were discovered, as well as a bone punch.

Mound 10 was a small circular mound, three feet high. It held one skeleton with four pots, two of which were under the head of the skeleton. Mound 11 was 35 feet in diameter and three and one-half feet high. Broken mussel shells and potsherds were found along with pots, skeletons, and clay pipes. Burned clay with the impression of split cane was found, suggesting the walls of a burned dwelling. Small trees stood on top and near the mound. [554]

Mound 12, circular, 25 feet in diameter and three feet high, contained skeletons, a clay disk, a clay pipe, and pots. Several small hardwood trees were growing on top.

It is unknown what James and Sam discovered on their trip. While James enjoyed his explorations and discoveries in the area, he was discontent during his stay in Osceola, lamenting that it was a shame that his "best years should be spent in this hole." [555]

James stayed in Osceola for another 17 months after discontinuing his diary. In 1879, he spearheaded the organization of the Mississippi County Medical Society. He also assisted the U.S. Corps of Engineers in a survey of the Mississippi River.

After leaving Osceola, James practiced medicine in St. Louis, Missouri, in 1880, and was a professor of chemistry at the St. Louis College of Physicians and Surgeons. He was associate editor of the *St. Louis Medical and Surgical Journal* and editor of the *National Druggist* from 1884 until his death. He became a member of the American Microscopical Society in 1882, [556] serving once as president. [557]

The "old folks" who left behind the artifacts Sam referred to were the Mound Builders, occupants of North America for a 5,000-year period who also left behind evidence of their way of life in the form of earthen constructions used for ceremonial, burial, religious, and residential purposes.

Spanish explorer and Conquistador Hernando de Soto's expedition provides the first records of the mound builders in the area, as they were still building mounds when he came through in 1541. However, by 1673, when Louis Jolliet and Jacques Marquette traveled into the area, the Mississippian towns that de Soto encountered were gone.

There were and are several mounds in Northeast Arkansas, one of which existed near some of Sam's property, and the rich artifacts and the chance to explore them brought others to the area before and after the turn of the century.

One of whom was Edward Palmer, a field assistant for the Smithsonian Institution's Bureau of Ethnology, Mounds Exploration Division from 1882 to 1884. The division conducted an exploration of mounds in the Eastern United States, and Arkansas was one of the areas studied intensively, with Palmer doing most of the research.

Palmer's notes on his travels in the area also offered a glimpse of life in Arkansas as he viewed it in the early 1880s. He described the town of Osceola, which served as a base of operations in 1881, as a "dirty, damp, expensive place to live." [558] Leaving there in a mule team, on October 27, he traveled first through the woods and over a new cut road toward Little River. Palmer noted that along the road were blazed trees and a few houses. He had to pass through cypress swamps up to his knees. After 10 miles, he came to the home of a man named Arnold, who had a "fine cotton crop." He crossed Little River at a spot that was a dry stream bed at this time, but noted that six months of the year, steamboats plied upstream.

On the other side of the river, Palmer stayed the night with Mr. Beggs, who lived in a "rude" log hut, while waiting for his house to be built. A windstorm roared throughout the night and felled some trees, blocking roads. He noted that those obstructions are not usually cleared if one can travel around them.

From there, Palmer traveled toward the Big Lake area, "a hunter's haven." On the way, Palmer and his group passed camps of hunters and a few log huts occupied by "long-haired, dirty, sickly people," mentioning that malarial fever is common. Some told him they had no food except what they shot. Cottonwood trees in the area had holes cut in them for collecting water, where the traveler might quench his thirst. [559]

On the 28th, Palmer visited Sam's farm on Pemiscot Bayou to explore the mound nearby. [560] It was 20 feet high and measured a quarter of an acre on top and originally a little larger at the base. The mound had been plowed over and searched for artifacts. Sam told Palmer that when he first cultivated the mound, its sides contained three ditches all around, at an equal distance from each other. Evidence of one of the ditches remained.

Palmer, who bestowed the title of esquire on Sam's name, possibly because Sam served as a judge, with voting held at his house, [561] surmised that since the mound was in an area that often overflowed, the ditches may have been built to prevent water from encroaching upon the mound, or possibly the ditches may have helped provide defense from enemies and a means of observation. Sam told him that when he first plowed over the mound, ashes, charcoal, and burnt clay with some bones and pottery were found. [562]

This mound is in Dell, Arkansas, where several early residents are buried, including Sam's daughter Matilda Perry.

Palmer and his group spent the night at a man named Peterson's house on the Pemiscot Bayou. Here, bees, cotton, fowl, cows, corn, and mules abound, he said. There were three women who met him at the door of the "poor and disorderly" house with "snuff sticks" in their mouths. Three men with guns had just returned from the hunt. "The place beggars of description. Its dirty appearance," he wrote, and the "clothing of the people would lead you to infer the people never wash."

Supper there that night consisted of black coffee, plain cornbread, and "abominably cooked wild goose." Speaking of Palmer exploring the mounds, the landlord or owner of the house told him that he did not "see the use of the nonsense" of opening graves and likened it to a sin. The farm had a horse-powered gin.

Three slept in one bed on the floor that night, along with the fleas and bedbugs. Breakfast the next morning consisted of black coffee, cornbread, and raccoon with a "little new made stinking butter," Palmer said, noting that they had seen the dogs licking the cream from the churn.

"We did not wait for dinner but left for Osceola," he wrote. [563]

John Peterson lived in the Big Lake area as early as 1860. In 1880, his household included him, 49, his wife, Mary J., daughters, Sarah Jane, 24, Manurvia L., 19, and Laura Ann, 16, and Mary's sons, A.B. Bishop, 30, and Andrew J. Bishop, 27. [564]

On October 31, Palmer would visit Chickasawba Mound, still located on the outskirts of what is now Blytheville. The mound had been previously dug, he noted, and it would not pay to open it. [565] The owner, H. B. Cooke, [566] did not want to have it dug into, as he was preparing to build a house upon it with a cellar because it was a dry spot.

The large mound was 25 feet high on one part and 30 feet high on another part. It was a quarter of an acre on top and had been dug many times in the past, he said. "I was informed that only a few things were found and those on the surface," said Palmer. He was told of one party digging 16 feet down and finding nothing, and another party digging from the side toward the center, finding "hewn timbers."

From the mound, Palmer noted that there was a "fine view" of the surrounding country and the Pemiscot Bayou. "For a wide distance around were the dwellings & graves of hundreds." Nearby, cotton was cultivated on a field covered with pottery and bone fragments. There were several elevations in the field where the owner told Palmer that, along with one skeleton in one place, ashes, charcoal, pots, and stone implements were found. Palmer dug into a post hole and recovered a small water vessel, striped red and white. [567]

Chickasawba is a multi-mound site that is mostly a late prehistoric, early pro-historic settlement, located on the Pemiscot Bayou, which had at least three mounds and a plaza area. Other small mounds existed. Burned daub and surface material suggest a sizeable village existed. Even though there were early components, the major occupation was late Mississippian. [568] The largest mound was probably the one Palmer wanted to explore.

The owner may not have been the first to build a home atop one of these mounds. It was told that the Chief Chickasawba, [569] for which the mound and the early settlement were named, built his hut on top of one of the mounds. [570]

Charles Bowen, whose family came to the area in 1828, recalled seeing Chickasawba carrying wild honey in a skin flung across his back on his way to Barfield Point to sell it. As late as 1836, Bowen said 40 Indian families were living in the vicinity of Chickasawba. [571]

Dr. James was one of those who had explored the Chickasawba area. In requesting funds to explore the "great Chickasawba mound" from Joseph Henry in November 1877, he wrote that in the 10 acres around it, "a spade can scarcely be thrust without turning up human remains and those, too, of a most interesting and valuable character." Some of the remains, he said, were up to seven feet six inches in height. Several skulls were artificially flattened and some were pointed. [572]

Sam accompanied James on more trips than the one to the Miller Mounds, James wrote in a footnote in his 1895 paper. He could have been with James when he first visited Chickasawba. "For, at the time spoken of, and several times subsequently, in company with Sam Hector (a half-breed Shawnee) [573] and alone, I opened many graves." The artifacts were sent to several institutions. [574] James did not keep records of his discoveries, so it is hard to know where his pieces came from or where they all went.

In 1876, James was "deputized" by Dr. Theo Hoerner, a chemist of Memphis, Tennessee, to assist in the collection of relics of the mound builders for the Museum at Vienna, Austria. In an article in *The Osceola Times,* residents of Mississippi County were encouraged to call on the doctor with any specimens they had on hand. James would receive and forward the artifacts with the names of the contributors and any information, as well as pay for the expense of transportation. [575]

One can still view the largest mound at the Chickasawba site in the middle of a crop field, where pottery shards can still be found in the plowed dirt. [576] The site has been explored many times over the years.

Palmer visited many other mounds in the area. Many mounds suffered damage from the 1811-1812 earthquakes, Palmer noted. At nearby Carson Lake, he examined three mounds that had been changed due to the earthquakes.

Other places Palmer visited while in the county in 1882 include Pecan Point, [577] "fishmouth," [578] the Jackson Mound, [579] the mounds on Frenchman's Bayou, [580] six miles west of the Golden Lake Post Office, and on the Mississippi River. [581]

Palmer's comments, with mound descriptions, offer some local color to Northeast Arkansas. While exploring the Forrest City area, Palmer noted that his driver referred to homemade tobacco as "Arkansas scrip." Here, turnips sold for one cent each, beef for 10 to 15 cents a pound, and small chickens at 25 cents each. The bread came from Memphis or Helena.

At the hotel in Harrisburg, one could stay for $1.50 per day. However, the food was "badly cooked," and drinking water had insects in it, Palmer said. In town was a brick courthouse with a jail, a doctor's office, a printing shop, and a post office. While saloons were prohibited, one could find "Kansas eggs," which were eggs filled with whiskey, sealed with white wax, and sold for 10 cents apiece. The grocery store had an inner room that received more traffic on Saturday than on other days.

In Osceola, the grand jury had two Black men, and the petit jury had one, but there was "some strong talk from some against it." Chinamen lived there at the time, earning their living by "burning bricks." He noted they were very industrious. He was there on July 4, 1882, when the Black residents held a festival that night, with ice cream and cake. During the day, they had a barbecue out of town, as did some White residents. With no saloons in town, "there was sobriety." [582]

When Palmer visited mounds at Pecan Point in the county, Dr. F.G. McGavock, whose land bordered Pecan Point, filled him in on some of his activities during the war, relating how he fed soldiers from both sides of the conflict. Federal gunboats were in front of his house while Confederates camped in the rear. The Confederates were calling for "contributions while the Federals had plenty."

Some of the laborers hired by McGavock after the war were 86 Irish girls from Castle Garden, New York. They were employed for one year, for $20 a month, and room and board. This was during the last year of the war, and cotton was selling between $1.40 and $1.80 a pound.

Unfortunately, when the floods came, part of the crop was unpicked, but upon promising the girls a new balmoral [583] and a pair of shoes, the crop was saved.

"All the teams were put in the field, four women on a side," and the rest of the cotton crop was pulled, loaded on the wagons, taken to a dry place, and saved. "They – barefooted with dresses between their legs," McGavock related to Palmer. [584]

Castle Garden was America's first official immigration center.

Without experience, the girls, who ranged in age from 14 to 45, helped the doctor realize a profit of $45,000 that year. Mindful of their comfort, he provided a corps of waiters, skilled cooks, and bakers to prepare their meals.

With their health in mind, he mixed a few drops of quinine into a barrel of whiskey, serving them two drams, three times a day. For their spiritual welfare, McGavock paid a Catholic Priest to visit them. [585]

The Irish women may have also entertained soldiers at times, as soldier Wilson Hay (Chapter 8) told of dancing with the girls at McGavock's on a visit in the fall of 1864.

Hay also told of how, in October, they received supplies from McGavock and issued them "to the men out in the field back of his house." They were often there to learn where the gunboats were, "and what was going on," he told, much like McGavock described his involvement in the Civil War to Palmer. [586]

The Irish women stayed there for two years. A few years later, McGavock hired 55 German men from Castle Garden and employed them on the Nodena plantation. The best workers were the Chinese he brought from Chicago to work at Shawnee Village. [587] The German men, however, were a "decided failure," he told Palmer.[588]

Between 1889 and 1894, histories of Arkansas were published by Goodspeed Publishing Company of Chicago, Illinois, Nashville, Tennessee, and St. Louis, Missouri. The histories were often supplemented by information from local citizens and public officials. *The Biographical and Historical Memoirs of Northeast Arkansas* was published in 1889 and covered Clay, Craighead, Fulton, Greene, Independence, Izard, Jackson, Lawrence, Mississippi, Poinsett, Randolph, and Sharp counties. [589]

The early history of Mississippi County in this volume was furnished by the Hon. H.M. McVeigh (Chapter 8) from a manuscript history he had written a few years before the Goodspeed publication. He studied sources of history for the area and interviewed old settlers, [590] including Sam.

He would later refer to Sam as an old friend when he shared some information in a letter about something Sam told him with Fay Hempstead, a historian. His information was used in the publication of *A Pictorial History of Arkansas, From the Earliest of Times to the Year 1890*. Hempstead was writing about the old French Fort St. Francis, which he said was believed then to be near the site of Wittsburg, in Cross County, and his footnote tells of how McVeigh told him about Sam. "'An old friend of mine, Sam Hector, part Indian, who spent his early life among the Indians, tells me he has often picked up iron musket balls on the bluff at Wittsburg, when a boy, living among the Indians,'" McVeigh said in a letter. [591]

Fort St. Francis was established in 1739. Dallas Herndon, in his *Centennial History of Arkansas*, said the site of the fort was concluded by some as near the site of Wittsburg, because of musket balls found there. However, he said, it was unlikely the fort was that far (40 miles) from the Mississippi River. He notes that "Monette" [592] says it was at the mouth of the St. Francis River, which would place it just north of Helena, Arkansas. [593]

McVeigh was appointed to the bar in Arkansas in 1865 and practiced law in Osceola. He was a member of the state legislature in 1873 and 1881.[594]

In the Goodspeed history, McVeigh described Sam as a "truthful, upright citizen of Big Lake." Sam told him that when he moved to the county in 1837, the Indians occupied the area.

Corn Meal (Chickalee) told Sam that there was once a town on his property and several others along the banks of Little River. The evidence of these occupations Sam witnessed in the numerous apple and peach trees he found growing in the woods. [595]

These types of fruit trees were introduced by Europeans, which would make the trees from later occupations than the mound builders

"In and around Mr. Hector's place on Big Lake, pieces of pottery and brick are often plowed up," Goodspeed's history continued. "The same material is found all along the banks of Little River, and there are everywhere through this part of Mississippi County relics of a once dense population." [596]

McVeigh, in his history of the area, told of how he believed the Casqui town, where the chief resided, and where de Soto visited after crossing the Mississippi River, was possibly the village site of Chickasawba. [597]

Casqui was one of the chiefs visited by de Soto and his men. They used the name to refer to the chief, as well as the town and the area where he ruled. A neighboring chief was Pacaha, with whom Casqui was at war. It is currently believed that Casqui may be the Parkin site, in Parkin Archaeological State Park in Cross County, Arkansas. During that time in June 1541, the residents of the town were experiencing a drought and requested de Soto's help. His men then constructed a huge cross and placed it atop a mound. [598]

A large wooden beam had been removed from the Chickasawba site, McVeigh said in his history. "Mr. Joseph Fassit, an old citizen of the county, states that a large wooden beam was taken from that mound a few years before" the Civil War. Leaving Casqui, the Spaniards traveled to Pacaha. Here, McVeigh writes that the chief town was situated on a lake with a stream of water flowing through it and to the Mississippi River. The lake, which came almost to the walls of the town, entered into a ditch that flowed almost around it. The country in and around Big Lake "still bears upon its surface traces of a wide" population. "And precisely such a ditch …," he wrote, "can now be traced near the home of Mr. Sam Hector of Big Lake." [599]

In 1939, years after McVeigh wrote his thoughts on de Soto's route, a detailed study of his route was commissioned by Congress, in recognition of the 400th anniversary of the army's landing in the United States. John R. Swanton of the Smithsonian Institution wrote a report largely based on the four surviving accounts of the expedition, the terrain over which the army would have marched, and archaeological information available at the time.

Ethnohistorian Charles Hudson of the University of Georgia led a restudy of the route for many years. His proposed route is different from Swanton's. His route is even more divergent west of the Mississippi from

Swanton's than east of the Mississippi. Due to differences, archaeologists across the Southeast renewed efforts to find the towns and places described in the original sources.

Only a few archaeological finds are available for study, with the best evidence of the route coming from artifacts found at Parkin. These items include a brass bell, remains of two other bells, lead shot, a Chevron bead, and possible remains of a cross. In 1966, archaeologists found what appeared to be remains of a cross, wrote Jeffrey M. Mitchem, Arkansas Archaeological Survey's Research Station Archaeologist for the Parkin Archaeological State Park, in an Arkansas Archaeological Survey publication. [600]

During a University of Arkansas Museum project, remains of the large wooden post were found. The workers collected a few samples of the wood at that time, and from the bottom of the pit. The remaining wood was covered with plastic sheeting, and the hole was filled in. In the 1990s, an analysis was done on wood samples. Findings showed the dates for the bald cypress wood between 1515 and 1633. Archaeologists then looked forward to the day they could dig down to the post and see if a tree ring date would show it was cut down in 1541. However, it wasn't until 2016 that the project became a reality. With a grant to cover costs, the excavation recovered a remnant of the post and some of the soil matrix. After sending it to an expert, it was decided that it was too broken to derive a tree ring date.

Radiocarbon analysis, however, showed calibrated date ranges of AD 1450-1650, which includes the year 1541. The archaeological context and dates, artifacts, and other archaeological information at Parkin offer a "compelling argument," said Mitchem, that this is a remnant of the cross raised by de Soto in 1541 at Casqui. [601]

A suggested alternative route by de Soto was offered by H. Terry Childs and Charles H. McNutt in a 2009 journal article, "Hernando De Soto's Route from Chicaça Through Northeast Arkansas: A Suggestion." This route would again take the expedition near Sam's home, as McVeigh had suggested. However, their route would differ from McVeigh's.

While noting historical accounts of a cross near Sam's home, the authors suggested the expedition may have erected crosses on more mounds, and "conversely, the presence of a cross on a mound does not necessarily identify Casqui."

After leaving the Casqui province, the de Soto expedition would travel across a swamp. The first major site on the other side of the swamp is the Chickasawba site. The site "conforms in many ways to the journal descriptions," the authors noted.

Compelling reasons to consider Chickasawba as Pacaha include it being a large town on the far side of a marsh, with a lake nearby; the use of mud and straw instead of wattle and daub compatible with descriptions of the stockade at Pacaha; the land being higher than surrounding areas, and at one time almost surrounded by water; and a possible water route to the Mississippi

---

River fits the description of Pacaha and others taking refuge on an island in a large river. The authors noted two possible sites within the range of travel in the journals. One would be in Southeast Missouri, where a Mississippian site exists, although not a lot is known about it. The other would be at Barfield Landing, where a large mound was lost to the Mississippi River in the mid-to-late 1800s. According to Charles Bowen, there were remains of an ancient fort at that site.

There is no evidence of a palisade at the time of their writing, which would add to the reasons for Chickasawba possibly being Pacaha. While necessary to establish the site at Pacaha, it is not absolutely needed for their interpretation. [602]

No matter where the actual expedition traveled in Arkansas, it remains that there once was a huge population along the waterways in the northeast part of the state. One is the Nodena site in Mississippi County. It was occupied from approximately AD 1400 to 1650. A collection of artifacts from the site is held at the University of Alabama Museum and its regional repository, the Arkansas Archeological Survey, and the Hampson Archeological Museum State Park in Wilson, Arkansas. Amateur archaeologist and owner of the Nodena plantation, Dr. James Hampson first surveyed the site in 1897. It wasn't until 1927 that the area was more extensively excavated, and then by the staff of the University of Arkansas and the Alabama Museum of Natural History. With the Parkin site described by many as Casqui, the Upper Nodena site, northeast of there, is believed by some to be Pacaha. [603]

Because of the numerous archaeological sites in the area, Sam would have had a large selection of pots to make his tea from the red leaves he gathered on this trip and other times.

In 1870, Sam and his wife Belona had three children in their household: Melissa, 16, James A., 6, and Nancy J., 3. His daughter Matilda had remarried John Perry. She had one son by her first husband James Daugherty, Thomas, 4. [604]

1873 was a year of depression for the county and the rest of the nation. Sam sold several pieces of property that year, maybe in response to the depression.

Recovery wasn't until later in 1880. James touches on it in his diary, noting how credit was not available for area planters in 1877. "Many and many of a family did without coffee, flour, and sugar (not to mention whiskey) this summer for the first time in their lives." [605]

By 1880, Sam and Belona had only one child at home, James, 16. Nancy J. had passed, and daughter Melissa had married Sam Bunch. The Bunch's were the parents of five-year-old twins, T.A. (Thomas) and J.A. (James), and Elizabeth, 2. [606] Matilda and her husband John Perry were the parents of four children, Balonia, Samuel, John W., and Edward T., besides her son, Thomas. [607]

William, son of old William and Jaley, died in 1875. [608] Sam's wife's half-brother, James East (James Alfred East Hector), was living in Hornersville with his wife, Mary, formerly Daugherty, and children, Annie, Julia, Samuel, Joseph, and Mary. [609]

These years would bring the beginning of big changes in the land and cause a longing for the days when it was a wilderness and not as populated for Sam.

Chapter 10
Where the Eagle Soars

The sky was dark this cold October morning, reminding Sam of the trip he and Dr. James made down the Little and St. Francis rivers to the Miller Mounds in Poinsett County more than 20 years ago.

Now, like then, there weren't dark clouds in the sky, but immense flocks of birds descending on Big Lake and other waterways. As they had for generations, they were traveling down the Mississippi Flyway to warmer climates for the winter.

The mallards were coming in droves and settling in with the wood ducks on the water. Large geese and the smaller cackling geese were making quite a chatter in the sky.

As Sam steadied his rifle and took aim at one of the ducks above, he lapsed into thoughts of his past when this area was a wilderness.

Like the birds heading to warmer climates, Sam had a desire to move on.

Lately, he had been troubled by the rapidly growing population of his little haven on earth. Although it would never be the same, he longed for the wilderness of his youth, where the buffalo roamed, where bear and elk were plentiful, and his kinsmen were nearby.

He was 70 years old and ready for a new frontier, just like his ancestors had been. He had been to Texas four times, seeking out an area where he could be more himself, where there were still wide-open spaces.

He had been in one spot too long.

Sam now understood a lot of how his father felt with one foot in the world of a White man and one in the world of an Indian. He had one foot in the wilderness and the other near the path of progression. The railroad was getting closer, and timber was being cleared at a fast rate. One foot walked the old paths with those who understood him and his traditions, and one foot was in the future world where many different ideas existed. He just wanted to live free, without encumberments.

He thought about the many times he had plied the waters of the lake, the Pemiscot Bayou, and the Little and St. Francis rivers through flooded times and drought; beginning in his childhood when he lived in the Indian village Chilletecaux and traveled south toward the Cherokee camps on the St. Francis River; on hunting trips with his father as he traversed the land between the rivers providing a shorter route to a place that would become Marked Tree; and his excursions.

Yes, he knew the waters well.

Here, one could still hear the panther scream, the wolves howl, and watch the otter dipping in and out of the water. Here, one could still find peace. The sky was alive, the tree limbs swayed under their weight, and the water shimmered in the sun as life beneath the surface broke through. Sam was born free, as much a creature of the wild as the buffalo that once roamed nearby or the eagle that soared above, perusing the land and water for his dinner.

The area was vastly and quickly changing. Way too many hunters came into the area for the joy of it, instead of for a living. Every day brought new hunters from faraway places. Before long, there would not be as many birds in the sky, no wolves to howl or cats to scream, and the deer would be scarce. The eagle would move on.

More and more settlers were moving into the area, and progress was about to roll on through. He could almost hear the whistle now.

While there were still remote areas where only the experienced could find their way, Sam foresaw the future of one of the best hunting spots in America, and it wasn't good for the wildlife or him.

A group of hunters from Memphis met up with Sam on a duck-hunting trip to Big Lake in November 1895. They referred to him as the "hermit of Big Lake" and a "presiding genius of the place."

They described Sam as "active and agile, as most people in the prime of life." He was a small, wiry fellow with a copper-colored complexion and long, black, glossy hair with some grey mixed in. [610]

Sam visited Osceola in mid-October that year, reporting to *The Osceola Times* about duck hunting. [611]

On another trip to Osceola a few years later in 1900, Sam's agility was noted in *The Osceola Times*. Having walked from his home at Big Lake "over a pretty tough road in time to eat his dinner" was impressive to the news writer. "When it is stated that Mr. Hector is 76 years old, the young men of this country will have no cause to sneer at his ability as a sprinter." [612]

How tough were the roads then? One might consider his ability to travel across the roads at his age a little hard, but when one hears how bad the roads could be at times, it seems a great feat.

An interesting story is told in Mabel Edrington's *History of Mississippi County, Arkansas,* about a trip some educators made from Osceola to Blytheville following the institution of the Peabody Normal Institute in the county in 1895. The program began to provide teacher training in each county each year. The first few institutes were held in Osceola, but with a majority of the teachers in the Blytheville area, it came time for the Osceola teachers to travel to Blytheville. Dressed in their best clothes, the educators left bright and early, a day early, "as the sun was casting its first long rays of the morning" to be "fit and fine" for the meeting. Riding in a two-horse hack, the finest the livery had to offer, the group expected to arrive with little resistance.

"The facts are; we struck deep mud between Osceola and Luxora," having just begun the trip, said Edrington. "Beyond Luxora to Sandy Ridge it was worse – between that point and Clear Lake we struck a snag or would have been if we had been steamboating," she said.

The years of overflows in the area took a toll on the roads. Add to that, driftwood and debris, and one had to be quite experienced to tell which way they were going, she said. "In the midst of these windings, we would come to a drain or a bayou, which seemed bottomless," continued Edrington. No one but the driver had any experience traveling the road, and at least two of them had never been in a swamp. However, they were making progress when they were suddenly halted - "the horses bogging, the vehicle hung on a cypress knee; water in every direction," she wrote.

Normal instructor, Professor D. B. Rivers, dressed in a light gray suit, Panama hat, and new tan toothpick shoes, following instructions from the driver to carry on with the trip until he could catch up, "gave one last look at his shoes and plunged in." The rest followed. Before long, the wagon caught up with them. They arrived at their destination around 4 p.m., where they were "greatly refreshed by a good meal and water to wash the mud out of our ears," said Edrington. [613]

The area had changed a lot since Sam had first settled there. He told the Memphis hunters how he had planned to leave because "'the country is getting too much settled up for me.'" When he came to Northeast Arkansas, one could see herds of buffalo right across the lake, he said, referring to Big Lake and what would be Buffalo Island. Elk and bears frequented the area. Even though only 20 families were living within 20 miles of him, it was getting too thickly populated for Sam. He planned to move to Texas "in hopes of finding a spot more remote from civilization than that which he now inhabits."[614]

While Sam was unhappy with the increasing population, Dr. James was discontent with the remoteness and left in 1878. He received a degree from the St. Louis College of Physicians and Surgeons, College of Medicine and Science in St. Louis, Missouri, in 1882. [615]

James was an instructor there from 1880 to 1881 when a young Joseph J. Kinyoun, the father of the National Institute of Allergy and Infectious Diseases, studied under the noted microscopist. [616] He was the editor of the pharmaceutical and scientific publication, *The National Druggist*, for 18 years. He wrote a book for students called "*Elementary Microscopical Technology*." [617] He died in 1907 in St. Louis. [618] A writer in the *National Druggist* wrote in his obituary that "his mind was like some storehouse of vast information and his conversational powers made his companionship much sought after by lovers of knowledge." [619]

Sam may have had moving on his mind when he ran an ad to sell his farm on the Pemiscot Bayou in December 1900 for $12 an acre. The area for sale featured 125 acres, with 50 acres in cultivation. The remainder could be easily cleared, read the ad. [620]

Belona had been in poor health for a few years, as reported in *The Osceola Times* on February 20, 1892, when their house burned. Sam was not home. "Mrs. Hector, who was old and an invalid, was left in charge of an old lady, a neighbor, who was almost as helpless as herself." Nonetheless, Belona was able to drag her neighbor out of the house. However, due to exhaustion, she couldn't drag her far, and her clothing and the bedclothes caught fire. The community of Osceola, when they heard the news, gathered "quite a collection of the necessities of life" for the Hectors, the article said.[621]

The area, then as it is now, is in the middle of the Mississippi Flyway, one of four routes used by migrating fowl from their northern breeding grounds to southern areas to winter. It follows the Missouri, Mississippi, and lower Ohio Rivers in the United States, the Great Lakes, and the McKenzie River and Hudson Bay in Canada. The route's destination is the Southern United States, Mexico, and Central and South America. The course narrows in the lower Mississippi Valley in the states of Missouri, Arkansas, Louisiana, and Mississippi. [622] This accounts for the large numbers of birds found in some areas, such as those in the Big Lake area.

In Sam's time, as news spread of the bounty in the area, the influx of hunters for sport and market escalated. "The fame of the place has spread wonderfully," Sam told the Memphis hunters. "'Every day brings new parties of duck hunters from Memphis, Louisville, St. Louis, Chicago, and even as far as Cincinnati and Pittsburgh,'" he said. [623]

In the winter of 1893-1894, one hunter in the Big Lake area sold 8,000 mallards, with the total number of ducks sent to market numbered at 120,000.[624] In 1880, *The Osceola Times* noted that ducks were brought in by the wagon load and sold for 25 cents a brace. One group, John B. Driver, T.C. Edrington, W.B. Edrington, and Henry Cook, killed 170 ducks in two days in the fall of 1879. Other instances in the *Times* included eight hunters in 1881, killing 110 ducks. And a party from Memphis taking 700 ducks.

They were also being shipped from there. An article on November 25, 1882, told of W.E. Moss shipping 400 ducks on board the Mark Twain. In February 1886, a party of hunters killed 500 ducks, 35 geese, and a swan, all shipped to the Memphis market. [625]

The Memphis hunters said that Sam spent all his time hunting and fishing, but never tilled the land. [626] While Sam was a hunter, before and after the turn of the century, census records from 1870 and 1880 note his occupation was farming. In the 1850 census, Sam was listed as a hunter, while his dad William, although employed as a hunter (See Moonshine and furs, Chapter 6), was listed as a farmer. In 1852, tax records in Mississippi County show William owning 50 head of cattle, [627] which could be the reason for this listing. James Hector (James Alfred East Hector) gave his occupation as a hunter in 1870, but as a farmer in 1880. [628]

Occupations on the census switched back and forth between hunting and farming. In 1895, Sam was involved in hunting, but had also cultivated his land at times, as he related in 1881 to Edward Palmer, field assistant for the Smithsonian Institution's Bureau of Ethnology (Chapter 9).

His 1900 ad in the newspaper noted that 50 acres of his land were in cultivation.

Besides census records, other records show Sam's activities during the late 1800s. In October 1895, Sam dropped in at *The Osceola Times* office and reported that "duck shooting" was "pretty good" earlier in the week on Monday. [629]

Sam may have spent time hunting with his son, James "Jim" Hector. In 1886, Jim Hector was the first to bring venison and "bar" meat to the market in Osceola that season. [630] In 1882, bear meat could be purchased on the market in Osceola for 10 cents per pound. [631]

In 1889, a James Hector, who could be Sam's son or his brother-in-law James, came into Osceola from Big Lake with two horse wagons loaded with venison headed to the Blytheville market. [632] A March 6, 1886, bounty act would allow counties to declare an amount to be paid for wolf, wild cat, or panther scalps from the treasury of the county. The scalps would be shown to a county authority, who would examine, destroy the scalps, and issue a certificate for which the hunter would be paid. [633]

In April 1890, Sam was paid $6 for a wild cat and a wolf scalp, and John Perry was paid $10 for two wolf scalps. [634] In April 1892, Sam and James[635] were paid $5 for wolf scalps. [636]

The red wolf, panther, and black bear were the three largest predators in Arkansas during historical times and ranged statewide. The red wolf, larger and more robust than the coyote, is tawny on its muzzle, ears, nape, and outer surface of the legs. The rest of the fur is cinnamon, buff, and tawny, mixed with gray and black. The wolves would range in packs or by themselves. By the turn of the century, their population, particularly in Eastern Arkansas, had decreased dramatically. As the coyote population grew, a hybridization occurred. Coupled with the hybridization and continued killing, the red wolf was extirpated in the 1970s.

The mountain lion or panther is pale brown to reddish brown above and dull white below. By 1900, most were killed or driven to remote areas, and were thought to have been extirpated from the state by the 1920s.

At the turn of the century, the black bear had been largely exterminated from the state. In 1959, a restocking program began, which re-established the bear population. [637]

While great numbers of birds flew over Sam's head, the land under his feet was rich beyond measure. To be able to harvest the land, it had to be reclaimed. The timber needed to be harvested, and a way to transport it needed to be built. To bring more agriculture to the land, it needed to be drained. One industry after another led to yet another, and all benefited the area.

Levee work in the county created a need for timber.

The great Chicago fire of 1871 has also been credited with providing an impetus for the harvesting of the rich woodlands in Northeast Arkansas and other places. [638]

In 1889, the lumber business was in its infancy in the county, as noted in Goodspeed's *Biographical and Historical Memoirs of Northeast Arkansas,* about Mississippi County. There were three sawmills at that time at Barfield. "The success of these three mills assure the development of great wealth from surrounding valuable timber in the near future." [639]

Robert E. Lee Wilson would capitalize on the sawmill and timber industry, as forecasted by Goodspeed's history for Barfield, and become one of those successes.

Born in the county, Wilson was orphaned at a young age when his father died in Memphis in 1870, and his mother a few years later during a yellow fever epidemic. At 15 years of age, in 1880, he returned to the area and "camped in the cypress swamp he inherited" while he harvested the timber. A few years later, in 1889, he began agricultural production, growing cotton for export, and employing more than 100 sharecroppers. In 1933, just before Wilson died, he had 14 plantations, employing 2,500, and ranked as the largest cotton producer in the South. [640]

In 1889, when Goodspeed's history was published, Wilson owned 2,700 acres and had built a sawmill on part of his land four miles from the river. From the mill, which could handle 14,000 feet per day, he would ship lumber to Chicago via the river. How did he transport it four miles from the mill to the river? He built a tramway at the mill extending six miles from the river into his timbered lands, with 30 employees engaged in lumbering. [641]

Robert E. Lee Wilson, III, described some of those trams in an interview for the 1986 book *Mississippi County, Arkansas: Appreciating the Past, Anticipating the Future.* He said the only way to get logs out of the swampy forests was by rail. As a child, he remembered going into the forest with his grandfather, Robert E. Lee Wilson, on a log tram. Instead of crossties, the tracks were built on logs that were cut as the tram went along. The logs were staked to keep them straight. When the train was not on them, the tracks floated. "'When the train would come along, the tracks would sink beneath the water. You couldn't see any tracks for two hundred yards in front or behind the train.'" [642]

At the turn of the century, Arkansas ranked among the foremost as a timber-producing state, wrote J.A. Fox of Osceola, assistant engineer of the St. Francis Levee District, in *The Garden Spot of the Mississippi Valley in the St. Francis Basin of Arkansas.* Most of the timber in the area was hardwoods, including elm, gum, ash, oak, hickory, walnut, pecan, and cottonwood, with cottonwood being the most in demand. Other varieties included cypress, sycamore, persimmon, and hackberry, but there was not as great a demand for those species. The Mississippi River provided a means of transportation that was economical. "There is a constant fleet of lumber and timber craft moving either crude material or sawed lumber to Cairo, Illinois, St. Louis, Louisville, and Cincinnati," he wrote. [643]

In 1902, 35 sawmills had been erected in the county "within the last five years," noted J.A. Fox. They were located "right in the heart of the forests," finding an outlet to the Mississippi River through "wooden and steel trams," varying in length from three to 10 miles. A bit of the process, then, described by Fox, was cutting the logs from the tree in lengths of 10 to 16 feet that were hauled to the tram on log wagons pulled by mules. From there, they were loaded onto cars on the trams by large cranes and taken to the mill or the river for shipment. At the river, the logs were loaded onto barges for shipment to Cairo, Illinois, where they were sawed into lumber, wrote Fox. Several large timber companies began to operate in the county just after the turn of the century. In 1902, the largest were the Chicago Mill and Lumber Company, the Three States Lumber Company, Wilson & Beall Lumber Company, and Moore & McFerrin. [644]

Just a few years before, in 1898, there were no railroads in the county, said Fox. The nature of the overflows prevented railroads from establishing permanent tracks. By 1902, though, there were three routes through the county. A branch of the Frisco came in from the south and connected to Luxora with the St. Louis and Southeastern Railroad, which extended to New Madrid, Missouri. The Jonesboro, Lake City and Eastern Railroad (J.L.C.&E. Railroad) came into the county from the west, traveling toward the Mississippi River. The Paragould Southeastern came in from the northwest and formed a link with the Cotton Belt Railroad, which connected with St. Louis. The last two railroads were still being built in the county at that time. Surveys for two other roads, the Cotton Belt Railroad and Decatur Egg Case, planned to begin work in the near future. The Cotton Belt planned to extend from the north of the county toward Memphis, and the Decatur Egg Case planned to enter the county on the west side of Big Lake and Little River and go to Osceola. [645]

The Decatur Egg Company, a corporation with headquarters in Cardwell, Missouri, just across the state line in Dunklin County, Missouri, had a tram road built to handle timber. The Paragould & Memphis Railroad Company would extend a line from Paragould to the southern part of Dunklin County, Missouri, to Manila, which was developed from that tram road. [646]

In 1899, an idea to build a railroad to Blytheville was conceived. By 1902, the trunk line provided a direct connection between St. Louis and Memphis. It would become part of the Frisco system and be known as the St. Louis, Memphis and Southeastern. The Paragould, Hornersville, and Southeastern, finished by 1902, provided a connection with the Cotton Belt Railroad at Paragould and opened a "new and rich scope of territory to the northwest," wrote Fox. The Jonesboro, Lake City and Eastern Railroad (J.L.C.&E. Railroad) provided a connection to the Iron Mountain Railroad at

Nettleton, near Jonesboro, and the Cotton Belt of Jonesboro, all providing a route to Little Rock and other areas across the state, said Fox. [647]

No railways had considered building into the sunken lands before any attempts at reclaiming the land had begun. Then, most travel was by waterway, and the few existing roads were often bogged down with water, except in drier seasons. However, the value of a reliable means of transportation into the area to tap the vast resources of timber was obvious, and in 1896, a group of Jonesboro businessmen decided to tackle the prospect of building a railroad in hopes of funneling the potential wealth into Jonesboro. On April 7, 1897, the Railroad Commission of Arkansas issued a charter to the Jonesboro, Lake City and Eastern Railroad (J.L.C.&E. Railroad) to build a railroad from Nettleton to Lake City. By late November, the tracks had been laid to Lake City, and the first train had arrived. [648]

The next obstacle for the railway was bridging the St. Francis River, a mile wide at that spot. By 1898, arrangements were made to build a bridge, and the railway was soon given authority to extend the line as far away as Leachville. At the end of 1899, the tracks had bridged the river, extending into "the vast forests of Buffalo Island." [649]

The line was also extended from Nettleton to Jonesboro that year. That fall, the railroad ran two passenger trains daily between Jonesboro and Lake City, with one going to Monette and Leachville. Besides providing passage for people, the resources from the area were opened up. That year, among other items, dressed fish at the rate of 2,000 pounds per day were transported from Lake City. The advent of the railroad started a change in population as more settlers began to settle in the area. Towns, such as Black Oak, formed around the tracks. And towns already established begin to grow. [650]

By December 1900, the rails had been laid to Manila. The next big obstacle in the railway's path was Big Lake. In 1902, a bridge was constructed over Big Lake, and the railway made its way eastward to Blytheville, reaching there that year. [651]

The route would take the tracks on the north side of where Sam may have lived at the time, [652] on land that had originally been part of his and his father's swamp land grants.

The Jonesboro, Lake City and Eastern Railroad (J.L.C.&E. Railroad) opened up to Blytheville, "that territory of untold wealth in and around Big Lake," said Fox. [653]

The railway would bring more people to the area, thus adding to Sam's fear of the area becoming too crowded for him. "All the towns along the line were swarming with new inhabitants - the loggers, sawmill men, 'blind tiger operators,'" [654] and other characters attracted by the plentiful jobs and available money of the timber towns," wrote Lee A. Dew in "The J.L.C. and E.R.R. and the Opening of the Sunk Lands of Northeast Arkansas," for an *Arkansas Historical Quarterly* publication. From the logging operations, radiated wagon trails, and tram railways to haul the logs to loading spurs. [655]

As more logging operations began, more people came into the area, and more trails were built from the logging areas. Just west of Sam, a lumbering camp on the route of the J.L.C.&E. Railroad, between the Dell and Manila offices, applied for a post office. Answering the questions sent by the Post Office Department, S. J. Matthews stated on December 3, 1903, that the office would serve 2,000 people. The site of the post office, in Section 9, to be called Big Lake, would serve the lumber camp and offices, a clubhouse, and fishing docks. The post office was in Section 10 at the railway station in Petteyville in 1905. [656] Stonewall J. Matthews would be the postmaster at Big Lake Post Office on April 15, 1904. [657]

In Section 12, the rail line would travel toward Dell on its way to Blytheville. Dell was a large settlement, as noted by J.B. Richardson on his application for a special post office on September 9, 1897, to be called Dell. The office was to be located in the northwest quarter of Section 8, Township 14 North, Range 10 East, on the Pemiscot Bayou, and would serve 200 people. [658] Richardson was appointed postmaster in October 1897.[659] Richardson applied for a change of site for the Dell Post Office to the southeast quarter of Section 5, north of the previous site, but still on the bayou, on December 6, 1898. [660] Richardson had a store on the bayou. After the J.L.C. & E. Railroad was located nearby, the owner of the land that had given the right of way to the railway, W.F. Rozell, of Holly Springs, Mississippi, laid out a plan for a new community named Rozell. Richardson moved his store and post office there. Others followed, and the community was called Dell/Rozell. However, there was another town in the county named Rozelle, and the community continued to be called Dell. [661]

The town of Dell was incorporated in 1905. [662] The railway station in that area is shown as Rozell Station in 1903 on a plat map. Dell P.O. is shown north of there on the map, along with a schoolhouse south of the post office.[663] By February 1904, the post office would once again be located in the northwest quarter of Section 8, on the north side of the railroad, 90 feet from the center of the track, and one-half mile from the bayou on the south side.[664] An annual report of the Railroad Commission of Arkansas showed the station as Dell in 1904. [665] Due to the influx of farmers after the timber was cut, Dell became a boom town. [666] In 1905, Dell boasted of five stores, a pool room, a barber shop, a blacksmith shop, three hotels, a schoolhouse, and a church. [667]

Ekron, northeast of Dell, applied for a special post office in October 1901. At that time, it was four and a half miles from Dell, "as the road runs," and was to serve 45 families. It was to be located in the southeast quarter of Section 27, Township 15 North, Range 10 East. [668]

In 1902, due to the railroad, Manila was growing rapidly and had been a contender with Blytheville for the county's second court seat in 1901. "This fertile territory was, until the construction of the railroad a few years ago, completely cut off from the outside world," noted Fox. [669] In its early years, the community of Manila was called Cinda, named for Lucinda, the sister of

Sam Bunch,[670] Sam's son-in-law, and the wife of the younger William Hector, who served in the Civil War (Chapter 8). Bunch was postmaster there from 1892 to 1894 and 1897. [671]

The post office requested a name and site change on August 31, 1900, to Manila, to be located three-eighths of a mile from the current post office. The nearest post office, but not on the same route, was Dell. The population to be supplied by the office was 1,000 and would be located in the southeast quarter of Section 31, Township 15 North, Range 9 East, 200 feet from the new railway station. [672] The town was incorporated on July 3, 1901, under the name of Manila, in honor of the recent victory of Commodore George Dewey in the Spanish-American War. [673]

While the area around Sam was becoming more "settled," as he told the Memphis hunters, the rest of the county was also growing.

Blytheville, described by Fox as a small village at the time, owed its growth to the fertility of the soil in the area, valuable timber, the levee system, the railroads, and its people. Blytheville also became a judicial district, called the Chickasawba District, when the county was divided into two judicial districts in 1901. A new courthouse had been built, and a school with seven rooms was under construction. [674] Blytheville was named for the Rev. Henry T. Blythe, a Methodist minister, who moved to the area in 1853, settling near Crooked Lake. By 1873, he had moved to the future Blytheville area. He laid out the village of "Blythesville" in 1880. He owned the first businesses, a sawmill and a cotton gin. He would soon be postmaster, staying in that position until 1889. In 1886, he was elected to the state legislature for one term. [675]

A mile west of Blytheville was the little town of Chickasawba, named for the chief who lived in the area in the early 1800s. In the future, the town, built around an ancient settlement, would be swallowed by Blytheville. In 1898, Chickasawba had four businesses, while "Blythesville" had six businesses. [676]

In 1902, Osceola had a population of 2,500 and boasted of one of the most modern opera houses in the state, said Fox. It had electric lights, waterworks, and several industries and businesses, including two banks, several churches, two newspapers, and a school with six teachers. It was the court seat for the southern portion of the county. [677] In 1899, a railroad reached Osceola. Walter Driver made the first shipment of 400 sacks of potatoes. [678] Growing Irish potatoes had been introduced in the county a few years before 1900, yielding "wonderful returns," said Fox. The variety of Irish potatoes called "Bliss Red Triumph" adapted well to the soil and climate in the county. [679]

Besides Manila, Dell, and Blytheville, the sawmills and railroads were partly responsible for the growth of other towns in 1902.

Golden Lake was a settlement on the river and the railroad. It was the sawmill site of Wilson & Beall Lumber Company. The lake, responsible for its name, dried up after the levee was built. In 1902, there were gins, stores, a church, and homes located there. [680]

Evadale owed its existence to the railroad. Located directly on the route of the Frisco Railroad, it was four miles from the river. It had a church, a schoolhouse, a gin, several stores, and a sawmill. [681]

With the changes in transportation from rivers to railroads to highways, little towns did not fare well in the future as the traffic changed.

Mail delivery was also affected by changing traffic and routes.

Mail service was erratic at times due to high water making areas inaccessible. An 1897 map shows postal routes. Cinda's route delivered mail three times a week, Dell by special supply, and Osceola had mail delivery six times a week. [682]

D.T. Waller, of Elmot, explained the positions of post offices in his area and delivery to the Post Office Department in 1883. Elmot was situated four miles above Osceola and 12 miles below Blytheville. On the Mississippi River, three mails upstream and three downstream were carried weekly by "Anchor Line." There were two mail deliveries each week, carried on horseback, to and from Clear Lake and Blytheville. The mail was regular "if not prevented by ice in the river, or overflows in the 'Miss' [sic] Bottom from Osceola to Blythesville." [683]

The postal service also moved around for various reasons. Some offices were discontinued, and some were re-established.

In 1900, when the post office to be called Archillion applied to be established, an explanation showed the offices of Clear Lake in the past and present, and why an office at Archillion was needed presently. Three Clear Lake offices were discontinued for abandonment of stores, and one because of death, "especially last year because of postmaster Grant Coble shooting his brother and absconding." To further complicate things, the bondsman temporarily moved the post to his store and later moved to Blytheville and rented it to a saloon keeper. "This place is not suitable for an office," noted the applicant. However, they did not care if they continued the Clear Lake office or not, as "we only want our office restored." From the maps included, it appears the second site of the Clear Lake office is where the Archillion office was to be located. [684] Reginold Archillion was postmaster at the Clear Lake office beginning November 25, 1881, and Rollo Archillion was postmaster there beginning March 12, 1883. [685]

Grant Coble was the postmaster at Clear Lake, beginning in April 1893. When Clear Lake was discontinued, the mail would go to Archillion effective March 31, 1902. John W. Conley was the postmaster at Archillion beginning on August 29, 1900. [686]

Mail service also took some time. Alice Marie Ross described a round trip made by her mother in 1899 to deliver mail from Blytheville to Osceola via a mail hack. The hack was like a two-seated surrey [687] drawn by two horses. Since it was very cold on the day of their return trip, they were given a bottle of whiskey and rock candy by Billy Hale. They would take a sip from the bottle and hand it to the driver. They left Osceola after an early breakfast, stopping in Sandy Ridge for lunch, yet it was still dark when they got home.[688] Hale was acquainted with Sam and old William (this chapter).[689]

Even in Osceola, when the mail was carried by boat, the mail could get delayed, due to floating ice on the river, for up to three weeks. Later, during the transition to the "new town," or the settlement of the town that moved closer to the railroad, the mail delivery was often a "bone of contention," as the post office "practically stayed on wheels," causing *The Osceola Times* to post items asking "where is the post office today?" [690]

Drainage improvements would impact the way people travelled, and mail was delivered in the county.

Mississippi County was probably the earliest in the state to "establish drainage districts under the old inadequate and unworkable drainage laws," said S.E. Simonson in an article, "Origin of Drainage Projects in Mississippi County," in 1946 for the *Arkansas Historical Society*. The first attempt in a petition headed by J.T. Coston of Osceola, R.E. Lee Wilson, C.M. Bell, J. W. Rhodes, and John B. Driver was filed in April 1902 and failed "largely on account of the impractical drainage laws." [691]

However, not to be deterred, the proponents for drainage, Coston, Wilson, Simonson, and L.I. Hidinger, President of Morgan Engineering Company of Memphis, met with the Hon. George B. Rose in Little Rock to formulate a plan. As a result, their efforts in the meeting were put before the legislature and enacted into law. Drainage District No. 7, or the Pemiscot Bayou Drainage District, was organized in 1905. By 1908, two more districts, Drainage District No. 8 and No. 9, were established. [692]

However, they faced a great deal of opposition from lumber companies and landowners who did not want to pay a tax for undertaking the projects.

Drainage opened the door to the next phase in the evolution of Mississippi County from Simonson's description as a "hopeless permanent mosquito and malarial ridden swamp" to an agricultural enterprise.

In 1918, the J.L.C.&E. Railroad announced that the final drainage work had begun, and by the next year, the area experienced a land boom. Wilson, who bought the railroad in 1911, would set the record for a single freight lading for the railroad when the railroad hauled 6,500 bales of cotton, valued at approximately one million dollars, to market in late 1919. [693]

Despite the timber being cut and the land being drained, farming still had its obstacles in the early years of agriculture in the county.

"In the Spring, when you were planting, it was a solid sea of stumps as far as you could look," told R.E.L. Wilson, III, in his later years. When the cotton got high, though, it looked clear. "Of course, it wasn't," he said. [694]

Progress, while beneficial to the area, was not part of Sam's dreams. Sam would not make it to Texas or Indian Territory to live, as he passed in mid-November 1904, at 80 years old. He would not live to see the county reach it's full potential as the number one county in rain-produced cotton in the world. He would not live to see all the fights over the birds that flew overhead. He would not live to see the land drained and reclaimed. He would not live to see the endless cotton fields. And, he would not live to see the greatest of floods in the area in 1927 and 1937.

His death was reported in *The Osceola Times* on December 3, 1904, and occurred about two weeks earlier. He "was reared among the Indians who occupied the country in the early years of his young manhood," read *The Osceola Times* article. [695]

Sam lost all of his immediate family before his death, except for one daughter, Melissa. She would pass less than a year after him. Melissa Bunch died September 25, 1905. *The Osceola Times* noted that "she was the last member of Sam Hector's family. [696] Belona Elizabeth, Sam's wife, passed sometime around the turn of the century. [697] Matilda had died shortly before Sam on September 9, 1904. [698] Nancy Jane had possibly passed at a young age. She was gone by the time Melissa passed, as Melissa was Sam's only surviving immediate family member.

Sam's son, James "Jim," died on November 1, 1901. [699] Jim had married Belle Hardin in 1882 and had three sons, Sam, Don, and Will, before she died in 1890. In March 1892, he was accused of murder in the death of Mr. Baker at Big Lake. According to an article in *The Osceola Times*, Jim had made a comment about Baker's daughter, and Baker slapped him. Jim went home and returned with a shotgun and shot Baker. He was arrested but later escaped. [700] He had a bond of $3,000 in May 1892. [701] The case was continued a couple of times. [702] Other details on the case remain unknown.

James "Jim" married again in 1896 to Parlee Gardner [703] and had three children, Harrison Gilbert, Hettie Jane, and James Harvey. In 1898, "Jim" served as a judge for East Big Lake. [704] He died four months before his last son, James Harvey, was born. [705]

In 1893, Sam would stop by *The Osceola Times* office on his way to Dr. McGavock's home as he was "interested in securing his claim as a member of the Cherokee Tribe." [706] W. J. Bowen of Osceola stated in an affidavit in the Guion Miller file of John W. Perry that he knew of Sam going to Indian Territory to try and "get land on account of his Indian blood." [707] Maybe the trip Perry was talking about was a result of that meeting with McGavock. Bowen, of Osceola, was the son of Charles Bowen (Chapter 8), and was a farmer. [708]

While it is unknown how Sam traveled to Texas before 1895, or Indian Territory, as Perry stated, a train ride may have made it more convenient at that time.

After he and his immediate family had all passed, some of his grandchildren and other family members continued the quest to be recognized by the Cherokee Nation when they filed applications to be listed on the Guion Miller rolls. The list was for Eastern Cherokee, wherein they applied for compensation as a result of a lawsuit with judgment in the tribe's favor. In 1902, the tribe sued the United States for monies due them under the treaties of 1835, 1836, and 1845. Claimants had to prove they were members of the tribe or prove they were descended from members at the time of the treaties.

Several of Sam's descendants made their application in which they were asked to give their name and their Indian name, place of birth, name of husband or wife, names of children, names of and places of birth and death dates of parents and grandparents, names and ages of brothers and sisters, and names of aunts and uncles. They were asked where their ancestors were in 1851 and allowed to use affidavits from others that could prove their ancestry.

All the applications filed by Sam's descendants and others, such as James East (James Alfred East Hector) and his descendants, were rejected. Rejected claims included those who left the Cherokee Nation in the East before 1835, illegitimate children, those who filed after the cutoff date, those with dual tribal ancestry, and those who failed to prove relationships with their ancestors.

The family could not provide a connection to the Eastern Cherokee because their ancestors left the East before 1835.

The applications from 1906-1909 provide a wealth of family history, as well as the history of some Indian families in Mississippi County. Each applicant would give, if they knew, the names of their parents, grandparents, aunts, uncles, and children; Cherokee names, and where they lived in 1851. Affidavits from locals provided additional information.

In the applications, there were differing opinions on the family Cherokee name of Chickalee. All that knew seemed to agree that the Moonshine name was assigned to old William Hector, Sam's father. Chickalee was the Hector Indian name, noted William Thomas, Samuel, and Don Hector, the three older sons of James, "Jim," Sam's only son. [709] Matilda Perry's children, John W., Samuel, and Charles H.L. Perry, would claim Chickalee as the Hector Indian name. [710] The exception was Thomas J. Daugherty, who claimed the name was assigned to his grandmother Hector. [711]

Melissa Bunch's children, Jane, Bertie, Sallie, and Nervie, would claim Moonshine as the Hector name and Chickalee as the Rice name. [712] However, there is confusion concerning the name. Sam Bunch stated in an affidavit in Nervie's application that he answered the questions for his minor children, Nervie, Willie, and Sallie. [713] He also answered questions for Pinkie, his grandson, as stated in this affidavit. [714]

While it all seems confusing concerning the name of Chickalee, James East, also known as James Alfred Hector (James Alfred East Hector), [715] the oldest applicant, and James Davis, aforementioned, helped undo the confusion for the Chickalee name in an affidavit filed by Isaac E. Daugherty in the John W. Perry application folder. [716] In Isaac Daugherty's application of June 1907, he claimed his great-grandmother was "Jaley Chockalee." The commissioners requested more information about Jaley. It is noted in Daughtery's file that his application should be grouped with Perry's application. [717]

In John W. Perry's application, a sworn statement by Daugherty, of August 25, 1908, retracts his statement made the previous year, concerning his great-grandmother, Jaley. He said he had deferred answering questions by the commissioners until he had more substantial proof. "Watha-Capa" [sic], was the name of his great-grandmother. "Jaby Chockalee [sic], as reported by me in my application was incorrect – a mere confusion of names on my part, regarding my ancestor's name," he said. [718]

Daugherty's statement included a sworn statement signed by James A. East (James Alfred East Hector) and James Davis, noting that they knew Daugherty and the ancestors of whom he spoke. [719] Jaley, East's mother, lived with him at least until 1870. [720]

East said in his application that he was the son of John East, a full-blood Cherokee, and Jaley, also part Cherokee. Jaley was also the mother of Sam's wife, Belona Elizabeth Rice. Jaley was born in 1802 at a station camp on the Little Duck River in Tennessee to Leonard Brown and Wathacape. "My mother was ¼ breed Cherokee," he said. James was born at Chilletecaux on July 4, 1837, "where there were 300 Indians and only two White families," he said on his application. James A. Davis, of Manila, provided an affidavit stating he had known John East since 1846 and that he was a full-blood Cherokee. East made his claim based on his relationship to John East. [721]

Thomas J. Daugherty likely based his claim concerning Jaley on Isaac's original claim.

In James' son Josiah W. East's application was an affidavit from F.M. Schultz supporting James' assertion that his father was Cherokee, as John East told Schultz "time after time" that he was Cherokee. Schultz, of Hornersville, had known John East since 1848, when "there were a great many Indians here." Also, in his application was an affidavit from Temperance Neal, born in 1818, who lived in Neal Township in Mississippi County in 1910, [722] stating that to her knowledge, James was born near Kennett. Josiah died during the application process, James noted in a letter to the United States Court of Claims in Josiah's file. [723] James was living in Lake City in 1908. [724]

John W. Perry's application had several affidavits, including one by James Davis. He said he knew (old) "Billy" Hector and Sam Hector and heard them claim Cherokee blood. To back up how well he knew them, he said, "I lived with them, worked, hunted, and fished with them." [725]

Sam was young when Native Americans were first beginning to be moved to the Indian Territory, but old enough to remember those he knew and loved leaving the village where he lived. He was old enough to hear the stories of those driven across the frozen Mississippi in the cold with barely a blanket. He was old enough to hear the tales of sorrow from the Trail of Tears. Yet, during a time when many would not proclaim their Native American heritage for fear, he was always proud to tell everyone he met that he was Indian.

When H.M. McVeigh (Chapter 9) wrote about Sam in the *Biographical and Historical Memoirs of Northeast Arkansas* publication of 1889, he noted that Sam was "proud of his Indian blood." [726] The personal accounts in the Guion Miller records by those who knew Sam also testified to Sam talking about his Indian ancestry. William P. Hale, of Osceola, told in an affidavit that he often heard Sam talk about his Indian blood. He also remembered Sam's father, "old Billy Hector," and his looks showed his Indian heritage "strongly." [727] Hale came to the county as a youth in 1855. He was in the mercantile business in Osceola in 1870. He had farmland and a gin and served as an alderman and a member of the school board for Osceola. He served as president of the first bank there. [728]

Sam's grandson, Thomas J. Daughtery, told of how Sam stayed with him sometimes after he had married and that he often talked about his Indian blood, and "he used to talk a good deal to us about his father Billy Hector."[729]

While all these applications noted their Cherokee ancestry, it remains that the family's ancestors left the Eastern Cherokee before 1835. A requirement for the Guion Miller roll was an ancestor on the 1835 roll. Chickalee, from whom the Hector family claims descent, was in Arkansas at least by 1813, when he and other Cherokee complained about nearby settlers.

A note in Sam's grandchild Bertie Holsclaw's (Bunch) application reads: "Rejected. Ancestor, this whom claim is made resided in Missouri in 34-35, so if Cherokees at all must have been old settlers." [730] Old Settlers was one of the terms used to describe the Cherokee who came to Arkansas before forced migration.

Other applications in the family included one by James East's (James Alfred East Hector) daughter, Julia East Joliff, [731] one by his granddaughter, Monte J. Pack East, [732] and some of Matilda's grandchildren by her daughter, Belona Jane Lott, who was deceased. This application was filed by John Perry, the grandfather and guardian of the children. The children included John W. Lott, Charley Lott, Robert C. Lott, Samuel G. Lott, and Minnie E. Lott. [733]

James East (James Alfred East Hector) died in 1922, when he was 85 years old, as a result of being hit by an automobile in Lake City, where he had lived for several years. "Uncle Alf Hector," as the article in the Arkansas Democrat called him on May 14, 1922, "spent most of his time in the St. Francis River bottoms in the eastern section" of Craighead County and "was a veritable storehouse of information about the early days." The article lamented the loss of early settlers, taking with them the stories of the past of exploration and early settlement in the area. Besides "Uncle Alf," Rufus Snoddy and Daniel O'Gwynne [sic] (Chapter 5) were mentioned. Snoddy, the article noted, hunted with the Indians during their fall hunts at Big Lake. Witnessing history slip away resulted in the preliminary arrangements for the organization of the Craighead County Historical Society. [734]

In his writings, Simonson would recall "old Sam Hector" as the "last Indian resident of Mississippi County" in another article for the *Arkansas*

Historical Quarterly in 1947 about high waters on the Mississippi River (Chapter 7). Recalling Sam, Simonson told of how Sam's son-in-law had killed a panther that was trying to drag a hog out of his fattening pen near his house. [735]

The area continued to have tremors and quakes, probably very similar to what is felt presently. The largest earthquake along the New Madrid Seismic Zone since the 1811-1812 earthquakes occurred in 1895. The quake was a 6.6 and centered at Charleston, Missouri. It was slightly larger than the 1843 earthquake. However, it most likely caused no damage in the Big Lake area, as it did not in neighboring Dunklin County, Missouri. A report from Malden afterward, sent to *The Republic*, a newspaper, noted that there was no damage in the county from "'the heaviest earthquake since 1812'" that lasted three minutes. "'There was a general scare, but no damage is known.'" [736]

In 1901, a new county township was named for the Hector family. Parts of the Chickasawba Township were given to Bowen and Hector townships.[737] The geographic subdivision, east of Little River, included the town of Dell. The township is listed in District 16 as "Hector, (new)" in a July 1901 story in *The Osceola Times* about apportioned road tax funds. [738]

In 1902, Hector Farm on Pemiscot Bayou, then under the ownership of John B. Driver, was being used to raise cattle, a newer enterprise for Mississippi County. The cattle farm was the only one of its kind in the county.[739]

Driver, of Luxora, was the first mayor of the incorporated town, first known as Elmot Landing; was a sheriff of the county from 1873, serving for six years; and an organizer of the St. Francis Levee District, serving as second president. He was a state senator for one term, elected in 1880, and circuit and county clerk in 1888. His obituary in the *Blytheville Courier News*, January 26, 1937, tells of him, at one time, owning a section of land in what is now Roseland. This would be in the neighborhood where Sam and his father's land were located on the Pemiscot Bayou. According to the article, Driver traded it for an interest in the J.L.C.&E. Railroad and later sold that to Robert E. Lee Wilson. [740]

An 1898 plat map for the county shows land with Sam's name in Section 12, Township 14 North, Range 9 East. This land is part of the land granted to him on May 9, 1855, and part granted to his father, William, on May 19, 1855. [741] William and his wife, July [sic] Ann, sold land adjacent to Sam's original swamp land grant to Sam in 1857. [742]

In December 1903 and January 1904, Proof of Loss [743] duplicate certificates were issued to and in favor of the heirs and legal representatives of William Hector, deceased, after Sam made a "diligent search" for the deeds to the unassigned lands of his father, who died in 1864 or 1865, intestate. He and his sister were the only heirs. [744]

In October 1903, Sam's sister, Docia Wells, of New Madrid, Missouri, would meet him in Osceola, as reported in *The Osceola Times*, [745] accompanied by her son, W.I. Wells. [746] Docia had lived in New Madrid at least as early as 1850 when she lived there with old William's sister, Elizabeth Magers, and husband James Magers, and was enumerated as Docia Mager.[747]

Her visit corresponded with a sale of land with Sam. On October 1, she and Sam signed a Quit Claim Deed as "the only children at law of William Hector, deceased" to W.B. Flanigan for $5,000. The sold land encompassed 1960 acres. [748]

Earlier in July 1903, for $1000, Sam signed a Quit Claim Deed to W. B. Flanigan, [749] as an heir of William Hector. In all, the land sale contained 1,040 acres, more or less. [750] In April, Sam sold 40 acres to W.J. Lamb. [751] These lands were part of the swamp land originally granted to William.

The land was constantly changing. One thing led to another, from levees to timber to railroad to agriculture, and from market hunting to conservation.

Competition for the abundance of unregulated wildlife beginning in the mid-1870s resulted in a conflict referred to as the Big Lake Wars, which pitted mostly poor local hunters against affluent northern sportsmen, mostly from St. Louis, Missouri. The sportsmen began leasing land to keep out other hunters, resulting in fights, shootings, and beatings, with some clubhouses and lodges being burned. Clubs signed leases and bought land. Numerous court actions resulted in legislation, some of which prohibited out-of-state residents from hunting in Arkansas. However, the wealthy would often pay the fines and continue hunting.

Dwindling wildlife was not only a concern in Arkansas but nationally as well. In 1913, the International Migratory Bird Treaty was passed by Congress, placing geese and ducks under federal control. New federal and state laws established hunting seasons and set daily limits on the taking of wildlife.[752]

In 1915, a portion of Sam's beloved refuge from the encroaching population and the continued evolution of the land became a protected and managed national refuge, thus promoting the preservation of the habitat for waterfowl in what would become a mostly agricultural area of Mississippi County.

The Big Lake National Wildlife Refuge encompasses 11,038 acres and is managed by the United States Fish and Wildlife Service. Several species of waterfowl spend the winter there annually. In January and February, peak numbers can exceed 200,000. Designated as a wilderness area are 2,100 acres, and 5,000 acres are designated as a National Natural Landmark. More than 225 bird species have been observed on the refuge. Other wildlife includes otters, beavers, turkeys, deer, and bobcats. [753]

Adjacent to the refuge is the Big Lake Wildlife Management Area, managed by the Arkansas Game and Fish Commission.

Big Lake Wilderness was established in 1976 and serves as a migration habitat for ducks and geese along the Mississippi Flyway. It is the state's smallest wilderness and the only one in Eastern Arkansas. The wilderness area consists of interspersed wooded swampland, which during times of flooding may be 99 percent covered in water. Pondweed grows there and supplies food for waterfowl. In 1993, the first bald eagle eggs hatched in a nest just south of the wilderness area. [754] Since that year, the eagles have raised their young there annually. [755]

While the refuge doesn't house all the wildlife that Sam knew and saw when he first settled in the area, there is little doubt that he would feel at home there and approve of the preservation of a portion of the area as it once was – a place where the eagle soars.

Endnotes

Endnotes, Chapter 1

[1] Some of this story is paraphrased, and some direct quotes from James' story. Frank L. James, PhD, MD, "Role of Superstition in Therapeutics," *St. Louis Medical and Surgical Journal*. United States, n.p, 1895, 68, No. 1, 12-14.

[2] *Biographical and Historical Memoirs of Northeast Arkansas: Comprising a Condensed History of the State, a Number of Biographies of Distinguished Citizens of the Same, a Brief Descriptive History of Each of the Counties Named Herein, and Numerous Biographical Sketches of the Prominent Citizens of Such Counties*. 452. The Goodspeed Publishing Company, 1889.

[3] Louis Houck, *A History of Missouri from its Earliest Explorations and Settlements Until the Admission of the State into the Union*, Vol. 1, 214, R.R. Donnelley & Sons Company, Chicago, 1908. According to Houck, the name "Chilliticaux," [sic] like Chillicothe, meant a place of residence; An article concerning the early history of the area causes one to wonder about the meaning of Chilletecaux. The article stated that the name change of the town was made during the first year of the county's representation in the state legislature and Mr. Horner brought about the name change because of his modesty concerning the definition of the word. Francis Valle Lesieur, *Early History: Biographical Sketches of the First Settlers of New Madrid – Their Descendents and Historical Events*, with excerpts by Godfrey Lesieur, Article IV, 20, *Missouri Historical Society*. These articles were originally printed in the *New Madrid Weekly Record* on August 26, 1893; A bill was signed in 1847 in the Missouri House of Representatives to change the name to Butler. In 1851, the name would be changed to Kennett. The name, Chilletecaux, was also said to be too hard and long for a county seat, Mary F. Smyth-Davis, *History of Dunklin County, Mo., 1845-1895. Embracing an Historical Account of the Towns and Post-Villages of Clarkton, Cotton Plant, Cardwell, Caruth, Gibson, Halcomb, Hornersville, Kennett, Lulu, Malden, Nesbit, Senath, Valley Ridge, Vincent, [sic] White Oak, and Wrightsville. Including a Department Devoted to the Description of the Early Appearance, Settlement, Development, Resources, and Present Appearance of the County. With an Album of its People and Homes Profusely Illustrated*, 121, Nixon-Jones Printing Co., St. Louis, Missouri, 1896.

[4] Pierre Menard, of Kaskaskia, Illinois, served as an Indian sub-agent from 1813 to 1833. He was also a fur trader and businessman and had served as Illinois' first Lieutenant Governor. "Research Sheds New Light on Pierre Menard," Press Release, August 12, 2004, *Illinois.Gov*. Accessed April 15, 2022. https://www.illinois.gov/news/press-release.3272.html.

[5] Chilletecaux was located where the city of Kennett, Missouri, now stands.

[6] S.G. Hopkins, New Madrid, Mo. to Genl. Wm. Clark, S.I.A., St. Louis, Mo., Letter, 8-12-1831, Vol. 6, 273-279, 276, William Clark Papers, *Kansas State Historical Society*, Topeka, Kansas. A census taken on August 12, 1831, put the number of those at the village at 76, as reported in a letter by S.G. Hopkins; William Myers noted in a letter dated August 7, same year, there were 92 persons to be removed. Col. Pierre Menard, U.S. Ind. Sub Agt., Kaskaskia, Ill. to Wm. Miers, Letter, July 18, 1831, William Clark Papers, *Kansas State Historical Society*, Topeka, Kansas, Vol. 6, 280, and William Myers to Col. Pierre Menard, U.S. Ind. Sub Agt., Kaskaskia, Ill., Letter,

August 7, 1831, William Clark Papers, *Kansas State Historical Society*, Topeka, Kansas, Vol. 6, 280.

[7] Watkins, of Jackson, Missouri, was a general in the Civil War, but must have been a general earlier, as this is 1831. He was a soldier in the War of 1812 and the Mexican War. He served in the state legislature and senate. He was also a half-brother to American Statesman Henry Clay. During the Civil War, his home in Jackson, Missouri, was burned by the federal troops, and he moved to Scott County. Margaret Cline Harmon, "Gen. N.W. Watkins – Missouri Statesman And a Lawyer of 60 Years active practice." Accessed October 22, 2020. http://www.rootsweb.ancestry.com/~moscott/articles-cem/page-001.htm.

[8] Francois Lesieur and Son, Point Pleasant, Mo. to Col. Pierre Menard, Kaskaskia, Ill., A.L.S. Letter, August 4, 1825, Richard Graham Papers, Missouri History Museum, *Missouri Historical Society*, St. Louis, Mo. S.G. Hopkins, Point Pleasant, Mo. to Major Richard Graham, Agent for Indian Affairs, St. Louis, A.L.S. Letter, August 6, 1825, Richard Graham Papers, Missouri History Museum, *Missouri Historical Society*, St. Louis, Missouri.

[9] John Miller, Missouri Gov. to William Clark, Letter, June 24, 1831, Vol. 6, 265, William Clark Papers, *Kansas State Historical Society*, Topeka, Kansas.

[10] R. Graham to Col. P. Menard, Kaskaskia, Ill., A.L.S. Letter, June 28, 1825, Richard Graham Papers, Missouri History Museum, *Missouri Historical Society,* St. Louis, Missouri.

[11] This would likely be Dr. Robert D. Dawson. Robert Sidney Douglass, AB, LLB, Publishers*, History of Southeast Missouri, A Narrative Account of its Historical Progress, Its People and its Principal Interests,* Vol. 1, 105. The Lewis Publishing Co., Chicago, Illinois and New York, New York, 1912.

[12] R. Graham to Col. P. Menard, Kaskaskia, Ill., A.L.S. Letter, June 28, 1825, Richard Graham Papers, Missouri History Museum, *Missouri Historical Society*, St. Louis, Missouri; Graham's letter says he enclosed a letter from a Doc. Dawson (who would be Dr. Robert D. Dawson, aforementioned, Endnote 11), noted that John R. Walker was the "authorized agent" who would receive the runaways and asked that he notify Dawson when he would visit the village.

[13] Francois Lesieur and Son, Point Pleasant, Mo. to Col. Pierre Menard, Kaskaskia, Ill., A.L.S. Letter, August 4, 1825, Richard Graham Papers, Missouri History Museum, *Missouri Historical Society*, St. Louis, Missouri.

[14] He is referring to the Little River. Little River flowed, as it does now, through Big Lake and joins the St. Francis River at Marked Tree, Arkansas.

[15] S.G. Hopkins, Point Pleasant, Mo., to Major Richard Graham, Agent for Indian Affairs, St. Louis, Mo., A.L.S. Letter, August 6, 1825, Richard Graham Papers, Missouri History Museum, *Missouri Historical Society*, St. Louis, Missouri.

[16] Chilletecaux's River, part of which was later named Varner's River. The map shows "Chitticas R" (river). David H. Burr, and John Arrowsmith. *Map of Mississippi, Louisiana & Arkansas exhibiting the post offices, post roads, canals, rail roads, &c.* [London: J. Arrowsmith, 1839] Map. Accessed July 31, 2022. Library of Congress. https://www.loc.gov/resource/g3935.rr001340/?r=0.572,0.028,0.178,0.085,0.

[17] Francois Lesieur and Son, Point Pleasant, Mo. to Col. Pierre Menard, Kaskaskia, Ill., A.L.S. Letter, August 4, 1825, Richard Graham Papers, Missouri History Museum, *Missouri Historical Society*, St. Louis, Missouri; Robert McCoy came to the area when it was still under Spanish rule, having obtained a grant, in the area of the city of New Madrid. He was a lieutenant under Spanish rule, who patrolled the river

with a company of soldiers, Lesieur, *Early History*, Article II, 4; McCoy settled in New Madrid in 1787 and engaged in Indian trade. He was an officer in command of a Spanish galley. In 1799, he was the commandant of New Madrid and Tywappity Bottom in 1800. Houck, *A History of Missouri,* Vol. II, 143.

[18] John Miller, Missouri Governor, City of Jefferson, Mo. to William Clark, S.IA., St. Louis, Mo., Letter, June 24, 1831, Vol. 6, 265-266, William Clark Papers, *Kansas State Historical Society*, Topeka, Kansas.

[19] Francois Lesieur and Son, Point Pleasant, Mo. to Col. Pierre Menard, Kaskaskia, Ill., A.L.S. Letter, August 4, 1825, Richard Graham Papers, Missouri History Museum, *Missouri Historical Society,* St. Louis, Missouri.

[20] Some of those whose names were on the petition to remove the Indians included Francis L. Lee, Thos. Neel Jr., Alexander Drury, Ephraim Snider, James Myers, Nathial Moyers, Morton Eubanks, James Neel, John Garner, William Hardin, Thomas Page, Jordan Garner, Peter Crytes, William Troy, Benjamin Taylor, John Eaker, Ligo Rise, John Wray, Soloman B. Jackson, Jacob Crytes, Lewis Mansker, Frederick Varner, Andrew Stroup, Lewis Lilbourn, William Bess, and Abraham Taylor. John Miller, Missouri Governor, City of Jefferson, Mo. to William Clark, S.IA., St. Louis, Mo., Letter, October 25, 1831, Vol. 6, 307-316, William Clark Papers, *Kansas State Historical Society*, Topeka, Kansas. Menard to Miers, William Clark Papers, *Kansas State Historical Society*, 280; N. W. Watkins to Gov. Miller, Letter, May 28, 1831, Vol. 6, 265-266, 273, William Clark Papers, *Kansas State Historical Society*, enclosed in Miller to Clark letter June 24, 1831, Endnote 18; Hopkins, claimed that 9/10 of these names were forged. Hopkins to Clark, William Clark Papers, *Kansas State Historical Society*, 275.

[21] Could this be the same Walker who visited the village in 1825 to seize Colbert's runaway slaves? In the correspondence, however, he is named as John R. Walker. R. Graham to Col. P. Menard, A.L.S. Letter, June 28, 1825, Kaskaskia, Ill., Richard Graham Papers, Missouri History Museum, Missouri Historical Society, St. Louis, Missouri; A John B. Walker was an early settler just north of Hornersville, Missouri. Smyth-Davis, History of Dunklin County, Mo., 41. He was the captain of a regiment in 1820. Letter signed Stephen Ross, Winchester, New Madrid County, to William Clark. A hunting party of Shawnee and Seminole committed a "wanton and cruel murder upon the person of a Mr. Davis of Tennessee" while wounding another whose "name is not now recollected." April 30, 1820, Box: 13, Folder: 4. Clark Family Collection, A0289. *Missouri Historical Society* Library and Research Center.

[22] William Myres [sic] was employed as a clerk for trader William Gillis at the James Fork and Swan Trading Posts from 1827 to 1829. Previously, he had been employed by Menard and Valle in late 1826 or early 1827 when he went with Col. Peter Menard to the James Fork Trading Post, operated by Gillis in the employ of Menard and Valle. Senator Emory Melton, "Delaware Town and the Swan Trading Post, 1822-1831," *White River Valley Historical Quarterly*, Vol. 6, No. 3, 1-11. Spring 1977. Accessed October 22, 2020. http://thelibrary.org/lochist/periodicals/wrv/V6/N3/Sp77d.htm.

[23] Myers would tell in a deposition in the early 1870s that when visiting Menard in St. Louis in early 1830, he was sent to Stoddard County, Missouri, "for removal of balance of Delawares." "Boyer, Francis and Charley, James Jr. by McGee, M.W. v Dively, Michael admin of will of Gillis, William (Deceased) and Donnelly, Bernard and Black F.M., executor of the will of Troost, Mary A. (Deceased)," Missouri Supreme Court Historical Database, 58 MO 510, Box 1112, Folder 4, *Missouri Digital Heritage*. Accessed January 13, 2025. https://www.sos.mo.gov/mdh/.

[24] Godair was paid $12 for his services as interpreter to the Delawares in 1831. H.R. Doc. No. 137, 22nd Cong., 2nd Sess. (1833); He settled in New Madrid in 1792. "Pemiscot County," Ramsay Place Names File, 1928-1945 (C2366)," Columbia Manuscript Collections, *The State Historical Society of Missouri.* Accessed March 24, 2022. https://collections.shsmo.org/manuscripts/columbia/C2366/pemiscot-county.

[25] Some of those who signed a petition in favor of the villagers included Robert McCoy, G.G. Alford, Thomas C. Powell, William Murphey, Thom Mosely Jr., Ephraim Campbell, Presley Phillips, A. Smith, A.E. Alford, James Eastwood, Napoleon Lesieur, J.F. Ross, John B. Ruddel, John D. Mercer, John Dumay, Peter Dumay, Thomas Bartlett, James McClure, Thomas James, F.G. Butler, L.W. Butler, Ebenezer Walker, Francois Maisonville, William Wells, and Charles Loignon. Hopkins to Clark, William Clark Papers, Vol. 6, 279; Several of these names can be found on the 1830 New Madrid Census. "1830 United States Federal Census," *Ancestry.com.* New Madrid, Missouri, Series: M19; Roll: 73; Family History Library Film: 0014854, Provo, Utah, USA: Ancestry.com Operations, Inc., 2010. Images reproduced by *FamilySearch.* Original data: Fifth Census of the United States, 1830. (NARA microfilm publication M19, 201 rolls). Records of the Bureau of the Census, Record Group 29. National Archives, Washington, D.C. Accessed January 3, 2025. https://www.ancestry.com.

[26] Possibly Dr. Thomas Varner, who settled in the 1830s near Chilletecaux. Smyth-Davis, *History of Dunklin County, Mo.*, 39.

[27] This would be Wapapilethe's village at Bloomfield.

[28] Godfrey Lesieur, New Madrid, Mo. to Gov. John Miller, Letter, October 6, 1831, Vol. 6, 311-312, William Clark Papers, *Kansas State Historical Society,* Topeka, Kansas.

[29] John Miller, Governor of Missouri to Clark, S.I.A., St. Louis, Mo., Letter, October 25, 1831, 309, William Clark Papers, *Kansas State Historical Society*, Vol. 6, 307-309.

[30] Smyth-Davis, *History of Dunklin County, Mo.,* 39.

[31] Chilitica, Indian Chief to John Miller, Governor of the state of Missouri, Memorial, October 1831, Vol. 6, 314-316, William Clark Papers, *Kansas State Historical Society*, Topeka, Kansas.

[32] Smyth-Davis, *History of Dunklin County, Mo.,* 120.

[33] Smyth-Davis, *History of Dunklin County, Mo.,* 22.

[34] Smyth-Davis, *History of Dunklin County, Mo.,* 224; The cabin had many cracks, and "with a word and a motion of his hand," he would send the cats outside, Smyth-Davis, *History of Dunklin County, Mo.,* 45.

[35] Chilitica to Miller, William Clark Papers, *Kansas State Historical Society*, 314-316.

[36] Smyth-Davis, *History of Dunkin County, Mo.,* 45.

[37] Smyth-Davis, *History of Dunkin County, Mo.,* 121.

[38] Godfrey Lesieur, to Miller, William Clark Papers, *Kansas State Historical Society*, Vol. 6, 311-312.

[39] Chilitica to Miller, William Clark Papers, *Kansas State Historical Society*, 314-16.

[40] The winter of 1830-1831 covered Southern Illinois in three feet of cold precipitation with winds that continued for 60 days, causing many to be snowbound in their homes. "The Deep Snow," *The Illinois Intelligencer*, January 28, 1968, as part of the Illinois Sesquicentennial Celebration. Accessed October 22, 2020.

http://www.illinoishistory.com/deepsnow.htm.

[41] William Clark, Diary, *Kansas State Historical Society,* United States Office of Indian Affairs, Central Superintendency, St. Louis, Missouri, Vol. 31, 123-124. *Kansas Memory.* Accessed March 26, 2022. https://www.kansasmemory.org.

[42] N. Prior, Cantonment Gibson to Gen. Wm. Clark, United States Office of Indian Affairs, Central Superintendency, St. Louis, Missouri. Letter, January 22, 1831, Vol. 6, 104, *Kansas State Historical Society, Kansas Memory*, Correspondence. Accessed March 26, 2022. https://www.kansasmemory.org.

[43] Col. Pierre Menard, U.S. Ind. Sub. Agt., Kaskaski, Ill. to Wm. Miers, [sic] Letter, July 18, 1831, Vol. 6, 280, and William Myers to Col. Pierre Menard, U.S. Ind. Sub Agt., Kaskaskia, Ill., Letter, August 7, 1831, Vol. 6, 280, William Clark Papers, *Kansas State Historical Society*, Topeka, Kansas.

[44] Smyth-Davis, *History of Dunklin County, Mo.*, 22.

[45] Lesieur, *Early History,* Article III, 10.

[46] Hopkins to Clark, William Clark Papers, Vol. 6, 280. The census taken by S.G. Hopkins, 276, placed the number of Indians at eight Shawnees, 25 Delawares, 18 Senecas, and 25 Creeks, for a total of 76. This is different than Myers' account of 13 Shawnees, 49 Delawares, 22 Senecas, and eight half-breed Shawnees and Creeks, for a total of 92 people just six days earlier, 281. Menard to Miers, and Myers to Menard, William Clark Papers, *Kansas State Historical Society*, Vol. 6, 280.

[47] James A. East - Application Number 40265; Eastern Cherokee Applications, 8/29/1906-5/26/1909, Record Group 123: Records of the U.S. Court of Claims, 1835-1984; M1104. National Archives at College Park, College Park, Maryland. Accessed March 20, 2022. www.archives.gov. In 1909, James East would state he was born in 1837 at an Indian camp (Chilletecaux) where there were 300 Indians and two White families. By 1837 there seemed to be few left in the village.

[48] Shawnee Indian "Chilitika" received $11.25 for provisions furnished for Delawares in 1831. "General Abstract of All Disbursements or Expenditures made by Pierre Menard, Indian Sub-Agent at Kaskaskia from the first October 1831 to the 30th September 1832, both dates inclusive," No. 33, 135, H.R. Doc. No. 137, 22nd Cong., 2nd Sess., *House Documents, Otherwise Publ. as Executive Documents*: 13th Congress, 2d Session-49th Congress, 1st Session. United States, 1832. Accessed December 7, 2024. https://books.google.com; Called "Chilc-ta-ca-la Shawe," he provided 350 pounds of beef at 2 ½ cents a pound and five bushels of corn at 50 cents a bushel. "Correspondence on the Subject of the Emigration of Indians, between the 30th November, 1831, and 27th December, 1833, with Abstracts of Expenditures By Disbursing Agents," GovInfo, Congressional Serial Set, 23rd Congress, No. 248, Senate Document No. 512, 501. Accessed December 7, 2024. Downloaded PDF. https://www.govinfo.gov/app/collection/serialset.

[49] Possibly Keshotte of which local stories exist.

[50] Menard to Miers, [sic] and Myers to Menard, William Clark Papers, *Kansas State Historical Society*, Vol. 6, 280.

[51] Sarcoxie, Sesarkoxy, or Sacoxy Anderson was a member of Chief William Anderson's tribe and was likely his son. Letter from William Myers to Pierre Menard says the greater part of those at the village were Delawares of Chief Anderson's family and relations. Menard to Miers, and Myers to Menard, William Clark Papers, *Kansas State Historical Society*, Vol. 6, 280; On October 16, 1830, Anderson, who was on his way at this time to Kansas, wrote Pierre Menard at Kaskaskia and mentioned that a small party of his nation had gone to the swamp. Pierre Menard, Kaskaskia, to Gen.

William Clark, Supt. Of Indian Affairs, St. Louis, Mo., Letter, November 2, 1830, William Clark Papers, *Kansas State Historical Society*, Vol. 6, 65-66. Accessed April 9, 2015. www.kansasmemory.org; This is probably the same John Sarcoxie who lived near Delaware Town on the White River. Melton, *Delaware Town and the Swan Trading Post,* Vol. 6, No. 3. 1-11.

[52] Thomas Turner, attorney in fact for Pierre Chouteau of St. Louis, Missouri to Sacoxy Anderson, of the Delaware Nation, August 12, 1831, permission to reside seven years on land granted to James Clarmorgan [sic] by the Spanish Government and conveyed to Chouteau on the "Grand Prairie," April 5, 1830, Vol. 6, 278, William Clark, *Kansas State Historical Society,* Topeka, Kansas.

[53] Clamorgan's grant, which was in what is now Southeast Missouri and Northeast Arkansas, below New Madrid, extended from the Mississippi River to the St. Francis River. *Title papers of the Clamorgan grant, of 536,904 arpens of alluvial lands in Missouri and Arkansas,* New York, printed by T. Snowden, 58 Wall Street, 1837, Internet Archive, Ebook and Texts Archive, Library of Congress. Accessed April 16, 2022. http://archive.org/details/titlepapersofcla01clam.

[54] Chouteau was named U.S. Agent for Indian Affairs west of the Mississippi River in 1804. He spent a lot of his time with the Osage Indians and established a trading post in the western part of their territory, near what is now Salina, Oklahoma, in 1796. In 1808, he was a negotiator for a treaty with the Osage in which they agreed to sell large portions of their lands in Arkansas and Missouri for federal annuities. "Jean-Pierre Chouteau," *Wikipedia,* Wikimedia Foundation. Accessed April 15, 2022. https://en.wikipedia.org/wiki/Jean-Pierre_Chouteau; This land included parts of Mississippi County, Arkansas.

[55] Sasa Coxie. "Correspondence on the Subject of the Emigration of Indians, between the 30th November, 1831, and 27th December, 1833, with Abstracts of Expenditures By Disbursing Agents," GovInfo, Congressional Serial Set, 23rd Congress, No. 248, Senate Document No. 512, 503. Accessed December 7, 2024. Downloaded PDF. https://www.govinfo.gov/app/collection/serialset.

[56] Brown was paid $65 for expenses during removal with a second voucher on December 7, 1832, for provisions. "Correspondence on the Subject of the Emigration of Indians, between the 30th November, 1831, and 27th December, 1833, with Abstracts of Expenditures By Disbursing Agents," GovInfo, Congressional Serial Set, 23rd Congress, No. 248, Senate Document No. 512, 108. Accessed December 7, 2024. Downloaded PDF. https://www.govinfo.gov/app/collection/serialset.; A John Brown Big Nose (Seneca) was listed with those who had obtained credit with Menard in Valle in St. Genevieve. Houck, *A History of Missouri*, Vol. I, 217.

[57] William Myers for his services in aiding and removing the Delawares, 128 days at $400 per annum, and his personal expenses during said trip, $77.88. "Correspondence on the Subject of the Emigration of Indians, between the 30th November, 1831, and 27th December, 1833, with Abstracts of Expenditures By Disbursing Agents," GovInfo, Congressional Serial Set, 23rd Congress, No. 248, Senate Document No. 512, 503. Accessed December 7, 2024. Downloaded PDF. https://www.govinfo.gov/app/collection/serialset.

[58] Moonshine was paid cash to defray the expenses of Delawares on a trip to the Kansas River in May 1832. "Correspondence on the Subject of the Emigration of Indians, between the 30th November, 1831, and 27th December, 1833, with Abstracts of Expenditures By Disbursing Agents," GovInfo, Congressional Serial Set, 23rd

Congress, No. 248, Senate Document No. 512, 12. Accessed December 7, 2024. Downloaded PDF. https://www.govinfo.gov/app/collection/serialset.

[59] Hector descendants would name their ancestor William Hector as William Moonshine in their Guion Miller applications in 1909. Nervie Bunch - Application Number 36058; Eastern Cherokee Applications, 8/29/1906-5/26/1909, Record Group 123: Records of the U.S. Court of Claims, 1835-1984; M1104. National Archives at College Park, College Park, Maryland. Accessed March 20, 2022. www.archives.gov.; Merriman, Jane Bunch - Application Number 36059; Eastern Cherokee Applications, 8/29/1906-5/26/1909, Record Group 123: Records of the U.S. Court of Claims, 1835-1984; M1104. National Archives at College Park, College Park, Maryland. Accessed March 20, 2022. www.archives.gov.

[60] Lesieur, *Early History*, Article III, 12.

[61] James, "Role of Superstition in Therapeutics," Vol. 68, 13-14.

[62] Yousery E. Sherif, Nasser M. Hosny, Ahmad H. Alghadir, and Rayan Alansari, "Phytochemicals of Rhus spp. As Potential Inhibitors of SARS-CoV-2 Main Protease: Molecular Docking and Drug Likeness Study," *Evidence-Based Complementary and Alternative Medicine, Hindawi*. Accessed August 29, 2022. https://www.hindawi.com/journals/ecam/2021/8814890/. This study explored the potential inhibitory effects of some active polyphenolic constituents of *Rhus spp* against the SARS-CoV-2 main protease enzyme (Mpro;6LU7) in which the conclusion shows potential in the treatment of COVID-19 and encourages further investigation as a preventative.

[63] Ibid.

Endnotes, Chapter 2

[64] James would later write about the wealth of artifacts along the Little River below Sam's home. "Appendix Q, A Memoir to accompany the map of Mississippi County, Arkansas," 229-235, Compiled by Frank L. James, MD, PhD, for the Mississippi River Commission, 1881, *Letter from the Secretary of War: Transmitting, in Compliance with the Requirements of the River and Harbor Act of August, 1882, a Report of the Mississippi River Commission with Accompanying Papers and Maps*, United States. Mississippi River Commission, U.S. Government Printing Office, January 1883. Accessed December 6, 2024. https://books.google.com.

[65] James, "Role of Superstition in Therapeutics," Vol. 68, 13-14.

[66] Meek, Seth Eugene, PhD, *A List of Fishes and Mollusks Collected in Arkansas and Indian Territory in 1894*, Vol. 15, 344-349 of Fishery bulletin, Government Printing Office, 1896. Accessed November 15, 2024. Google Books. https://books.google.com.

[67] James, "Role of Superstition in Therapeutics," Vol. 68, 13-14.

[68] James, Appendix Q, A Memoir to accompany the map of Mississippi County, Arkansas, 231.

[69] James, "Role of Superstition in Therapeutics," Vol. 68, 13-14. James, who had been a physician in Osceola, Arkansas in 1877 and 1878, said that Sam told him this story about killing a buffalo just before an earthquake. James alluded to the event being the 1811-1812 earthquakes, however, Sam would not have been born at that time. In consideration, it would seem more likely that the earthquake Sam was referring to was the January 4, 1843 earthquake centered near Marked Tree, which is estimated to be a 6.0 magnitude earthquake. In this article, James said the trip was in 1872 or 1873. Another clue to the year of the earthquake was Sam saying that he was about the age of his "little gal." Melissa, Sam's youngest daughter, would have been approximately 19-20 in 1872-1873. Sam would have been 18 in 1843.

[70] Charles Lyell, *A Second Visit to the United States of North America*, United Kingdom, Harper & Brothers, 1849, 237. Accessed March 24, 2022. https://books.google.com. Lyell was told about six buffalo being killed in 1844 on Buffalo Island from a herd of 300 to 400. "Bison survived in significant numbers only where inaccessibility hindered successful hunting. Bison found some protection in the thick canebrakes and sunk lands of the St. Francis River Basin in eastern Arkansas where they were reported as late as 1848"; Bison were reported in the St. Francis River Basin in the canebrakes and sunk lands as late as 1848. Joseph Patrick Key, "Indians and Ecological Conflict in Territorial Arkansas," *Arkansas Historical Quarterly*, Vol. LIX, No. 2, Summer, 2000, 135; However, bison may have been in the swamps as late as 1865. Smyth-Davis, *History of Dunklin County, Mo.*, 26.

[71] Lesieur, *Early History*, Article III, 10. Indians in the area had flint-lock rifles supplied by Col. Menard of Kaskaskia, Illinois. They were manufactured by Dickert and Gill of Philadelphia and were ornamented with brass escutcheons.

[72] Francis Parkman, *Prairie and Rocky Mountain Life; Or, The California and Oregon Trail, United States,* George P. Putnam, 1852, 388. Accessed August 2, 2022. https://books.google.com.

[73] Riley Clarkston told of how he could ride on his horse, clear under a tree on which a buffalo would hang up its hair on a limb. Smyth-Davis, *History of Dunklin County, Mo.*, 176.

[74] Harry Lee Williams, *The History of Craighead County, Arkansas*, 25, Parke-Harper Co., Little Rock, Arkansas, 1930. Williams told of the behavior of buffalo before

crossing a river or stream. He said that they appeared to dread crossing the water, and after devouring the food nearby, they would gather at a crossing and wait until they were hungry. They would then get in a close circle and move round and round, the inside animals crowding the outer circle of animals closer to the water until one was pushed out into the water and forced to swim. Then the rest of the herd would follow.

[75] W. Bowling Guion, U.S. Civil Engineer, "A report of the survey of the St. Francis River as called for by a resolution of the Senate of the 28th of Feb. 1837," *Public Documents Printed By Order Of The Senate Of The United States, Second Session Of The Twenty-Fourth Congress Begun And Held At The City Of Washington In Three Volumes,* Volume III, 4-5, n.p., 1837. Accessed August 2, 2022. https://books.google.com.

[76] Numerous sandblows resulted from the eruption of water and sand to the surface of the land during the 1811-1812 earthquakes. This phenomenon is known as liquefaction.

[77] Sheila McCall, "Beneath the Delta – Local man discovers rich history," *Blytheville Courier News*, October 6, 1996. The photo with the article shows tree trunks near the Pemiscot Bayou near Yarbro, Arkansas. The trees, discovered by Marion Haynes when sand was dug from a "'borrow pit,'" were most likely buried when the banks of the bayou fell in during the 1811-1812 earthquakes. The five sycamore tree trunks, all in a row as if on the banks of the bayou, were preserved because they were below the existing water table; One of the 1811-1812 earthquakes was centered near Yarbro. James Fletcher, "letter to the *Pittsburgh Gazette* (1812," Feb. 14, 1812, Eyewitness Accounts, New Madrid Compendium, The University of Memphis, Center for Earthquake Research and Information. Accessed September 25, 2013. https://www.memphis.edu/ceri/compendium/. Fletcher tells of seeing and being told of how the "little river Pemisece" (Pemiscot Bayou) was filled with sand.

[78] Lyell, *A Second Visit to North America,* Volume 2, 231. Accessed March 28, 2022. Google Books, https://books.google.com. Louis Bringier told Lyell, of how in 1811, while traveling in an area near New Madrid, he witnessed the trees bending and interlocking. Louis Bringier was a French explorer from New Orleans, Louisiana.

[79] Or 1873. James couldn't recall the exact date of this trip. James, "Role of Superstition in Therapeutics," *St. Louis Medical and Surgical Journal*, 13-14.

[80] Lesieur, *Early History,* Article IV, 20. F.V. Lesieur told of how he and commissioners appointed to survey and locate a plank road in southeast Missouri were on an expedition when an earthquake occurred. Describing the earthquake that lasted a few seconds, "water and sand was blown up on the vegetation some three to five feet from the force of the subterranean gases." The article states this happened in 1853. This was a phenomenon that happened in a larger earthquake.

[81] James, "Role of Superstition in Therapeutics," *St. Louis Medical and Surgical Journal*, 13-14. The Gar Hole is located at the foot of Big Lake; Another report told of a lake formed during this earthquake. *The Weekly Globe,* Containing Political Discussions, Documentary Proofs, Etc., Blair and Rives, editors, Washington, D.C., February 1843, Vol. 2, No. 9, 134. Accessed September 24, 2013. https://books.google.com. The report told of how a hunter from the St. Francis in Arkansas reported that a deep lake had formed by the earth's sinking on that river, and some hunter companions had disappeared and had not been heard from since; Could there possibly be some confusion here as to the actual spot of the newly-widened lake. A lake was formed on the St. Francis River during the 1811-1812 earthquakes.

[82] "Big Lake, National Wildlife Refuge," U.S. Fish & Wildlife Service. Accessed March 28, 2022. https://www.fws.gov/refuge/big-lake.

[83] Also donic, a colloquial term for a small island.

[84] W. Bowling Guion, U.S. Civil Engineer, "A report of the survey of the St. Francis River as called for by a resolution of the Senate of the 28th of Feb. 1837," *Public Documents Printed By Order Of The Senate Of The United States, Second Session Of The Twenty-Fourth Congress Begun And Held At The City Of Washington In Three Volumes,* Volume III. n.p., 1837, 5. Accessed August 2, 2022. https://books.google.com. This area was referred to as Buffalo Island as early as 1837.

[85] Smyth-Davis, *History of Dunklin County, Mo.*, 26. Accessed March 28, 2022. https://www.sos.mo.gov/mdh. Buffalo roamed the swamps in Southeast Missouri until 1865. See endnote 70.

[86] James, "Role of Superstition in Therapeutics," 13. James referred to Sam as "half-breed Shawnee."

[87] S. E. Simonson, "The St. Francis Levee and High Waters on the Mississippi River." *The Arkansas Historical Quarterly*, Vol. 6, No. 4, 419–429, Arkansas Historical Association, 1947. Simonson referred to Sam as the last Indian resident of Mississippi County.

[88] Mable F. Edrington, *History of Mississippi County, Arkansas, Ocala Star-Banner*, Ocala, Florida, 1962, 91. Mississippi County had grown from the shipping of 149 cotton bales and 1,973 sacks of cotton seed to Memphis by four farmers to the largest county in the world for rain-grown cotton in 1960.

[89] During the Mesozoic Era. Approximately 300 million years ago.

[90] Crowley settled near Walcott, Arkansas in 1821.

[91] Seismic evidence questions the fluvial origin of the ridge by the Mississippi and Ohio rivers due to uplift along the ridge bounding faults, which may be ongoing. "Crowley's Ridge," *Wikipedia*, Wikipedia Foundation, Last modified January 25, 2022. Accessed August 1, 2022. https://en.wikipedia.org/w/index.php?title=Crowley%27s_Ridge&oldid=1067926854.

[92] James, "Appendix Q, A Memoir to accompany the map of Mississippi County, Arkansas, 232.

[93] Michael B. Dougan, *Arkansas Odyssey, The Saga of Arkansas from Prehistoric Times to present*, 12, Rose Publishing Company, Inc., Little Rock, Arkansas, 1994.

[94] Ibid, 12-13.

[95] "Eaker Site," *Wikipedia*, Wikimedia Foundation, Inc. Accessed March 28, 2022. http://en.wikipedia.org/wiki/Eaker_Site.

[96] Jeffrey M. Mitchem, PhD. "The Expedition of Hernando de Soto in Sixteenth-Century Arkansas," *Arkansas Archaeological Survey*. Accessed March 28, 2022. https://archeology.uark.edu/wp-content/uploads/2015/06/Expedition-of-Hernando-de-Soto.pdf.

[97] The Michigamea were a tribe of the Illinois Confederation. When Marquette and Jolliet descended the Mississippi, they described a village on the west side of the river, near a lake. It has been believed to be that of Big Lake in Arkansas, which was changed by the New Madrid earthquakes. Later, the Michigamea were driven out of the area by the Quapaw or Chickasaw and joined the Kaskaskia tribe.

[98] Smyth-Davis, *History of Dunklin County, Mo.*, 22. Accessed April 14, 2022. https://www.sos.mo.gov/mdh.

[99] Houck, *A History of Missouri*, Vol. I, 208.

[100] Louis Lorimier, credited with founding the city of Cape Girardeau, Missouri, first came to the area of Bois Brule, Missouri, in 1787 with a contingent of Shawnee and Delaware as their agent. In 1791, he and his family moved to the area that would become Cape Girardeau. His wife, Charlotte Penampieh Bouganville, was half Shawnee.

[101] Houck, *A History of Missouri,* Vol. I, 217.

[102] Melton, "Delaware Town and the Swan Trading Post, 1822-1831, Vol. 6, No. 3, 1-11. Menard and Valle was a fur trading firm organized by Jean Baptiste Valle and his cousin Pierre Menard of Kaskaskia in 1817. The firm dealt with the government in supplying Indian tribes with rations and also purchased furs and peltries. Accessed March 28, 2022. http://thelibrary.org/lochist/periodicals/wrv/V6/N3/Sp77d.htm.

[103] Houck, *A History of Missouri,* Vol. I, 217. This is probably Chilletecaux.

[104] Ibid, Vol. I, 219. In mentioning the Creek living among the Shawnee, Houck referenced "Flint's *Mississippi Valley,*" *footnote* 173, Vol. i, 159.

[105] Weston Arthur Goodspeed, editor, *The Province and the States: A History of the Province of Louisiana under France and Spain, and of the Territories and States of the United States Formed Therefrom*, Vol. I, 437, Western Historical Association, Louisiana, 1904. Accessed March 29, 2022. https://books.google.com.

[106] Ibid, 437.

[107] "Peoria people," *Wikipedia*, Wikimedia Foundation, Inc. Accessed March 29, 2022. http://en.wikipedia.org/wiki/Peoria_tribe.

[108] The New Madrid Seismic Zone (NMSZ) is a major fault zone that stretches from Marked Tree, Arkansas to Cairo, Illinois. The currently active zone is located in Southeastern Missouri, Southern Illinois, Western Tennessee, Western Kentucky, and Northeast Arkansas.

[109] Lesieur, *Early History*, Article V, 25.

[110] Similar to the effect one gets when one moves their feet in the sand close to the water at a beach, liquefaction in an earthquake is the process by which the soil loses its strength and stiffness in response to applied pressure and liquefies.

[111] Martitia P. Tuttle, Eugene S. Schweig, John D. Sims, Robert H. Lafferty, Lorraine W. Wolf, and Marion L. Haynes, "The Earthquake Potential of the New Madrid Seismic Zone," *Bulletin of The Seismological Society of America.* Vol. 92, 2080-2089. 10.1785/0120010227, August 1, 2002. Downloaded PDF. Accessed March 29, 2022. researchgagte.net. https://www.researchgate.net/publication/241444348_The_Earthquake_Potential_of_the_New_Madrid_Seismic_Zone.

[112] Lesieur, *Early History*, Article IV, 23.

[113] *Biographical and Historical Memoirs of Northeast Arkansas*, 447.

Endnotes, Chapter 3

[114] In the William Clark Papers, "Chilitica" is the spelling used for the principal chief and the village of Chilitica. John Miller, Governor of Missouri to William Clark, S.I.A., St. Louis, Missouri, Letter, October 25, 1831, Vol. 6, 307-309. William Clark Papers, *Kansas State Historical Society*, Topeka, Kansas. The local spelling of the village and the original name for the town now called Kennett, Missouri, was a French version of the chief's name, Chilletecaux, and is the version that has been used since. In 1845, when Dunklin County was formed, Chilletecaux was the county seat. The local version of this name will be used in this writing.

[115] This is a reference to the village of Wapapilethe, a Shawnee village, near Bloomfield, Missouri, near where Sam's family lived in 1828 when he was three years old. The chief would sit in the center of a circle and make music by beating a rawhide stretched over a keg with sticks. Draper, Lyman Copeland, Draper Manuscripts, Draper Mss. 1-5YY129, (microfilm edition) State Historical Society of Wisconsin.

[116] Draper Mss. 1-5YY129.

[117] Fay Hempstead, *A Pictorial History of Arkansas, from Earliest Times to the Year 1890*, 91, *footnote*. N.D., Thompson Publishing Company, 1890, St. Louis and New York. Downloaded book from Google Books, February 26, 2020. Note: The footnote referred to reads, "Hon. H.M. McVeigh, of Osceola, has kindly furnished by letter the following information on this point, to-wit 'An old friend of mine, Sam Hector, part Indian, who spent his early life among the Indians, tells me he has often picked up iron musket balls on the bluff at Wittsburg, when a boy, living among the Indians.'" At the writing of this book, the St. Francis fort area referred to was the site of Wittsburg. The site of the fort is however, further down the river, closer to Helena. The area near Wittsburg is the site of one of the earliest Cherokee settlements in Arkansas. Most of the Cherokee moved westward after the New Madrid earthquakes. No doubt they returned to the area many times afterward to hunt. The balls described were made of iron. Musket balls were made of lead. Is it possible the iron balls were from some sort of cannon shot? Possibly, Sam picked up these balls at another place along the river, closer to the old site of Fort St. Francis. Also, nearby on the river is Parkin, an archaeological site of a Mississippian-era village. It is believed to be on the path of Hernando de Soto's travels in Arkansas in 1541.

[118] Who is William? He is likely the son of Gilbert Hector, who received a Spanish Land Grant for land in the Cape Girardeau, Missouri area and settled there during the Spanish occupation in 1799. "U.S., Indexed Early Land Ownership and Township Plats, 1785-1898," Township 31 North, Range 13 East, 591, Township 32 North, Range 13 East, 597, Missouri, Fifth Principal Meridian, *Ancestry.com*. Provo, Utah, USA: Ancestry.com Operations, Inc., 2011. Accessed January 11, 2025. https://www.ancestry.com; Both Gilbert and William were residents of Byrd Township, Cape Girardeau, Missouri. William: State Vs Hector, William, Reel C21015, Circuit Court Case File, Cape Girardeau County, Missouri State Archives, Jefferson City, Missouri and Gilbert: Hector, Gilbert, Byrd Township, Territorial Taxes in the county of Cape Girardeau, C3677, Cape Girardeau County, Missouri, Tax Lists, 1812, 1814, *Missouri Historical Society*, Missouri; Gilbert Hector was in Ohio County, West Virginia, before moving to the Cape Girardeau area where a court case involving him in 1801, from an incident early in 1799, noted that he had "absconded." Melba Pender Zinn, *Monongalia County, (West) Virginia: Records of the District, Superior, and County Courts*, Vol. 2, 193-194, 1800-1902, 1990; William was born in Virginia in approximately 1791, "1850 United States Federal Census," Big Lake,

Mississippi, Arkansas, Roll: 28, 353b *Ancestry.* Ancestry.com Operations, Inc., 2009, Lehi, Utah. Accessed March 21, 2022. https://www.ancestry.com; Gilbert's wife was Ann Dixon. Some of her family lived in the Cape Girardeau area, as well as in the West Virginia area, where Gilbert formerly resided. *Abstracts of Cape Girardeau County Deeds*, Books A/B-F, 1796-1826, Cape Girardeau County Genealogical Society, Jackson, Missouri, 2000, 152, Abstracted by Bill Eddleman and Jane Randol Jackson, December 14, 1822. Mentioned are heirs of Zilla or Drusilla Dickson, including Ann, wife of Gilbert Hector, Lewis Dickson, Frederick Dickson, Nathaniel Dickson, Hezekiah Dickson, Jonathan Purdy and his wife Unis, David Brady and his wife Ester, and Arthur Burns and his wife Polly; Purdy, also lived in Ohio County, West Virginia, as early as 1790. Jonathan Purdy, New York, Revolutionary War Pension and Bounty Land Warrant Application File S. 5, 996, Record Group 15: Records of the Department of Veteran's Affairs, 1773-2007, Case Files of Pension and Bounty-Land Warrant Applications Based on Revolutionary War Services, ca. 1800-ca.1812, Fold3, M804, Roll 1985, ARC Identifier 144211314, National Archives, Washington, D.C. Accessed August 24, 2022. https://catalog.archives.gov; In Ohio, across the river from the West Virginia Northern panhandle were settled the Shawnee Indians and some of those from Ohio settled Cape Girardeau, along with founder, Louis Lorimier; William's descendants would claim he and Sam were Cherokee in their Guion Miller applications for enrollment in the Eastern Cherokee tribe, (Chapter 10); William was not noted as Cherokee when he was enumerated as Moonshine in 1831 in the village of Chilletecaux. Those enumerated at the village in 1831 were either Shawnee, Delaware, Seneca, or Creek, or half Muscogee, or half Shawnee. Myers to Menard, William Clark papers, Kansas State Historical Society, Vol. 6, 280-281; Frank James also noted that Sam was "a half-breed Shawnee," possibly indicating that his mother or father was at least part Shawnee (Chapter 9). Perhaps there was a mixture of Native American Heritage in the Hector line. Records show that William went by the names of Moonshine and William Hector at different times (Chapter 3). Records also show that the Cherokee lived at Chilletecaux village in 1835. Thomas Moseley Jr., New Madrid, Mo., to Gen. Wm. Clark, S. Int. Indian Affairs, St. Louis, Missouri, Letter, July 4, 1835, *The Foreman Transcripts, Commissioner of Indian Affairs*, Seven Volumes, Vol. 1, 53-55, Western Superintendency, Miscellaneous and schools. Accessed July 28, 2022. https://www.okhistory.org/research/foremantranscripts. Chilletecaux is spelled Chilitecau in this letter; Other residents of Missouri related to William include Henry Hector of New Madrid County, Missouri, Ezekiel Hector of Cape Girardeau County, Missouri, and Elizabeth Magers of New Madrid County, Missouri. Elizabeth Magers Estate, 1859, New Madrid County Probate Court, Box 0011, Folder 0120, Missouri Judicial Records Historical Database, Collections, *Missouri Digital Heritage*, John R. Ashcroft, Missouri Secretary of State. Accessed August 24, 2022. https://www.sos.mo.gov/mdh/. Elizabeth is Elizabeth Hector, previously married to William Long (Endnote 162).

[119] Called by the French, Grand Marias, Big Swamp was a bottom about three miles wide just south of Cape Girardeau, according to Houck. Houck, *A History of Missouri,* Vol. II, 154; In *The Spanish Regime in Missouri,* Houck noted that Terance Dyal lived in the Big Swamp about six miles southwest of Cape Girardeau. Louis Houck, *The Spanish Regime in Missouri: A Collection of Papers and Documents Relating to Upper Louisiana Principally Within the Present Limits of Missouri During the Dominion of Spain, from the Archives of the Indies at Seville, Etc., Translated from the Original*

Spanish Into English, and Including Also Some Papers Concerning the Supposed Grant to Col. George Morgan at the Mouth of the Ohio, 407 and 413. The Congressional Library. (1909). United States: R. R. Donnelley & sons. Accessed August 2, 2022. https://books.google.com. Dyal had land in Township 30 North, Range 13 East. "U.S., Indexed Early Land Ownership and Township Plats, 1785-1898," Township 30 North, Range 13 East, 564, Missouri, Fifth Principal Meridian, *Ancestry.com.* Provo, Utah, USA: Ancestry.com Operations, Inc., 2011. Accessed January 11, 2025. https://www.ancestry.com.

[120] It is unknown whether the grandmother Sam referred to as teaching him about herbs was on his mother's or father's side. James, "Role of Superstition in Therapeutics," 13-14.

[121] Various spellings of Wapapilethe exist, Ouppileene, Wappapello, Wappillessee, and Wabepelathy, all of which seem to belong to this Shawnee chief. Wapapilethe, Draper, Draper Mss., 1-5YY129 (microfilm edition).

[122] Wabepelathy told in a speech in 1815 at Portage des Sioux, Missouri, during treaty negotiations, that he had been in Missouri for 30 years, "Talks," Wabepelathy, *American State Papers,* Vol. 2, Senate, 14th Congress, 1st Session Indian Affairs, 11. Accessed December 9, 2024. https://www.hathitrust.org; Among those settled on Apple Creek was Wappillessee, Houck, *A History of Missouri,* Vol. I, 212. He was a war chief and his name meant White Bird. Houck also says, 208, that the Shawnee and Delaware first settled in Southeastern Missouri around 1784; Ouapipelene (Wapepillose) and his small band of Shawnees arrived in Cape Girardeau on February 25, 1794. "Journal of Lorimier during the Threatened Genet Invasion of Louisiana 1793`1795," *The Spanish Regime in Missouri,* Vol. II, 74.

[123] Grant Foreman, *Indians and Pioneers, The Story of the American Southwest Before 1830,* 214. Yale University Press, 1930.

[124] Houck, *A History of Missouri,* Vol. 1, 220.

[125] Draper Mss., 1-5YY129.

[126] Draper Mss. says he was found on the banks of the St. Francis River. Draper Mss. 1-5YY129; Houck, *A History of Missouri,* Vol. I, 232, says he was found on Crowley's Ridge; *Biographical and Historical Memoirs of Northeast Arkansas,* 452, says Little George was found at the foot of Buffalo Island in Mississippi County.

[127] Edwin James, *Account of an expedition from Pittsburgh to the Rocky Mountains,* Vol. 3, 146. Botanist and geologist to the expedition of U.S. Army explorer Stephen Harriman Long. Accessed August 2, 2022. https://books.google.com. James compiled this account from the notes of Long and others of the expedition party.

[128] Houck, *A History of Missouri,* Vol. I, 231.

[129] Ibid.

[130] Draper Mss., 1-5YY129. Delaware Camp was a name for a place where the Delaware Indians camped near the city of Bloomfield; "Stoddard County," Ramsay Place Names Files.

[131] Jacobs had land in Township 30 North, Range 13 East. "U.S., Indexed Early Land Ownership and Township Plats, 1785-1898," Township 30 North, Range 13 East, 564, Missouri, Fifth Principal Meridian, *Ancestry.com.* Provo, Utah, USA: Ancestry.com Operations, Inc., 2011. Accessed January 11, 2025. https://www.ancestry.com.

[132] State Vs Jones, Samuel, Reel C21015, Circuit Court Case File, Cape Girardeau County, *Missouri State Archives,* Jefferson City, Missouri.

[133] State of Missouri versus Samuel Jones, on Indictment for Larceny, August 15, 1823, "Cape Girardeau, Missouri, United States Records," images, Court Records V, A-D, 1815-1824, *FamilySearch*. Accessed December 5, 2024. https://www.familysearch.org/en/united-states/.

[134] Andrew Ramsay will. Missouri Probate Records, 1750-1998, images, Cape Girardeau, Letters testamentary, wills, 1807-1867, Vol. A-C, *Missouri State Archives*, Jefferson City, Missouri, *FamilySearch*. Accessed September 22, 2014. https://www.familysearch.org/en/united-states/; Jacobs was a brother-in-law to Andrew Ramsay, *The Spanish Regime in Missouri,* Vol. II, 408.

[135] "Early Lutheranism in Missouri," *Theological Quarterly,* Volume 3, 338. Concordia Publishing House, St. Louis, Missouri, 1899. Google Books. Accessed March 29, 2022. https://books.google.com; This Big Swamp settlement may have encompassed more of an area just southwest of Cape Girardeau, possibly along the road to Bloomfield, based upon the settlement of several others in this group. Two of those settlers were Benjamin and Jacob Taylor, who came from North Carolina in 1825 and lived three miles east of Bloomfield. *Goodspeed's History of Southeast Missouri: embracing an historical account of the counties of Ste. Genevieve, St. Francios, Perry, Cape Girardeau, Bollinger, Madison, New Madrid, Pemiscot, Dunklin, Scott, Mississippi, Stoddard, Butler, Wayne and Iron, and including a department devoted to the preservation of personal, professional and private records,* 304, Goodspeed Publishing Company, 1888; Also found among this group was William Lorimier, son of Louis Lorimier who maintained a store at the Shawnee Village. Draper Mss., 1-5YY129.

[136] Smyth-Davis, *History of Dunklin County, Mo.,* 38.

[137] Ibid, 39.

[138] James A. East, Eastern Cherokee application 40265. James A. East, also known as James Alfred Hector, (James Alfred East Hector) said that his mother, Jaley Brown Rice, also known as Jaley Hector, was ¼ Cherokee, and her mother was Wathacape.

[139] Smyth-Davis, *History of Dunklin County, Mo.,* 248. Abijah and Jaley Rice's son, Pascal, would tell of being in camp at Chilletecaux; Robert Sidney Douglass, *History of Southeast Missouri, 306.*

[140] *American State Papers*, House of Representatives, 24th Congress, First Session, Public Lands: Volume 8, 303. Chilletecaux was called Chiletican in this report.

[141] Possibly the village at Chilletecaux. R. Graham, U.S. Indian Agent, to Francois Lesieur and son, License to trade for one year with the Shawnees and Delawares on St. Francis River, November 17, 1824, Godfrey Lesieur Papers, *Missouri History Museum Archives,* St. Louis, Missouri.

[142] Hypolite Tirard or Tirart was an early settler north of Little Prairie, Missouri, on the Pemiscot Bayou, earlier referred to as Pemiscon Bayou. Houck, *A History of Missouri,* Vol. 2, 160.

[143] Henry Goder, or Godair, of Vincennes, Indiana, settled on Open Lake near Portage Bay in Missouri around 1795. Houck, *A History of Missouri,* Vol. 2, 161-162.

[144] Most likely Jean Baptiste Valle, co-partner in Menard and Valle fur trading firm.

[145] A Francois Maisonville settled on Open Lake near Portage Bay. He was the Maisonville who previously lived at the Shawnee village on Apple Creek and married a sister of Tecumseh. Houck, *A History of Missouri,* Vol. 2, 161-162; He was found in the "Papers of Original Claimants (1777-1851) submitted before the First Board of Land Commissioners to determine the validity of the French and Spanish land grants made before the Louisiana Purchase." Missouri Secretary of State Office, Missouri

Digital Heritage Web Pages, RG 951 U.S. Recorder of Land Titles, RG951.01 First Board Papers of Original Claimants, 1777-1851, 93. Accessed March 29, 2022. https://www.sos.mo.gov.

[146] Houck, *A History of Missouri,* Vol. II, 161. Houck says Godair was once a resident of Cape Girardeau and later of New Madrid, where he had a concession; He was found in "Papers of Original Claimants (1777-1851)," RG 951, RG951.01, 58.

[147] He may have been related to Antoine Gamlin, a French Canadian who settled in New Madrid in 1791. He was a trader among the Indians in Indiana and had been an interpreter and Indian agent for George Rogers Clark. Houck, *A History of Missouri,* Vol. II, 139.

[148] A trading firm involved in Indian trade in Missouri and Arkansas. The house, built in 1818 and used as headquarters for the firm, still stands on Merchant Street in St. Genevieve. Tours are offered at the house, which features a stocked mercantile store and upstairs living quarters. The house was the home of Felix and Odile Valle in 1824. "Felix Valle, State Historic Site." Accessed April 2, 2022. https://www.visitstegen.com/felix-valle-state-historic-site/.

[149] Points were lines woven into the side of a blanket and were an indication of the size of the blanket.

[150] Most likely on the Meramec River, where Shawnee Chief Lewis Rogers had established a village.

[151] Francis Lesieur and son, New Madrid, Mo. to Richard Graham, U.S. Indian Agent, St. Louis, Mo., Letter, September 24, 1825, Richard Graham Papers, Missouri History Museum, *Missouri Historical Society*, St. Louis, Missouri.

[152] N.W. Watkins, New Madrid Co. to Major Richard Graham, St. Louis, Mo. Letter, March 17, 1825, Richard Graham Papers, Missouri History Museum, *Missouri Historical Society*, St. Louis, Missouri.

[153] R. Graham to Adam Rittenhouse, Letter, April 9, 1825, Richard Graham Papers, Missouri History Museum, *Missouri Historical Society*, St. Louis, Missouri.

[154] S.G. Hopkins, Point Pleasant, New Madrid County, Mo. to Richard Graham, Letter, February 4, 1826, Richard Graham Papers, Missouri History Museum, *Missouri Historical Society*, St. Louis, Missouri.

[155] Ibid.

[156] R. Graham, St. Louis, to Capt. Samuel G. Hopkins, New Madrid, Mo., A.L.S. Letter, February 16, 1826, Richard Graham Papers, Missouri History Museum, *Missouri Historical Society*, St. Louis, Missouri.

[157] Samuel Goode Hopkins, New Madrid, Mo. to Major Richard Graham, Indian Agent at St. Louis, Mo., Letter, January 29, 1826, Richard Graham Papers, Missouri History Museum, *Missouri. Historical Society*, St. Louis, Missouri.

[158] Correspondence relative to St. Francis Indians and licenses to trade, Sample Invoice to be filled out in applying for license to trade with the Indians, 1826. Richard Graham Papers, Missouri History Museum, *Missouri Historical Society*, St. Louis, Missouri.

[159] Hopkins to Clark, William Clark Papers, Vol. 6, 276.

[160] Sir Charles Lyell, *A Second Visit to North America,* Vol. 2, 237. Accessed March 28, 2022. Google Books. https://books.google.com.

[161] Fred W. Allsopp, *Folklore of Romantic Arkansas*, The Grolier Society, 1931, Vol. 1, 156.

[162] "Missouri Probate Records, 1750-1998," New Madrid Probate Packets, images, Drawer 4, No. 94-109, *FamilySearch*. Missouri State Archives, Jefferson City,

Missouri. Accessed March 30, 2022. https://www.familysearch.org/en/united-states/; A William Long is also on this list.

[163] "Missouri Probate Records, 1750-1998," New Madrid Probate Packets, images, Drawer 6, No. 155-159, *FamilySearch*, Missouri State Archives, Jefferson City, Missouri. Accessed March 30, 2022. https://www.familysearch.org/en/united-states/.

[164] Douglass, Robert Sidney, *History of Southeast Missouri,* 291.

[165] Henry Sanford Vs. Hector, William, Reel C11873, Justice of the Peace Case Files, Cape Girardeau, *Missouri State Archives*, Jefferson City, Missouri.

[166] A William Long was married to Elizabeth Hector and was likely Hector's brother-in-law. Elizabeth Hector and William Lang [sic], November 17, 1818, "Missouri County Marriage, Naturalization, and Court Records, 1800-1991 *FamilySearch.* Accessed January 11, 2025. https://www.familysearch.org/en/united-states/.

[167] State of Missouri Vs Hector, William, Reel C21015, Circuit Court Case File, Cape Girardeau County, *Missouri State Archives*, Jefferson City, Missouri.

[168] He was possibly enumerated twice, as there are two William Hectors on the 1830 Cape Girardeau, Missouri census. "1830 United States Federal Census," Cape Girardeau, Missouri, Roll 72, 433, Provo, Utah, U.S.A., *Ancestry*, Ancestry.com Operations, Inc., 2010. Images reproduced by FamilySearch. Original data: Fifth Census of the United States, 1830. (NARA microfilm publication M19, 201 rolls). Records of the Bureau of the Census, Record Group 29. National Archives, Washington, D.C. Accessed August 2, 2022. https://www.ancestry.com; "1830 United States Federal Census," Cape Girardeau, Missouri, Roll 72, 453, Provo, Utah, U.S.A., *Ancestry*, Ancestry.com Operations, Inc., 2010. Images reproduced by FamilySearch. Original data: Fifth Census of the United States, 1830. (NARA microfilm publication M19, 201 rolls). Records of the Bureau of the Census, Record Group 29. National Archives, Washington, D.C. Accessed August 2, 2022. https://www.ancestry.com.

[169] Sherida K. Eddlemon, "New Madrid County, Missouri, Delinquent Tax List, 1833," Capitol Fire Documents, Box 16, Folder 1062, 164. *Missouri Genealogical Records and Abstracts, Vol. 2: 1752-1839*, Heritage Books, Inc., Bowie, Maryland, 1990.

[170] Listed as "Bill Moonshine (Indian)" in Elias Hopkins Probate records, New Madrid County, Missouri. "New Madrid, Missouri, United States Records," images, Missouri. County Court (New Madrid County). Image group 007630841, *FamilySearch.* Accessed September 22, 2022. https://www.familysearch.org/en/united-states/.

[171] State of Missouri vs William Hector & Jaily Ann Rice, Indit, Laciviously Abiding & Cohabiting together, "Stoddard, Missouri, United States Records," Stoddard County Circuit Court, October 1837, images, *FamilySearch.* Accessed September 18, 2022. https://www.familysearch.org/en/united-states/.

[172] The State of Missouri vs William Hector and Jaily Ann Rice, Indictment, Stoddard County Circuit Court, October 1837, "Stoddard, Missouri, United States Records," Stoddard County Circuit Court, images, *FamilySearch.* Accessed September 18, 2022. https://www.familysearch.org/en/united-states/.

[173] "United States Census, 1840," William Huton [sic], Mississippi, Arkansas, United States, *FamilySearch.* Accessed June 10, 2022. https://www.familysearch.org/en/united-states/; The name is misspelled and should be William Hector.

Endnotes, Chapter 4

[174] Lesieur, *Early History,* Article III, 10. After Godfrey Lesieur sent to the "reservation" for Chickalee (Chookalee in this version). He and others of the Shawnee and Delaware tribes received permission to hunt in the area and did so in 1837. Lesieur doesn't say to which tribe Chickalee belongs.

[175] Ibid.

[176] As Moonshine, Hector traded furs with Godfrey Lesieur in and around 1850, substantiated by a notation on the back of a memo describing a strip of land between the swamps, part of which would be Buffalo Island. In what appears to be scribbling, summing up monetary amounts is a notation under the heading of Moonshine and lists more than one hundred skins, including coon, mink, bear, and deer skins. Memo, description of strip of land between swamps on west Little River and Castor swamps in Missouri and the swamps in Arkansas, P. Chouteau Jr. to Godfrey Lesieur and his son G.A. Lesieur, Point Pleasant, Mo., LS Letters, October 14, 1850 to January 29, 1851, Lesieur Collection, Godfrey Lesieur Papers, *Missouri History Museum Archives*, St. Louis, Missouri.

[177] John East was Cherokee. James A. East, Eastern Cherokee application 40265; In 1860, he was listed on the Mississippi County Census in Little River Township. He is designated as Indian. John East, 1860 United States Federal Census, Little River, Mississippi, Arkansas; Roll: M653_46, 740; Family History Library Film: 803046, Ancestry.com. [database on-line]. Provo, Utah, USA: Ancestry.com Operations, Inc., 2009. Images reproduced by FamilySearch. Original data:1860 U.S. census, population schedule. NARA microfilm publication M653, 1,438 rolls. Washington, D.C.: National Archives and Records Administration, n.d.

[178] Lou Curtwright and Maggie Miller, of Manila, Arkansas, claimed to be descendants of Big Knife and made Guion Miller, Eastern Cherokee applications in 1908. In the file for Curtwright is an affidavit by James A. East (James Alfred East Hector) attesting that Miller's statements, are to the best of his beliefs and knowledge, true and correct. An affidavit for Lou Curtwright stating her statements are true and correct is signed by S.W. Bunch and B.A. Ashabranner. Lou Curtwright, Application number 36064, and Maggie Miller, Application number 36063, Eastern Cherokee Applications, 8/29/1906-5/26/1909, Record Group 123: Records of the U.S. Court of Claims, 1835-1984; M1104. National Archives at College Park, College Park, Maryland. Accessed April 3, 2024. www.archives.gov.

[179] It is unknown where Chickalee is buried. Traditionally, the Indians buried their dead soon after death, so it seems reasonable that he would have been buried at Pt. Pleasant or nearby. For this narrative, I have them taking Chickalee to be buried at Chilletecaux, where Moonshine was living part of that year. Moonshine and his family moved to Mississippi County in late 1837, *Biographical and Historical Memoirs of Northeast Arkansas,* 452; Moonshine, as William Hector, left Stoddard County, Missouri, later Dunklin County, by October. The State of Missouri vs William Hector and Jaily Ann Rice, Indictment, Stoddard County Circuit Court, October 1837, "Stoddard, Missouri, United States Records," images, Stoddard County, Missouri Circuit Court, *FamilySearch.* Accessed September 18, 2022. https://www.familysearch.org/en/united-states/.

[180] Lesieur, *Early History,* Article IV, 38. Lesieur described Point Pleasant from his memory as a youth.

[181] Lesieur, *Early History,* Article III, 10. Lesieur said Chickalee was also known as Corn Meal.

[182] *Biographical and Historical Memoirs of Northeast Arkansas,* 452. Possibly the Kechotowais from Chilletecaux's village, enumerated in 1831. In stories of the capture of Little George, the name of Corn Meal is used as the pursuer; An embellished story about Little George and his capture is also told in Williams, *The History of Craighead County, Arkansas,* 156-169.

[183] Lesieur, *Early History,* Article III, 10. Godfrey Lesieur's point in requesting Chickalee return to the area was to show him where the legendary lead was located. Chickalee was apparently living in Indian Territory and traveled back with the Shawnee and Delaware, who had moved west. Even though he was Cherokee, it appears that Chickalee was still associated with the Shawnee, with whom he may have been associated at Wapapilethe's village in August 1820.

[184] Williams, *The History of Craighead County, Arkansas,* 139. Corn Meal, Buckeye, and another Indian visited Ben Crowley and were requested to reveal the location of the lead mine from which they obtained their lead. They did not reveal its location.

[185] Robert A. Myers, "Cherokee Pioneers in Arkansas: The St. Francis Years, 1785-1813," *The Arkansas Historical Quarterly,* Vol. LVI, Summer 1997, 130.

[186] The son of Little Carpenter (Attakullakulla), Dragging Canoe was a war chief who lived from 1738 to 1792. He served as the war chief of the Chickamauga Cherokee from 1777 until his death. "Dragging Canoe," *Wikipedia,* Wikimedia Foundation, Inc. Accessed April 3, 2022. https://en.wikipedia.org/wiki/Dragging_Canoe.

[187] "Chickamauga Cherokee," *Wikipedia,* Wikimedia Foundation, Inc. Accessed January 5, 2021. http://en.wikipedia.org/wiki/Chickamauga_Cherokee.

[188] Myers, "Cherokee Pioneers in Arkansas," 130. Others in this group included Dick Justice, The Glass, Bloody Fellow, The Terrapin, Fool Charles, The Badger, Will Elder, Pumpkin Boy, Black Fox, and John Watts.

[189] Ibid, 133.

[190] Houck, *A History of Missouri,* Vol. 1, 220-221.

[191] Myers, "Cherokee Pioneers in Arkansas," 134.

[192] Houck, *The Spanish Regime in Missouri,* Vol. I, 100, "Fourth Spanish Detailed Statistical Report of the Products of St. Louis and Ste Genevieve for 1775," letter, from Francisco Cruzat to Don Luis de Unzaga y Amezaga, Spanish Governor of Louisiana at the time, mentions the Cheraquis [sic] Indians in a report.

[193] Houck, *The Spanish Regime in Missouri,* Vol. II, "CXXVI, Statistical Census of New Madrid of 1797," 402. Tison lived among the Cherokee in July of the year before the 1796 New Madrid census in what is now Dunklin County.

[194] Myers, "Cherokee Pioneers in Arkansas," 141-142.

[195] "John and James Pettigrew & Heirs of," *Reports of Committees, 16th Congress, 1st Session – 49th Congress,* Vol. 3, Report No. 406, 1-4, March 22, 1832. Accessed April 2, 2022. https://books.google.com.

[196] Zebulon M. Pike, Fort Pickering, Chickasaw Bluff to David Henley, Knoxville, Letter, June 3, 1800, *Papers of the War Department, 1784-1800*, Roy Rosenzweig Center for History and New Media, Fred Manning Collection of Documents from Various Series, RG217. Accessed April 2, 2022. https://wardepartmentpapers.org/s/home/item/76187.

[197] Myers, "Cherokee Pioneers in Arkansas," 127, 152-153. His name is spelled Connetoo in this article.

[198] Born in France, Bringier was the eldest son of Emanuel Marius Pons Bringier, a prominent and wealthy citizen of early Louisiana. Bringier lived among the Indians, possibly the Osage, during his travels in Arkansas from 1810 to 1812. W. D. Williams,

and Louis Bringier. "Louis Bringier and His Description of Arkansas in 1812." Vol 48, No. 2, 108-136, *The Arkansas Historical Quarterly*, Arkansas Historical Association, 1989. Accessed August 2, 2022. *JSTOR*. https://www.jstor.org.

[199] *The American Journal of Science and Arts*, Biodiversity Heritage Library, Carnegie-Mellon University. University Libraries, S. Converse, New Haven, Connecticut, 1821, 39-41. Accessed August 23, 2022. https://books.google.com.

[200] "Great Comet of 1811," *Wikipedia*, Wikimedia Foundation, Inc. Accessed April 1, 2022. https://en.m.wikipedia.org/wiki/Great_Comet_of_1811. Possibly this comet, which was visible to the naked eye for approximately 260 days and in October 1811 was at its brightest.

[201] *The American Journal of Science and Arts,* 39-41.

[202] Myers, "Cherokee Pioneers in Arkansas," 155; Toluntiskee to Col. Return J. Meigs, Agent for the Cherokee, Letter from Arkansas, March 14, 1813, Correspondence and Miscellaneous Records, 1813, Records of the Cherokee Indian Agency in Tennessee, 1801-1835, 124-128, M208. Accessed January 2, 2021. https://www.fold3.com.

[203] Duane Huddleston, "Some Indian Incidents Along White River 1813-1814," Vol. 15, No. 4, 37-38, *Independence County Chronicles*. Chikilly in this version.

[204] Zoalkqua. Could this be Skawqua, the Cherokee prophet on the St. Francis River?

[205] Huddleston, "Some Indian Incidents Along White River," Vol. 15, No. 4, 37-38.

[206] Myers, Robert. "Nick Trammell: The Making of an Old Southwest Legend." *The Arkansas Historical Quarterly*, Vol. 74, No. 4, 352-378, Arkansas Historical Association, 2015. *JSTOR*. http://www.jstor.org/stable/26281833.

[207] Ibid.

[208] Gary L. Pinkerton, *Trammel's Trace, The First Road to Texas From the North*, Preface, 5, Texas A&M University Press, College Station, Texas, 2016.

[209] John Sullivan to Gov. Clark, Letter, July 9, 1816, United States Office of Indian Affairs, Central Superintendency, St. Louis, MO, Vol. 3, 44-45, Miscellaneous letters and documents, 1815-1817. *Kansas Historical Society,* Topeka, Kansas. Accessed April 3, 2022. Kansas Memory www.kansasmemory.org.

[210] Most likely, the settlement that is presently Batesville, Arkansas. The town has also been known by the names Napoleon and Poke Bayou. "Batesville, Arkansas," *Wikipedia*, Wikimedia Foundation, Inc. Accessed April 4, 2022. https://en.wikipedia.org/wiki/Batesville,_Arkansas.

[211] An early ferry on the White River was Shield's Ferry, located by the farm of Nathaniel and James Shield, upriver from what is now Batesville near Chataunga Mountain. Most likely, one of these men was the Mr. Shields, whom Sullivan enlisted to recover his horses. Duane Huddleston, Pat Wood, and Sammie Rose. *Steamboats and Ferries on the White River: A Heritage Revisited,* 157, New ed., Fayetteville: University of Arkansas Press, 1998; Chataunga Mountain, mentioned in the boundaries of the 1817 treaty with the Arkansas Cherokees as a boundary for the land, was about seven miles upstream from Batesville on the south side of the river. W.R. Jones, "Marion County, Arkansas, Some Marion County History Articles from the *Mt. Echo* newspaper," 1929, transcribed by Gladys Horn Brown. Accessed April 1, 2022. www.argenweb.net/marion/stories/marion-co-ar-wr-jones.html.

[212] As of 1814 and a few years thereafter, Asa Musick owned the old mill, originally owned by John Hadley on Spring Creek just above Poke Bayou, later Batesville, Arkansas. George E. Lankford, "Losing the Past: Draper and the Ruddell Indian Captivity," *The Arkansas Historical Quarterly*, Vol. 49, No. 3214-3239, Arkansas

Historical Association, 1990, *JSTOR*. Accessed December 5, 2024. https://doi.org/10.2307/40030798.

[213] Lovely was named Indian agent to the Arkansas Cherokee in 1813. He bought land from the Osage in 1816 to use as a buffer between the Osage and Cherokee. This land would become known as Lovely's Purchase and was not recognized by the government.

[214] Meridith Martin-Moats, "Chickalah (Yell County)," *CALS Encyclopedia of Arkansas*. Accessed April 4, 2022. https://encyclopediaofarkansas.net/entries/chickalah-yell-county-7006/. Chickalah is an unincorporated community in Yell County, Arkansas, on Highway 27, nine miles west of Dardanelle, Arkansas.

[215] "Copies of Accounts, Receipts And Disbursements, 1801-20," Records of the Cherokee Indian Agency in Tennessee, 1801-1835, 114. Accessed November 30, 2020. https://www.fold3.com.

[216] Ibid, 124.

[217] Ibid, 116.

[218] Gary E. Moulton, *John Ross, Cherokee Chief*, 10, University of Georgia Press, 1978.

[219] Ron Street, John D. Kiefer, and Jerry L. Raisor, "Assessing the Felt Reports of the 1811-12 New Madrid Earthquakes in the Central United States," (2008). Kentucky Geological Survey Report of Investigations. Accessed April 1, 2022. Downloaded PDF. https://uknowledge.uky.edu/kgs_ri/22.

[220] Norman W. Caldwell, "Fort Massac: Since 1805." *Journal of the Illinois State Historical Society (1908-1984)*, Vol. 44, No. 1, 47-60, University of Illinois Press, 1951. Accessed December 5, 2024. http://www.jstor.org/stable/40189112.

[221] "Correspondence and Miscellaneous Records, 1813," Records of the Cherokee Indian Agency in Tennessee, 1801-1835, 120. Accessed January 2, 2021. https://www.fold3.com.

[222] "Invoice of merchandise forwarded to that part of the Cherokee Nation removed to the river Arkansas in charge of John Ross, 1812 Nov. 30," MS2033, Penelope Johnson Allen, Special Collections Library, The University of Tennessee, Knoxville, Tennessee, presented in the Digital Library of Georgia. Accessed April 4, 2022. https://dlg.usg.edu.

[223] William L. Lovely to Col. Return Meigs, April 10, 1813, Correspondence and Miscellaneous Records, 1813," Records of the Cherokee Indian Agency in Tennessee, 1801-1835, 158, M208. Accessed November 14, 2020. https://www.fold3.com.

[224] Carter, Clarence Edwin, ed., "William Russel to Delegate Hempstead," *The Territorial papers of the United States,* Vol. 14, 1806-1814, 720, *Hathi Trust Digital Library*. Accessed April 4, 2022. https://www.hathitrust.org.

[225] Carter, Clarence Edwin, ed., "William Lovely to the Cherokee," *The Territorial papers of the United States,* Vol. 14, 1806-1814, 721, *Hathi Trust*. Accessed April 4, 2022. https://www.hathitrust.org.

[226] John D. Chisholm, Cherokee Village on the River Arkansas, the 23d May, 1814, May 23, 1814, Correspondence and Miscellaneous Records, Records of the Cherokee Indian Agency in Tennessee, 1801-1835, M208, 120-122. Chickelley in this document. Accessed November 5, 2018. https://www.fold3.com.

[227] Hoig, Stan, *Jesse Chisholm: Ambassador of the Plains*, University of Oklahoma Press, Norman, Oklahoma, 2005, 13.

[228] Tol-Lon-Tis-Kee, Head Chief of the Arkansas Cherokee to Jeremiah Evarts, Esq., *The Panoplist, and missionary herald,* Vol. 14, 391. 1818. Accessed April 4, 2022. https://www.hathitrust.org.

[229] Charles Russell Logan, *The Promised Land: The Cherokee, Arkansas and Removal, 1794-1839,* 1-69, 15, *Arkansas Historic Preservation Program.* Downloaded PDF. Accessed November 15, 2024. https://www.arkansasheritage.com.

[230] Return J. Meigs to the Arkansas Cherokee Chiefs, Letter, June 14, 1819, Correspondence and Miscellaneous Records, Records of the Cherokee Indian Agency in Tennessee, 1801-1835, 126-128, M208. Che.kil.lee in this document. Accessed January 1, 2022. Downloaded PDFs. https://www.fold3.com.

[231] Logan, *The Promised Land: The Cherokee, Arkansas and Removal,* 15.

[232] Meigs to the Arkansas Cherokee Chiefs, Records of the Cherokee Indian Agency in Tennessee, 1801-1835, 126-128. Tolontiskee in this document.

[233] Searcy held various positions in territorial Arkansas. Besides being secretary to the territorial legislature in 1820, he was county clerk to Lawrence and Independence counties, judge in the First Judicial District, postmaster at Davidsonville, and lawyer based in Batesville. Erica Eaves, "Richard Searcy (1794-1832)," *CALS Encyclopedia of Arkansas.* Accessed April 1, 2024. https://encyclopediaofarkansas.net.

[234] William Clark wrote to Arkansas Territorial Governor James Miller in early November 1820 concerning the Osage prisoners, "who may be among the Shawnee and Dellaways of this territory." Governor William Clark, St. Louis, Missouri, to Governor James Miller, Osage Indian Affairs, Transcript, November 10, 1820, L.C. Gulley collection, *Arkansas State Archives,* Little Rock, Arkansas. Accessed April 4, 2024. https://www.arkansasheritage.com/arkansasstatearchives/home.

[235] This is an example of the Cherokee traveling to the Southeast Missouri and Northeast Arkansas area after leaving the area.

[236] Richard Searcy, White River, Arkansas, to Governor James Miller, Cherokee Indian Affairs, Transcript, November 21, 1820, L.C. Gulley collection, *Arkansas State Archives,* Little Rock, Arkansas. Accessed April 4, 2024. https://www.arkansasheritage.com/arkansasstatearchives/home.

[237] An old oak stands on the banks of the Arkansas River in Dardanelle and is believed by some to be the setting of the council. The huge oak was standing when the author visited in 2016. The location of the meeting, however, is debatable. This meeting was not a treaty-making event. Ann M. Early, "Treaty of Council Oaks," *CALS Encyclopedia of Arkansas.* Accessed April 4, 2022. https://encyclopediaofarkansas.net/entries/treaty-of-council-oaks-4833/.

[238] Dutch, also known as Tachee, was the son of Skyugo, a noted Cherokee chief born at Turkey Town on the Coosa River in 1790 in Alabama. At the age of five, he accompanied his mother and an uncle named Thomas Taylor to the St. Francis River in Arkansas. Carolyn Thomas Foreman, "Dutch, the Cherokee," *The Chronicles of Oklahoma,* Vol. 27, No. 3, 252-255, Autumn 1949; Oklahoma City, Oklahoma, The Gateway to Oklahoma History. Accessed December 5, 2024. https://gateway.okhistory.org.

[239] *Biographical and Historical Memoirs of Western Arkansas: Comprising a Condensed History of the State, a Number of Biographies of Distinguished Citizens of the Same, a Brief Descriptive History of Each of the Counties Mentioned, and Numerous Biographical Sketches of the Citizens of Such Counties,* A Southern Publishing Company, Chicago, Illinois, 1891 Southern Historical Press, 118. Accessed August 2, 2022. https://books.google.com.

[240] Hempstead, Fay, *Historical Review of Arkansas,* Vol. I, 61-62.

[241] Takotaka, also spelled as Tiketoke, Ta-Ka-To-Kuh, De'gata'ga, Degadoga, was likely a member of the group led west by Talonteskee. This group left the St. Francis River valley after the 1811-1812 earthquakes. He was chosen to travel to Washington, D.C. to meet with the government, however, he died en route at the home of Pierre Menard in Illinois. Susan Martinez Heinritz, "Takatoka (1755?-1824)," *CALS Encyclopedia of Arkansas.* Accessed April 2, 2022. https://encyclopediaofarkansas.net/entries/takatoka-4288/; Tik-ki-do-ke was a Cherokee signer in a treaty with the Osage in 1818. "A Treaty of Amity and Friendship," United States Office of Indian Affairs, Central Superintendency, St. Louis, Missouri, Miscellaneous letters and documents, 1813-1825, Vol. 2, 93-95. *Kansas Historical Society*, Kansas Memory, Topeka, Kansas. Accessed April 2, 2022. www.kansasmemory.org.

[242] Chih-kil-leh in Washburn's account. Cephas Washburn and James Wilson Moore. *Reminiscences of the Indians*, 185, United States, Presbyterian committee of publication, 1869. Accessed April 2, 2022. https://books.google.com.

[243] Chekeli in this treaty. "Documents relating to the negotiation of an unratified treaty of August 9, 1822, between the Cherokee and Osage Indians," National Archives, August 9, 1822, 5. *University of Wisconsin Digital Collections* (UWDC), The History Collection. Accessed April 2, 2022. http://digital.library.wisc.edu/1711.dl/History.Unrat1822no4. Cherokee signers also included Thomas Maw, J. Martin, and James Rogers. Osage signers included Tally, the blind chief, and others.

[244] Foreman, *Indians and Pioneers*, 85-86.

[245] Clarence Edwin Carter, ed., "Cherokee Council to Reuben Lewis and William Bradford," February 10, 1820, *The Territorial papers of the United States*, Vol. 19, 1819-1825, 151-152, *Hathi Trust* Digital Library. Accessed April 4, 2022. https://www.hathitrust.org.

Endnotes, Chapter 5

[246] "Map of Missouri showing Aboriginal Trails and Warpaths," Shawnee trail. Houck, *A History of Missouri,* Vol. 1, 226.

[247] There was a pine tree in the southern portion of what became Holcomb Township in Dunklin County, south of Holcomb, that had long served as a landmark to Indians and hunters. It was a lone pine, not native to the area. "Dunklin County," Ramsay Place Names File.

[248] Later, in this area, there would be a ferry called Brown's Ferry. Even later, there would be a bridge there. "Dunklin County," Ramsay Place Names File. The bridge connects Holcomb, Missouri, to Piggott, Arkansas.

[249] Spicewood or spicebush fruit was dried and used by Native Americans as a spice. The leaves were used for tea.

[250] Poke Sallet, or Poke weed, is a perennial plant that grows in North and Central America and is commonly found in Northeast Arkansas and Southeast Missouri. Its young shoots were and are cultivated in the spring to eat. Its roots were cultivated in the fall, sliced and dried, and used medicinally. Parts of the plant are poisonous. The berries have been used as a dye.

[251] Friedrich Gerstacker. *Wild Sports in the Far West*, 365-366, United States, Crosby, Nichols, 1859. Accessed April 4, 2022. https://books.google.com.

[252] Williams, *The History of Craighead County, Arkansas*, 217, 137. Lake City was also known as Old Town and was an early Indian encampment, 217. Later, Indians had a village there, 137.

[253] Ibid, 137.

[254] "Dunklin County," Ramsay Place Names File. The entire stream had formerly been called Chilletecaux's River, but the upper portion came to be called Varner's River after early settler Thomas Varner. He settled near the source of the river in 1835.

[255] "Plat of Township 18 North, Range 9 East," 1848, April 3, 1848, Missouri Department of Agriculture, Land Survey Program, Land Survey Index, GLO (General Land Office). A campground on Varney's River in Section 20 is noted. Downloaded PDF, February 3, 2016. https://agriculture.mo.gov/weights/landsurvey/.

[256] Nicholas, "rugged character of the backwoods," was an Indian trader on the St. Francis River in the 1830s. Williams, *The History of Craighead County, Arkansas*, 382.

[257] Maumelle Prairie was first settled in 1838 on an ancient Indian campground on the west side of the St. Francis River. Charles A. Stuck, *The Story of Craighead County, A Narrative of People and Events in Northeast Arkansas,* 111, Charles A. Stuck, publisher, 1960.

[258] Williams, *The History of Craighead County, Arkansas*, 382. Local Indians had given Amanda Snoddy, who had family living at Deep Landing, a pair of deerskin moccasins.

[259] The road westward from Cotton Plant across Buffalo Creek and towards the St. Francis River, a few years before 1895, was "scarcely more than a bridle path." Smyth-Davis, *History of Dunklin County, Mo.,* 54.

[260] Smyth-Davis, *History of Dunklin County, Mo.,* 18.

[261] See John Brown, Chapter 1.

[262] Indian Camp Slough, "Dunklin County," Ramsay Place Names File.

[263] Ibid. Kinamore Slough.

[264] Ibid. John Ease's Camp.

[265] Bowlin Island, or Boland Island in some cases, was named for Capt. Nathaniel Bowlin, who settled there following the Civil War, and operated a ferry. H.B. Crowley, *History of Greene County,* as written in 1906, Ninth Edition. Transcribed by Sandy Hardin. The Highway 412 bridge crosses the river near here. Accessed April 26, 2022. http://www.argenweb.net/greene/AUTHORSSHOWCASE/greenecohbhcrh.htm.

[266] Smyth-Davis, *History of Dunklin County, Mo.*, 175.

[267] Hamblen, Mack, Greene County Historical Society, "Greene County," *CALS Encyclopedia of Arkansas.* Accessed August 12, 2022. https://encyclopediaofarkansas.net/entries/greene-county-772/.

[268] Postmaster Appointments for Greene County Arkansas Territory, Record Group 28: Records of the Post Office Department, 1773-1971, Records of Appointment of Postmasters and the Establishment of Post Offices, 7/1/1931 - 10/31/1971; National Archives at College Park, College Park, Maryland [online version available through the Archival Research Catalog (ARC identifier 7872653) at www.archives.gov; Ancestry 2018. Image 1. Accessed August 12, 2022. www.archives.gov. John M. Mitchell was the postmaster on April 13, 1842.

[269] Smyth-Davis, *History of Dunklin County, Mo.,* 176.

[270] Ibid, 25-26.

[271] Ibid, 114-115.

[272] Bowling, "A report of the Survey of the St. Francis River," 1-5.

[273] "Plat of Township 16 North, Range 5 East," Greene County, Arkansas Survey Plat, 1825, U.S. Department of the Interior, Bureau of Land Management, General Land Office Records. Accessed April 5, 2022. https://glorecords.blm.gov.

[274] *Early History*, Article III, 9.

[275] "Trace from Davidsonville to the mouth of the St. Francis, via Delaware village." "Plat of Township 16 North, Range 4 East," 1825, Greene County, Arkansas, U.S. Department of the Interior, Bureau of Land Management, General Land Office Records. Accessed April 5, 2022. https://glorecords.blm.gov.

[276] Ibid. Crowley's home was near the springs at the present Crowley's Ridge State Park; He settled in Section 4, Township 16 North, Range 4 East; Hon. Benjamin Crowley, "Reprint of a Historical Writing on Greene County," Spring, 1966, Vol. 2, No. 2, 12-16, *The Greene County Historical Quarterly,* Vols. 1-3, 1965-1967, Paragould, Arkansas.

[277] Williams, *The History of Craighead County, Arkansas,* 193.

[278] Williams, *The History of Craighead County, Arkansas,* 139-140.

[279] H.B. Crowley, "History of Greene County, as written in 1906 by H.B. Crowley," Fourth Installment. *The Greene County Historical Quarterly*, Vols. 1-3, 1965-1967, Winter 1967, Vol. 3, No. 1, 19-24, *The Greene County Historical Society*, Paragould, Arkansas. The meeting place was north of the Wiley Crowley home. Wiley Crowley settled on Sections 33 and 34 in Township 17 North, Range 4 East. The "supposed location" for the mine was in Section 10, Township 16 North, Range 4 East. Hanover gained some notoriety as a justice of the peace in Lawrence County, following the Civil War. He met an untimely death at the hands of several men who shot him as he sat in a chair, too old to stand, in a field picking cotton. Ibid, First Edition.

[280] Dan F. Morse, Phyllis A. Morse, *Archaeology of the Central Mississippi Valley*, 32, Academic Press, Inc., San Diego, California, 1983.

[281] Postmaster Appointments for Greene County, Arkansas Territory, 1.

[282] Mike Polston, "Greensboro (Craighead County)," *CALS Encyclopedia of Arkansas.* Accessed August 4, 2022.

https://encyclopediaofarkansas.net/entries/greensboro-craighead-county-7919/.

[283] Postmaster Appointments for Greene County, Arkansas Territory, 1.

[284] Walnut Camp, a small community on the eastern side of Crowley's Ridge, had a post office in 1844. Johnny H. Wilson, Isaac A. Bratcher, Don Evans, and James O. Jeffers, *35 Degrees 24 Minutes North – 91 Degrees West: A Town Called Hickory Ridge,* 127, Trafford, Victoria, B.C., 2004.

[285] Wittsburg developed near the intersection of the roads on Crowley's Ridge, the St. Francis River, and the Military Road from Memphis, Tennessee, to Little Rock, Arkansas. It was incorporated in 1848. It was a county seat from 1862 to 1865 and again from 1868 to 1884. Derek Allen Clements, "Wittsburg (Cross County)," *CALS Encyclopedia of Arkansas.* Accessed August 24, 2022. https://encyclopediaofarkansas.net/entries/wittsburg-cross-county-6202/.

[286] Postmaster Appointments for St. Francis County, Arkansas; Record Group 28: Records of the Post Office Department, 1773-1971, Records of Appointment of Postmasters and the Establishment of Post Offices, 7/1/1931 - 10/31/1971; National Archives at College Park, College Park, Maryland [online version available through the Archival Research Catalog (ARC identifier 78727324) at www.archives.gov; HMS/MLR Entry Number, A1 322; Ancestry 2018, 1. Accessed July 27, 2022. www.archives.gov.

[287] Williams, *The History of Craighead County, Arkansas*, 133.

[288] Puryear's family first settled at Buck Snort in 1840 before moving to Jonesboro in 1859. When Craighead County was created, his store served temporarily as the first seat of justice. Williams, *The History of Craighead County, Arkansas,* 579-580.

[289] The McDaniel settlement was southwest of Jonesboro and had its beginning in 1839. Williams, *The History of Craighead County, Arkansas*, 438.

[290] Bolivar was established in 1838 as a seat of government in Poinsett County, Arkansas. Mike Polston, "Bolivar (Poinsett County)," *CALS Encyclopedia of Arkansas.* Last updated December 7, 2021. Accessed August 29, 2022. https://encyclopediaofarkansas.net/entries/bolivar-poinsett-county-7386/.

[291] One of the early settlers of the Big Creek Settlement, north of Jonesboro, was W.Q. Lane, who came to the county in 1837-1838. Williams, *The History of Craighead County, Arkansas,* 390-391.

[292] The Broadway settlement was established in 1841 when William and Yancy Broadway settled there. It was west of Jonesboro. Williams, *The History of Craighead County, Arkansas*, 434.

[293] Matthew Love came to Craighead County in 1844 and settled on the Jacksonport/Gainesville road in Big Creek Township, northwest of Jonesboro. Williams, *The History of Craighead County, Arkansas,* 393.

[294] Early pioneers in Craighead County settled in an area that was first called the Grinder settlement in the 1830s. It was west of Jonesboro. Other early pioneers settled west of Grinder near the Cache River. Williams, *The History of Craighead County, Arkansas*, 427.

[295] Jacksonport was/is located near the confluence of the White and Black rivers, and along a trail that became the Old Southwest Trail. The town was established when a riverboat captain saw the potential and established a store there in 1833. Adam Miller, "Jacksonport (Jackson County)," *CALS Encyclopedia of Arkansas.* Accessed August 26, 2022. https://encyclopediaofarkansas.net/entries/jacksonport-jackson-county-2804/.

[296] Davidsonville, founded in 1815, was an early settlement in Northeast Arkansas. It was the site of the first post office in what would become Arkansas, the first state courthouse, and the territory's first federal land office. Mike Polston, "Davidsonville (Randolph County)," *CALS Encyclopedia of Arkansas*. Accessed August 26, 2022. https://encyclopediaofarkansas.net/entries/davidsonville-randolph-county-6090/.

[297] Lester Landing was named for Phil Lester, a farmer, after he and Jesse Morgan came to Craighead County sometime after the Civil War and settled on the banks of the St. Francis River, approximately six miles above Lake City (Old Town). Stuck, *The Story of Craighead County*, 251.

[298] Between the time Maumelle Prairie (Endnote 257) was settled in 1838, and Varner (Chapter 6) located on the opposite side of the St. Francis River in 1844, Old Town was settled at the narrowest point to cross the river for miles. Later, this settlement would take on the name of Lake City when the county created a second county seat in 1883. Stuck, *The Story of Craighead County,* 111-112.

[299] Arnold Stotts moved to some high land on Buffalo Island in 1853. At the time, there was but one other family nearby, the Varners (Chapter 6), and some Indians who remained at High Banks, an old settlement, opposite what became Mangrum. Williams, *The History of Craighead County, Arkansas*, 457.

[300] See Endnote 287.

[301] Charles A. Stuck, "The Creation of Craighead County," *Craighead County Historical Quarterly*, Vol. XIII, No. 2, 12-17, Spring, April 1, 1975, Jonesboro, Arkansas; The map was drawn by William V. Davidson, Geography Department of Arkansas State University, reconstructed from a manuscript map attached to the 1860 census reports for Craighead County, Arkansas.

[302] Bono, at one time Bonnerville, was established when the Frisco Railway wanted a station that would serve the Big Creek farming community, Stuck, *The Story of Craighead County*, 246.

[303] Ibid, 253.

[304] Holcomb wrote down some of his history in a letter shared by his great-great-granddaughter, Mrs. Dell Robinson of Corning, Arkansas, to the *Piggott Times*. Henry Holcomb, Record Spotlight, *SEMO Record*, Dunklin County, Missouri Genealogical Society, Vols. 1-3, 1983-1985, Vol. III, No. I, January 1985.

[305] J.M. Lewis, Commissioner of Immigration, Gainesville, Greene County, Arkansas, August 26, 1868, State of Arkansas, Commissioner of State Lands, History and Archives, 1868 Report. Accessed April 5, 2022. https://history.cosl.org.

[306] Ford, Clyde, "Poinsett County," *CALS Encyclopedia of Arkansas.* Accessed April 5, 2022. https://encyclopediaofarkansas.net/entries/poinsett-county-799/.

[307] *SEMO Record,* Dunklin County Genealogical Society, Kennett, Missouri, Vol. 1-3, 1983-1985, Vol. III, No. I, January 1985. Holcomb refers to Big Knife as Butcher Knife.

[308] "United States Census, 1840," Joseph Raotiford, [sic] Greenfield, Poinsett, Arkansas, United States; 122, *FamilySearch*. Accessed June 10, 2022. https://www.familysearch.org/en/united-states/.

[309] *Combined Personal Tax Assessment Lists of Greene County, Arkansas, 1834-1840*, 3-8, compiled by James Logan Morgan, Arkansas Records Association, Newport, Arkansas, 1972.

[310] Williams, *The History of Craighead County, Arkansas*, 428-429.

[311] Ibid, 382.

[312] Ibid, 389.

[313] Ibid, 130-132.

[314] Ibid, 131.

[315] Snoddy bought 80 acres from a soldier of the War of 1812 in 1830 in what would become Jonesboro. This land was between Matthews, Nettleton, Culberhouse, and Floyd streets. When he first settled there, some Indians lived southwest of him. Williams, *The History of Craighead County, Arkansas*, 382.

[316] *Biographical and Historical Memoirs of Northeast Arkansas,* 591.

[317] Thomas Ashley Stone, *Recollections of Early Life in Poinsett County*, 7-8, Poinsett County, Arkansas, 1927.

[318] Big Knife was sometimes used to refer to Americans. Lesieur, *Early History*, Article III, 12-13. F.V. Lesieur, a Creole, author of *Early History,* was born in 1826 and was a child when most Indians left the area. According to his articles, he was a subagent and later an agent of the American Fur Company from 1840 to 1858. Lesieur, *Early History*, Article III, 8-9.

[319] "As late as the early 40s (1840s) Indians named Big Knife, Keshotee, Corn Meal, Buckeye, John East, Moonshine, and Chuckalee resided on Buffalo Island and hunted on Maumelle Prairie and the ridge near Jonesboro; alternating their hunting expeditions from Big Lake to the L'Anguille bottoms southwest of Jonesboro and camping at Martin Spring." Williams, *The History of Craighead County, Arkansas*, 139.

Endnotes, Chapter 6

[320] Big Knife had been in the area as early as December 1811 when flatboat pilot John Wiseman came across him on the banks of a bayou near New Madrid following an earthquake. Wiseman called him a defunct Indian chief named Wapacapa or John Big Knife. Wiseman said Big Knife told him the "Great Spirit ke-chi-monito, whisky too much; heap drunk, bine-by he make all gone Injun hunten ground." Lesieur, *Early History*, Article V, 31.

[321] "United States Census, 1860," Entry for Thomas S. James and Laura James, Sixth Ward, City of Mobile, Mobile, Alabama, United States, *FamilySearch*, Accessed March 6, 2024. https://www.familysearch.org/en/united-states/.

[322] "1860 U.S. Federal Census - Slave Schedules," Thomas S. James, Mobile Ward 7, Mobile, Alabama, The National Archives in Washington, D.C.; Washington, D.C., USA; Eighth Census of the United States 1860; Series Number: M653; Record Group: Records of the Bureau of the Census; Record Group Number: 29. *Ancestry.com.* Lehi, Utah, USA: *Ancestry.com* Operations Inc., 2010. Accessed January 10, 2025. https://www.ancestry.com.

[323] James tells of visiting the opera and eating in fine restaurants in his diary. He also mentions a variety of publications and books, such as *Popular Science Monthly* and *The Devil's Pulpit*. Baird, *Years of Discontent,* 45.

[324] See Chapter 10, Endnote 610.

[325] James was concerned about his weight, having noted that he didn't mind his "fatness," but being fat seemed to be a "constant object of coarse remark" in the country, so he ordered some Fucus Vesiculus to take in January 1878 to reduce his obesity. Baird, *Years of Discontent, footnote* 221, notes that Fucus Vesiculosus was a common seaweed first recommended for obesity in 1862.

[326] Gloria Young, Heritage Trail Partners Board of Directors, "The Benge Detachment of Cherokees on the Trail of Tears," *Northwest Arkansas Heritage Trail Partners,* Springdale, Arkansas. Accessed April 6, 2022. http://www.heritagetrailpartners.com/2015/06/benge-route/. On a personal note, the author experienced vehicle problems north of the Arkansas border of Randolph County, Arkansas, in Ripley County, Missouri, with her husband and four small children. A kind family along that route (not sure where) assisted in continuing our journey. There was a family gathering that day, and while the men assisted with the car and our children played with their children, the adults sat with the author outside and talked. One of the stories they told was how the land had been in the family for generations and how their grandfather remembered his ancestors telling about the Cherokee traveling across their land.

[327] Logan, "The Promised Land: The Cherokee, Arkansas and Removal," 48.

[328] "Native American Removal Routes in Arkansas, (Cherokee, Chickasaw, Choctaw, Creek, and Seminole)," Staff, Arkansas Historic Preservation Program, The Cherokee, *Arkansas Heritage*, Arkansas Historic Preservation Program, Publications, Trail of Tears Native American Removal Routes in Arkansas. Accessed April 6, 2022. Downloaded PDF. http://www.arkansaspreservation.com.

[329] Postmaster Appointments for St. Francis County, Arkansas Territory, 1.

[330] Kitty Sloan, "Trail of Tears," *CALS Encyclopedia of Arkansas*. Accessed April 5, 2022. http://www.encyclopediaofarkansas.net/encyclopedia/entry-detail.aspx?entryID=2294.

[331] "Native American Removal Routes in Arkansas, (Cherokee, Chickasaw, Choctaw, Creek, and Seminole)," *Arkansas Heritage,* http://www.arkansaspreservation.com.

[332] Christopher D. Haveman, "The Removal of the Creek Indians from the Southeast, 1828-1838," dissertation, 2009, Auburn University's database of Master's theses and PhD Dissertations, Auburn University, Alabama. Accessed April 6, 2022. Downloaded PDF. https://etd.auburn.edu/handle/10415/2184.

[333] "Memphis to Little Rock Road - Henard Cemetery Road Segment" Properties, National Register of Historic Places, *Arkansas Heritage*, Arkansas Historic Preservation Program. Accessed April 6, 2022. PDF. http://www.arkansaspreservation.com.

[334] "Journal of Edward Deas – Creek Removal, 1837," *Sequoyah National Research Center*, Trail of Tears, Eyewitness Accounts, University of Arkansas at Little Rock. Accessed April 6, 2022. http://ualrexhibits.org/trailoftears/eyewitness-accounts/journal-of-edward-deas-creek-removal-1837/.

[335] Daniel S. Buttrick, *The Journal of Rev. Daniel S. Butrick, May 19, 1838, to April 1, 1839,* Cherokee Removal, The Trail of Tears Association, Oklahoma Chapter, The Association for Core Texts and Courses, Saint Mary's College of California. Accessed April 6, 2022. PDF. https://www.coretexts.org/old/cherokeelessons/unit5/downloads/Butrick%20Journal%20cherokee_removal_1.pdf.

[336] "Osage War, 1837," Abstract of Wars & Military Engagements: War of 1812 through World War I, Missouri Digital Heritage, John R. Ashcroft, Missouri Secretary of State. Accessed July 28, 2022. https://www.sos.mo.gov/archives/soldiers/abstract; Robert A. Glenn, "The Osage War," *Missouri Historical Review*, Vol. 14, No. 2, 201-210, January 1920, State Historical Society of Missouri. Accessed January 1, 2025. https://digital.shsmo.org/digital/collection/mhr.

[337] Another spelling of Chilletecaux or Chilitica.

[338] "Stoddert [sic] County," *American State Papers,* House of Representatives, 24th Congress, First Session, Public Lands, Vol. 8, 302-303. Accessed April 6, 2022. https://memory.loc.gov/ammem/amlaw/lwsp.html.

[339] Chapter 4, Endnote 191.

[340] East's Eastern Cherokee application says he was the son of John East, a Cherokee. James A. East (James Alfred East Hector), Eastern Cherokee application 40265; The 1860 Census lists John East's race as Indian (Native American). John East, "1860 United States Federal Census," Little River, Mississippi, Arkansas*;* Roll: M653_46; 740. *Ancestry,* Ancestry.com Operations, Inc., Provo, Utah, 2009. Accessed April 14, 2022. https://www.ancestry.com.

[341] Thomas Moseley Jr., New Madrid, Mo., to Gen. Wm. Clark, S. Int. Indian Affairs, St. Louis, Missouri, Letter, July 4, 1835. *The Foreman Transcripts*, Commissioner of Indian Affairs, Seven Volumes, Vol. 1, Western Superintendency, Miscellaneous and schools, 53-55. Accessed July 28, 2022. https://www.okhistory.org/research/foremantranscripts. Chilletecaux is spelled Chilitecau in this letter.

[342] Wm. Clark, Superintendency of Indian Affairs, St. Louis, Mo., to Gen. Geo Gibson, Commissary Genl. of Substinence, Washington, D.C., Letter, August 5, 1835. *The Foreman Transcripts*, Commissioner of Indian Affairs, Seven Volumes, Vol. 1, 59, Western Superintendency, Miscellaneous and schools. Accessed July 28, 2022. https://www.okhistory.org/research/foremantranscripts.

[343] Williams, *The History of Craighead County, Arkansas*, 451.

[344] Stuck, *The Story of Craighead County,* 72-73.

[345] The Clements family moved to land near Big Lake from Tennessee in 1840. Four years later, they moved to the Little River neighborhood, finally settling near Varner. Mrs. Clements died in 1845, and her husband in 1849. Their son, George, would later be found in the William Hector household on the census in 1850, listed as a farmer. Later, he would become a pioneer farmer, stock raiser, and cotton ginner of Cane Island. He was raised in "rude surroundings." Williams, *The History of Craighead County, Arkansas,* 455; George Clemens, "1850 United States Federal Census," Big Lake, Mississippi, Arkansas, Roll: 28, 353b *Ancestry.* Ancestry.com Operations, Inc., 2009, Lehi, Utah. Accessed July 28, 2022. https://www.ancestry.com.

[346] Williams, *The History of Craighead County, Arkansas*, 453.

[347] "Plat of Section 6, Township 13 North, Range 7 East," Original Survey Plat, Craighead County, Arkansas, April 21, 1848, General Land Office Records, Bureau of Land Management, U.S. Department of the Interior. Accessed August 4, 2022. https://glorecords.blm.gov.

[348] Williams, *The History of Craighead County, Arkansas,* 451.

[349] Thomas Varner, "1850 United States Federal Census," Big Lake, Mississippi, Arkansas, Roll: 28, 353b, *Ancestry.* Ancestry.com Operations, Inc., 2009, Lehi, Utah. Accessed July 28, 2022. https://www.ancestry.com.

[350] Howard Moore and his family, of Virginia, were the first White settlers in Dunklin County, settling near Malden in 1829. Douglass, *History of Southeast Missouri,* Vol. 1, 306.

[351] Smyth-Davis, *History of Dunklin County, Mo.*, 223-224.

[352] Williams, *The History of Craighead County*, Arkansas, 454.

[353] W.T. Buffaloe, "'Uncle France' Varner," *The Craighead County Historical Quarterly*, Vol. 2, Spring 1964, No. 2, 4-14; W.T. Buffaloe, "'Uncle France' Varner," *Arkansas Historical Quarterly*, Vol. 20, No. 2, Summer 1961, 151-171.

[354] Williams, *The History of Craighead County, Arkansas,* 451.

[355] William Hector, "1850 United States Federal Census," Big Lake, Mississippi, Arkansas, Roll: 28, 353b, *Ancestry.* Ancestry.com Operations, Inc., 2009, Lehi, Utah. Accessed July 28, 2022. https://www.ancestry.com.

[356] Lyell, Sir Charles, *A Second Visit to the United States of North America*, 237.

[357] Joseph Patrick Key, "European Exploration and Settlement, 1541 through 1802," *CALS Encyclopedia of Arkansas*. Accessed July 29, 2022. https://encyclopediaofarkansas.net/entries/european-exploration-and-settlement-1541-through-1802-2916/.

[358] Lesieur, *Early History*, Article 1, 1-2; John Thomas Scharf, *History of Saint Louis City and County: From the Earliest Periods to the Present Day: Including Biographical Sketches of Representative Men,* Vol. 1, 287-288. Accessed July 29, 2022. https://books.google.com/books.

[359] P. Chouteau Jr. to Godfrey Lesieur and his son G.A. Lesieur, Point Pleasant, Mo., Letters, LS, October 14, 1850 to January 29, 1851, Memo, Lesieur Collection, Godfrey Lesieur Papers, *Missouri History Museum Archives*, St. Louis, Missouri.

[360] P. Chouteau Jr. to Godfrey Lesieur and his son G.A. Lesieur, Point Pleasant, Mo., Letter, December 30, 1850, LS Letters, October 14, 1850 to January 29, 1851, Lesieur Collection, Godfrey Lesieur Papers, *Missouri History Museum Archives*, St. Louis, Missouri.

[361] P. Chouteau Jr. to Godfrey Lesieur and his son G.A. Lesieur, Point Pleasant, Mo., Letter, November 14, 1850, Letters, LS, October 14, 1850 to January 29, 1851, Lesieur

Collection, Godfrey Lesieur Papers, *Missouri History Museum Archives*, St. Louis, Missouri.

[362] P. Chouteau Jr. & Co., St. Louis, Mo. to Mr. Godfrey Lesieur, Point Pleasant, Mo., Letter, February 6, 1849, Lesieur Collection, Godfrey Lesieur Papers, *Missouri History Museum Archives*, St. Louis, Missouri.

[363] According to stories about the area, Oil Trough received its name from a time when hunters stored bear oil in troughs for transport down the White River to New Orleans. The area was settled as early as 1817. Nancy Griffith, "Oil Trough, (Independence County)," *CALS Encyclopedia of Arkansas.* Accessed July 28, 2022. https://encyclopediaofarkansas.net/entries/oil-trough-independence-county-5603/.

[364] Gerstaecker, *Wild Sports in the Far West*, 199.

[365] Copal or copalm is from the liquidambar or sweetgum tree. John Francis McDermott, *A Glossary of Mississippi Valley French 1673-1850*, 56, Washington University, St. Louis, Missouri, 1941. Downloaded PDF. Accessed July 29, 2022. https://archive.org; The Sweetgum tree has medicinal and beneficial properties. Jody M. Lingbeck, Corliss A. O'Bryan, Elizabeth M. Martin, Joshua P. Adams, Phillip G. Crandall. "Sweetgum: An Ancient Source of Beneficial Compounds with Modern Benefits." *Pharmacognosy Reviews,* Vol. 9, Issue 17, Jan-Jun, 2015. Accessed January 3, 2025. Downloaded PDF. https://www.phcogrev.com/content/pharmacognosy-reviews-vol-9-issue-17-jan-jun-2015.

[366] Most likely John B. Sarpy, a business associate, as Chouteau referred to him as "Our Mr. Sarpy," in his letter (Endnote 361). Sarpy was a partner with Auguste Chouteau, and later a member of the firm of P. Chouteau Jr. and Reuben Gold Thwaites, *Early Western Travels, 1748-1846: A Series of Annotated Reprints of Some of the Best and Rarest Contemporary Volumes of Travel, Descriptive of the Aborigines and Social and Economic Conditions in the Middle and Far West, During the Period of Early American Settlement. United States*, 165, Footnote 116, A. H. Clark Company, 1906. Accessed August 28, 2022. https://books.google.com.

[367] P. Chouteau Jr. & Co., St. Louis, Mo., to Mr. Godfrey Lesieur, Point Pleasant, Missouri, Letter, March 9, 1849, Lesieur Collection, Godfrey Lesieur Papers, *Missouri History Museum Archives*, St. Louis, Missouri.

[368] P. Chouteau Jr. & Co., St. Louis, Mo. to Godfrey Lesieur, Point Pleasant, Missouri, Letter, December 31, 1849, Lesieur Collection, Godfrey Lesieur Papers, *Missouri History Museum Archives,* St. Louis, Missouri.

[369] J.A. Davis, Affidavit, John William Perry, Application Number 34708; Eastern Cherokee Applications, 8/29/1906-5/26/1909, Record Group 123: Records of the U.S. Court of Claims, 1835-1984; M1104. National Archives at College Park, College Park, Maryland. Accessed March 20, 2022. www.archives.gov.

[370] The river begins in Mississippi County, south of Osceola, and flows into the St. Francis River near Parkin. It was rerouted, channelized, and ditched following the formation of levee and drainage districts. Cindy Grisham, "Tyronza River," *CALS Encyclopedia of Arkansas.* Accessed July 29, 2022. https://encyclopediaofarkansas.net/entries/tyronza-river-7456/.

[371] *Biographical and Historical Memoirs of Eastern Arkansas*, 423-424.

[372] 1840, "Mississippi, Arkansas, United States Records," images, 357, Arkansas Tax Records, Mississippi County, 1834-1869, *FamilySearch.* Accessed April 26, 2024. https://www.familysearch.org/en/united-states/; 1842, Ibid, 395; 1843, Ibid, 404; 1852, Ibid, 451; 1853, Ibid, 470; 1854, Ibid, 498; 1856, Ibid, 554.

Endnotes, Chapter 7

[373] Today, the pondberry is a federally endangered shrub. In the St. Francis Sunken Lands Natural Area, a portion of the largest known Arkansas population is located. "St. Francis Sunken Lands Natural Area," *Arkansas Heritage*, Arkansas Natural Heritage Commission, Little Rock, Arkansas. Accessed April 12, 2024. https://www.arkansasheritage.com/arkansas-natural-heritage/naturalareas/find-a-natural-area/st-francis-sunken-lands-natural-area.

[374] Meek, *A List of Fishes and Mollusks,* 347.

[375] Ibid, 345.

[376] Lesieur, *Early History*, Article VI, 34, from a description of a flood.

[377] James was the Mississippi County Surveyor from 1872 to 1874. Edrington, *History of Mississippi County, Arkansas*, 175.

[378] James, "Appendix Q, A Memoir to accompany the map of Mississippi County, Arkansas," 229-235.

[379] Harry Lee Williams, "The Old Delaware Indian Trails," *Craighead County Historical Quarterly*, Vol. I, No. 4, 33-36, Autumn, 1963.

[380] A local corruption of the L'Anguille River. French for "the eel."

[381] S.D. Flora, "The Great Flood of 1844 Along the Kansas and Marais Des Cygnes Rivers," *The Kansas Historical Quarterly,* Vol. XX, No. 2, 73-81, May 1951, published by Kansas State Historical Society, Topeka, Kansas, *Kansas Memory.* Accessed August 23, 2022. https://www.kansasmemory.org.

[382] William Franklin Switzler, *Switzler's Illustrated History of Missouri, From 1541 to 1877*, 257, C.R. Barns, Editor and Publisher, St. Louis, Missouri, 1879. Accessed August 12, 2022. https://books.google.com.

[383] S.K. Turner and S.A. Clark, *Twentieth Century History of Carroll County, Missouri,* Vol. I, 434-436, B.F. Bowen, Indianapolis, Indiana, 1911, *Missouri Digital Heritage*, Collections: Missouri County Histories. Accessed August 12, 2022. https://www.sos.mo.gov/mdh/.

[384] *History of Boone County, Missouri: Written and Comp. from the Most Authentic Official and Private Sources; Including a History of Its Townships, Towns, and Villages. Together with a Condensed History of Missouri; the City of St. Louis... Biographical Sketches and Portraits of Prominent Citizens ...,* 345-347, Western Historical Company, St. Louis, Missouri, 1882. Accessed August 12, 2022. https://books.google.com.

[385] Walter Barlow Stevens, *Missouri: the Center State,* Volume II, 567-570, S.J. Clarke Publishing Company, Chicago, Illinois, 1920. Accessed August 12, 2022. https://books.google.com.

[386] "Great Flood of 1844," *Wikipedia*, Wikimedia Foundation, Inc. Last edited, February 20, 2022. Accessed August 12, 2022. https://en.wikipedia.org/wiki/Great_Flood_of_1844.

[387] Lesieur, *Early History*, Article 1, 2.

[388] Phyllis A. Morse, "History of the Buffalo Island Area," Chapter 4, 23-31, 27, *An Archaeological Survey Initial Site Testing and Geomorphic Study of Ditches 7, 13, and Lower Buffalo Creek,* April 1988. Accessed December 6, 2024. https://apps.dtic.mil/sti/tr/pdf/ADA263200.pdf. Downloaded PDF.

[389] Williams, *The History of Craighead County, Arkansas*, 552.

[390] Buffaloe, "'Uncle France' Varner," *Arkansas Historical Quarterly,* Vol. 20, No. 2, 161-163.

[391] Williams, *The History of Craighead County, Arkansas,* 552.

[392] Williams, *The History of Craighead County, Arkansas*, 205.

[393] Firmin A. Rozier, *Rozier's History of the Early Settlement of the Mississippi Valley*, 98, G.A. Pierrot & Son, Printers, St. Louis, Missouri, Publisher, 1890.

[394] Lesieur, *Early History*, Article VI, 36.

[395] *History of the Organization and Operations of the Board of Directors St. Francis Levee District of Arkansas 1893-1945*, 15, West Memphis, Arkansas. Accessed August 12, 2022. *Hathi Trust Digital Library*. https://babel.hathitrust.org.

[396] Lesieur, *Early History*, Article VI, 36.

[397] Stone, *Recollections of Early Life in Poinsett County*, 7, 8.

[398] *History of the Organization and Operations of the Board of Directors St. Francis Levee*, 15-17.

[399] "Mississippi River floods." *Wikipedia*, Wikipedia Foundation, Last modified September 15, 2018. Accessed January 30, 2021. https://en.wikipedia.org/w/index.php?title=Mississippi_River_floods&oldid=859630702.

[400] Smyth-Davis, *History of Dunklin County, Mo.,* 30-31.

[401] Floyd M. Clay, PhD, *A Century on the Mississippi, A History of the Memphis District U.S. Army Corps of Engineers 1876-1976*, 28-29, U.S. Army Corps of Engineers, Memphis District, Memphis, Tennessee, January 1976.

[402] Ibid, 29-33.

[403] Lesieur, *Early History*, Article VI, 33-34.

[404] *Biographical and Historical Memoirs of Northeast Arkansas*, 459.

[405] Buffaloe, "'Uncle France' Varner," *The Craighead County Historical Quarterly*, Vol. 2, No. 2, 4-14; Buffaloe, "'Uncle France' Varner," *Arkansas Historical Quarterly*, 161-163.

[406] Edrington, *History of Mississippi County, Arkansas*, 231.

[407] Buffaloe, "'Uncle France' Varner," *The Craighead County Historical Quarterly*, 161-163.

[408] Simonson, "The St. Francis Levee," 419–429.

[409] Simonson, S. E., "Origin of Drainage Projects in Mississippi County." Vol. 5, No. 3, 263-273, *The Arkansas Historical Quarterly*, Arkansas Historical Association, 1946.

[410] Williams, *The History of Craighead County, Arkansas*, 140. Having been born in approximately 1841, Irwin would have been eight years old in 1849. He was four years old when his family moved to the county in 1845. Williams, *The History of Craighead County, Arkansas*, 383.

[411] Charles A. Stuck, "W.W. Nisbett and Minnie Nisbett Armour," *Craighead County Historical Society*, Vol 2, No. 4, 13-15, Autumn, 1964. Mary Nisbett, the wife of W.W., was a daughter of Ed. Mattix, II.

[412] "Swamp Lands in Missouri and Arkansas," February 28, 1849, Second Session, Thirtieth Congress, House of Representatives, *Reports of Committees: 16th Congress, 1st Session - 49th Congress, 1st Session*, United States, 1848, Vol. I, Report No. 130, 1-16. Accessed January 4, 2025. http://books.google.com/.

[413] Mary C. Suter, "Swamp Land Act of 1850," *CALS Encyclopedia of Arkansas*. Accessed July 20, 2021. http://www.encyclopediaofarkansas.net/encyclopedia/entry-detail.aspx?entryID=7402.

[414] Robert W. Harrison and Walter M. Kollmorgen. "Land Reclamation in Arkansas under the Swamp Land Grant of 1850." *The Arkansas Historical Quarterly*, 1947, Vol. 6, No. 4, 369-418. Accessed August 29, 2022. *JSTOR*.

https://doi.org/10.2307/40027472.

[415] William Hector, certificates 1885, 1886, 1887, 1888, 1926, 1927, 2027, and 2857. Sam Hector, certificate 1892. Historical Documents, Maps and More, Swamp Lands (1850), Entry Books, Book 1, North-East, 390-391, 392-393, 394-395, and 428-429. State of Arkansas, Commissioner of State Lands, History and Archives. Accessed April 14, 2022. https://www.cosl.org.

[416] Harrison, and Kollmorgen. "Land Reclamation in Arkansas," 369-418.

[417] Clay, *A Century on the Mississippi,* 12-13.

[418] *History of the Organization and Operations of the Board of Directors St. Francis Levee,* 1-3.

[419] Ibid, 173.

[420] Dallas Tabor Herndon, *Centennial History of Arkansas*, Vol. 1, 520-521, The S.J. Clarke Publishing Company, 1922. Accessed August 8, 2022. https://books.google.com.

[421] Wood, Stephen E. "The Development of Arkansas Railroads Part 1," *The Arkansas Historical Quarterly*, Vol. 7, No. 2, 103-140. Summer 1948. Accessed December 10, 2024. *JSTOR.* https://doi.org/10.2307/40027484.

[422] James, "Appendix Q, A Memoir to accompany the map of Mississippi County, Arkansas," 235.

[423] *The Osceola Times*, Osceola, Arkansas, June 14, 1879, 3, *Newspapers.com* by *Ancestry.* https://www.newspapers.com.

[424] James, "Appendix Q, A Memoir to accompany the map of Mississippi County, Arkansas," 235.

[425] The 1927 flood was the "most destructive and costly flood in Arkansas history," as well as the nation. Nancy Hendricks, "The 1927 Flood," *CALS Encyclopedia of Arkansas.* Accessed August 23, 2022. https://encyclopediaofarkansas.net/entries/flood-of-1927-2202/; The 1937 flood may have been the worst in Arkansas. John Spurgeon, "Flood of 1937," *CALS Encyclopedia of Arkansas.* Accessed August 23, 2022. https://encyclopediaofarkansas.net/entries/flood-of-1937-4878/.

[426] J.A. Fox, *The Garden Spot of the Mississippi Valley in the St. Francis Basin of Arkansas*, 17, (Edited and published by J.A. Fox, assistant engineer St. Francis Levee Board, Osceola, Arkansas), 1902.

Endnotes, Chapter 8

[427] *The Osceola Times*, Osceola, Arkansas, July 31, 1875, 2, *Newspapers.com* by *Ancestry*. https://www.newspapers.com. James is referred to as Capt. F.L. James, when the newspaper reprints an article he forwarded to the *Memphis Appeal*.

[428] *Selma Dollar Times,* Selma, Alabama, October 7, 1871, 2, *Newspapers.com* by *Ancestry*. https://www.newspapers.com. Referred to as Captain James, he used a Navy Colt in a shooting following an attack by a group of men at Dr. F.G. McGavock's home. The man died as a result.

[429] Le Havre is a port city in Northern France.

[430] "Necrology, Frank L. James, Ph.D., M.D." *Transactions of the American Microscopical Society,* Vol. 28, 1908, 207-209. Accessed March 19, 2024. Google Books. https://books.google.com.

[431] Census records from 1850 show three-year-old Matilda in the Sam Hector household, making a marriage date of 1846 likely. "1850 United States Federal Census," Big Lake, Mississippi, Arkansas, Roll: 28, 353b, *Ancestry*. Ancestry.com Operations, Inc., 2009, Lehi, Utah. Accessed March 21, 2022. https://www.ancestry.com.

[432] James A. East, Eastern Cherokee application 40265. (James Alfred East Hector).

[433] Jaley and William were indicted for lasciviously abiding and cohabiting together in October 1837 in Stoddard County, Missouri, which then encompassed Dunklin County. William Hector and Jailey Ann Rice, Indictment, lasciviously abiding and cohabiting together, Stoddard County, Missouri Circuit Court, October 1837. Court Records 1836-1844, Book A, 25, 26. *FamilySearch*. Accessed September 18, 2022. https://www.familysearch.org/en/united-states/.

[434] Clements' family, Chapter 6, Endnote 345.

[435] "Post Route," The Congressional Globe, Senate, 31st Congress, First Session, Part 2, 1559. *A Century of Lawmaking for a New Nation: U.S. Congressional Documents and Debates, 1774-1875.* Accessed February 23, 2022. Downloaded PDF. https://memory.loc.gov/ammem/amlaw/.

[436] Township 14 North, Range 9 East, Mississippi County, Arkansas, original survey plat, "road from Osceola, Ark. to Grand Prairie, Mo.," DM ID 5613, 3-17-1848, General Land Office Records, U.S. Department of the Interior Bureau of Land Management. Accessed August 12, 2022. https://glorecords.blm.gov.

[437] "Map of Mississippi County, Arkansas," James Anthony.

[438] Soloman Wyatt was the first postmaster. Postmaster Appointments for Dunklin County, Missouri; Record Group 28: Records of the Post Office Department, 1773-1971, Records of Appointment of Postmasters and the Establishment of Post Offices, 7/1/1931 - 10/31/1971; National Archives at College Park, College Park, Maryland [online version available through the Archival Research Catalog (ARC identifier 78753540) Ancestry 2018. Image 1. Accessed February 24, 2022. www.archives.gov.

[439] Postmaster Appointments for Mississippi County, Arkansas, Record Group 28: Records of the Post Office Department, 1773-1971, Records of Appointment of Postmasters and the Establishment of Post Offices, 7/1/1931 - 10/31/1971; National Archives at College Park, College Park, Maryland [online version available through the Archival Research Catalog (ARC identifier 78726975); Ancestry 2018. Image 1, 2. Accessed February 22, 2022. www.archives.gov.

[440] Thomas A. DeBlack, "Civil War through Reconstruction, 1861 through 1874," *CALS Encyclopedia of Arkansas*. Accessed March 6, 2020.

https://encyclopediaofarkansas.net/entries/civil-war-through-reconstruction-1861-through-1874-388/.

[441] Smyth-Davis, *History of Dunklin County, Mo.*, 33. James A. Walker was elected colonel.

[442] William A. Hecter, [sic] Record Group 109: War Department Collection of Confederate Records, 1825-1927 Series: Carded Records Showing Military Service of Soldiers Who Fought in Confederate Organizations, 1903-1927 File Unit: [Missouri] Hecter, William A - Age [Blank], Year: [BLANK] - State Guard, H-Hi, National Archives Catalog, Images 1, 2. Fold3 2016, ARC Identifier 32147063. Accessed December 7, 2019. https://catalog.archives.gov. Dooley is shown as captain.

[443] J.E. Dooley, Record Group 109: War Department Collection of Confederate Records, 1825-1927 Series: Carded Records Showing Military Service of Soldiers Who Fought in Confederate Organizations, 1903-1927 File Unit: [Missouri] Dooley, J E – Age [Blank], Year: 1861 - State Guard, Cu-E, Images 1-3. ARC Identifier 32143364, Fold3, National Archives Catalog. Accessed December 7, 2019, at https://catalog.archives.gov.

[444] Smyth-Davis, *History of Dunklin County, Mo.*, 31-34.

[445] "Reports of Brig. Gen. M. Jeff Thompson, Missouri State Guard, of the advance from Piketon and skirmishes at Big River Bridge and Blackwell Station," HDQRS First Military District, Mo. S.G., Camp Spring Hill, Mo., October 11, 1861, *The War of the Rebellion: A compilation of the Official Records of the Union and the Confederate Armies,* Vol. III, 223-225, 1881, Chapter X - Operations in Missouri and Arkansas, Kansas and Indian Territory, May 10-November 19, 1861, (Vol. 3, Chapter 19). Accessed August 13, 2022. Hathi Trust. https://babel.hathitrust.org/cgi/mb?a=listis&c=1930843488.

[446] Lesieur, *Early History*, 10; Douglass, *History of Southeast Missouri,* 43.

[447] *The Morning Democrat,* October 18, 1861, Davenport, Iowa. *Newspapers.com* by *Ancestry*. Accessed April 26, 2024. https://www.newspapers.com.

[448] Joseph A. Hector, Record Group 109 War Department Collection of Confederate Records, 1825-1927 Series: Carded Records Showing Military Service of Soldiers Who Fought in Confederate Organizations, 1903-1927 File Unit: [Missouri] Hector, Joseph Alford - Age 28, Year: 1862 - Seventh Cavalry, E-K. ARC Identifier 31975210, Fold3. Accessed August 12, 2022. https://catalog.archives.gov. James was called Joseph Alford Hector in this record.

[449] Ibid; William A. Hecter, [sic] Record Group 109: War Department Collection of Confederate Records, 1825-1927 Series: Carded Records Showing Military Service of Soldiers Who Fought in Confederate Organizations, 1903-1927 File Unit: [Missouri] Hecter, William A - Age [Blank], Year: [BLANK] - State Guard, H-Hi, National Archives Catalog, Images 1, 2. Fold3 2016, ARC Identifier 32147063. Accessed December 7, 2019. https://catalog.archives.gov.

[450] Mark K. Christ, "Engagement at Plum Point Bend," *CALS Encyclopedia of Arkansas.* Accessed April 11, 2024. https://encyclopediaofarkansas.net/entries/engagement-at-plum-point-bend-15748/.

[451] *Chicago Tribune*, Chicago, Illinois, April 19, 1862, 1, *Newspapers.com by Ancestry*. Accessed April 11, 2024. https://www.newspapers.com.

[452] "Map of the Mississippi River, from Cairo to the Gulf of Mexico, Showing the Positions of the Rebel Fortifications at the Mouth of the River, Those Already Taken and Those Remaining to be Captured, Etc.," *Frank Leslie's Illustrated Newspaper,*

May 10, 1862, Murray Hudson Antique Maps, Globes, Books & Prints, Halls, Tennessee. Original newspaper map in the Author's collection.

[453] Hamblen, "Green County," *CALS Encyclopedia of Arkansas*.

[454] Samuel S. Hildebrand, *Autobiography of Samuel S. Hildebrand, the Renowned Missouri 'Bushwacker' and Unconquerable Rob Roy of America, Being his Complete Confession,* Compiled by James W. Evans and A. Wendell Keith, MD, of St. Francois County, Missouri. State Times Book and Job Printing House, Jefferson City, Missouri, 1870. Ebook, Project Gutenberg. Accessed April 14, 2022. https://www.gutenberg.org.

[455] Fred R. Poole, Major, Commanding Expedition to Col. [J.B.] Rogers, Commanding Cape Girardeau, Mo., Letter, Sept. 7-30, 1863, "Report of Maj. Frederick R. Poole, Second Missouri State Militia Cavalry, Sept. 7-30, 1863, Expedition to Big Lake, Mississippi County, Ark., Headquarters, Camp Lowry, October 1, 1863, *The War of the Rebellion: a compilation of the official records of the Union and Confederate armies,* Series 01, Vol. 22, Part 01, 616. Accessed August 13, 2022. *HathiTrust.* https://babel.hathitrust.org/cgi/mb?a=listis&c=1930843488.

[456] James Bunch, Record Group 109: War Department Collection of Confederate Records, 1825 - 1927 Series: Carded Records Showing Military Service of Soldiers Who Fought in Confederate Organizations, 1903 - 1927. Missouri, Bunch, James, Age 30, Year: 1862, Seventh Cavalry, A-D. Images 1-10. ARC Identifier 31973585, Fold3 2016. Accessed August 12, 2022. https://catalog.archives.gov.

[457] David Sesser, "Conscription," *CALS Encyclopedia of Arkansas.* Accessed February 5, 2020. https://encyclopediaofarkansas.net/entries/conscription-5013/.

[458] James Bunch, War Department Collection of Confederate Records, 1825-1927. https://catalog.archives.gov.

[459] James Bunch is buried in Sec. 19, Site 9800, *U.S. Department of Veterans Affairs*, National Cemetery Administration, grave locator. Accessed August 13. 2022. https://www.cem.va.gov/index.asp.

[460] The 1850 census shows a James Bunch in the Walter Bunch household, along with Sam Bunch. Neighbors are the William and Sam Hector families. Bunch, Walter, "1850 United States Federal Census," Big Lake, Mississippi, Arkansas, Roll: 28, 353b, *Ancestry.* Ancestry.com Operations, Inc., 2009, Lehi, Utah. Accessed March 21, 2022. https://www.ancestry.com.

[461] "Report of Maj. John W. Rabb, Second Missouri Light Artillery," Report No. 1, Headquarters Post, New Madrid, Mo., April 10, 1864, and "Report of Capt. Valentine Pruiett, First Military Cavalry," Report No. 2, April 5-9, 1864 – Expedition from New Madrid and skirmishes in the swamps of Little River, near Osceola, and on Pemiscot Bayou, Ark., Series I, Vol. 34, Pt. 1, 872-875, *The War of the Rebellion: A compilation of the Official Records of the Union and the Confederate Armies,* Accessed August 13, 2022. *HathiTrust.* https://babel.hathitrust.org/cgi/mb?a=listis&c=1930843488.

[462] Mark Walker, "1850 United States Federal Census," Big Lake, Mississippi, Arkansas, Roll: 28, 352b, *Ancestry.* Ancestry.com Operations, Inc., 2009, Lehi, Utah. Accessed April 14, 2022. https://www.ancestry.com.

[463] Mark Walker, "1860 United States Federal Census," Big Lake, Mississippi, Arkansas; Roll: *M653_46, 734. Ancestry,* Ancestry.com Operations, Inc., Provo, Utah, 2009. Accessed April 14, 2022. https://www.ancestry.com.

[464] Mark Walker, "U.S. Census Mortality Schedules, Arkansas, 1850-1880;" Archive Roll Number: *1;* Census Year: *1870;* Monroe, Mississippi, Arkansas, *Ancestry.com,*

Provo, Utah, Ancestry.com Operations, Inc., 2010. Accessed April 14, 2022. https://www.ancestry.com.

[465] Historical Documents, Maps and More, Swamp Lands (1850), Entry Books, Book 1, North-East, 429, State of Arkansas, Commissioner of State Lands, History and Archives. Accessed April 14, 2022. https://www.cosl.org; This land was near a "Road from Grand Prairie, Mo. to Osceola, Ark." Plat of Township 15 North, Range 9 East, U.S. Department of the Interior, Bureau of Land Management, *General Land Office Records*, Survey Plats and Field Notes, Arkansas. Accessed April 14, 2022. https://glorecords.blm.gov.

[466] Reports 1, 2, Rabb and Prueitt, *The War of the Rebellion,* 872-875.

[467] "15th Arkansas Infantry Regiment (Josey's)," *Wikipedia*, The Free Encyclopedia, Wikimedia Foundation, Inc. Accessed March 2, 2020. https://en.wikipedia.org/wiki/15th_Arkansas_Infantry_Regiment_(Josey%27s).

[468] Edrington, *History of Mississippi County, Arkansas,* 282.

[469] L.R. Strange, (2016). The Civil War and Reconstruction in Mississippi County: The Story of Sans Souci Plantation. Graduate Theses and Dissertations. https://scholarworks.uark.edu/etd/1694.

[470] J. H. Atkinson and Elliott Fletcher. "A Civil War Letter of Captain Elliott Fletcher Jr." *The Arkansas Historical Quarterly*, Vol. 22, No. 1, 49-54. 1963.

[471] *Biographical and Historical Memoirs of Northeast Arkansas*, 496.

[472] Strange, The Story of Sans Souci Plantation, 28.

[473] "Ninth Arkansas Infantry Regiment," *Wikipedia*, Wikimedia Foundation, Inc. Accessed April 14, 2022. https://en.wikipedia.org/wiki/9th_Arkansas_Infantry_Regiment.

[474] Charles Bowen, Age [Blank], Year: 1865 - Miscellaneous, Arkansas, A-I, 7, Compiled Service Records of Confederate Soldiers Who Served in Organizations from the State of Arkansas. National Archives and Records Administration, Washington, D.C. Accessed February 8, 2020. https://catalog.archives.gov.

[475] Ibid. Charles Bowen to Major T.H. Mangum, Letter, requesting leave.

[476] "Captain Bowen Tells of Early Days in Mississippi County." *Delta Historical Review,* Fall 1996, 4-13.

[477] Rice, Paschal, Confederate Soldier from the State of Mississippi, Twenty-fifth Infantry. Record Group 109, War Department Collection of Confederate Records, 1825-1927, Roll 319, Carded Records Showing Military Service of Soldiers who fought in Confederate Organizations, 1903-1927. ARC Identifier 143380267, Fold3 2019. Accessed August 14, 2022. https://catalog.archives.gov.

[478] East, John, Confederate Soldier from the State of Mississippi, Twenty-fifth Infantry. Record Group 109, War Department Collection of Confederate Records, 1825-1927, Roll 319, Carded Records Showing Military Service of Soldiers who fought in Confederate Organizations, 1903-1927. ARC Identifier 145379110, Fold3 2019. Accessed August 14, 2022. https://catalog.archives.gov; East, John, Ninth Infantry, D-G, Record Group 109, War Department Collection of Confederate Records, 1825-1927, Roll 319, Carded Records Showing Military Service of Soldiers who fought in Confederate Organizations, 1903-1927. ARC Identifier 30357535, Fold3. Accessed August 14, 2022. https://catalog.archives.gov.

[479] "Itinerary of the District of Saint Louis," Report No. 1, commanded by Brig. Gen. Thomas Ewing Jr., U.S. Army, and "Reports of John T. Burris, Tenth Kansas Infantry," Report No. 2, July 18-August 6, 1864 – Operations in Southeast Missouri and Northeastern Arkansas, with skirmishes at Scatterville, Ark. (July 28), at Osceola,

Ark. (August 2), and at Elk Chute, Mo. (August 4), *The War of the Rebellion: A compilation of the Official Records of the Union and the Confederate Armies*, Series 1, Vol. 41, Part 1, 77-81. Accessed August 13, 2022. *HathiTrust.* https://babel.hathitrust.org/cgi/mb?a=listis&c=1930843488.

[480] *Biographical and Historical Memoirs of Northeast Arkansas,* 457.

[481] Charles Bowen, 1865 - Miscellaneous, Arkansas, A-I, 18, Compiled Service Records of Confederate Soldiers Who Served in Organizations from the State of Arkansas. National Archives and Records Administration, Washington, D.C. Accessed February 11, 2020. https://catalog.archives.gov.

[482] *Biographical and Historical Memoirs of Northeast Arkansas,* 471.

[483] Ibid, 533.

[484] Itinerary, Ewing and Report No. 2, Burris, *The War of the Rebellion*, 77-81.

[485] "Pemiscot County," "Ramsay Place Names File, 1928-1945 (C2366)," Columbia Manuscript Collections, *The State Historical Society of Missouri.* https://collections.shsmo.org/manuscripts/columbia/C2366. One story says the place was named for the skins left to dry in the trees after early settler, J.H. Walker, slaughtered hundreds of cattle before shipping to New Orleans, Louisiana.

[486] Itinerary, Ewing and Report No. 2, Burris, *The War of the Rebellion*, 77-81.

[487] *Biographical and Historical Memoirs of Northeast Arkansas,* 457.

[488] Strange, The Story of Sans Souci Plantation, 29.

[489] Ibid, 40; *Biographical and Historical Memoirs of Northeast Arkansas,* 531.

[490] Robert Gray, *The McGavock Family: A Genealogical History of James McGavock and His Descendants from 1760 to 1903*, 48-49. United States: W. E. Jones, 1903. Accessed December 6, 2024. https://books.google.com.

[491] *Biographical and Historical Memoirs of Northeast Arkansas*, 528-529.

[492] Edrington, *History of Mississippi County, Arkansas,* 114-115.

[493] F.G. McGavock, Louisiana, 1864, 3/3/1863-8/28/1866, Papers relating to citizens, War Department. The Adjutant General's Office. 1821-4/28/1904; War Department. Provost Marshal General's Bureau. Record Group 109, War Department Collection of Confederate Records, 1825-1927, ARC Identifier 28066782, Fold3 2014, Images 1-7. National Archives Catalog. Accessed August 12, 2022. https://catalog.archives.gov.

[494] William Hector, 1860 United States Federal Census, Mitchells, Poinsett, Arkansas; Roll: M653_48, 566; Family History Library Film: 803048, Ancestry.com. 1860 United States Federal Census, Provo, Utah, USA: Ancestry.com Operations, Inc., 2009. Accessed April 14, 2022. https://www.ancestry.com. In the Hector household were Louisa, minors James, John, and Joseph, and M.M. Cowib.

[495] Necrology, James, *Transactions of the American Microscopical Society*, Vol. 28, 207-209.

[496] Kelly, Howard Atwood, *A Cyclopedia of American Medical Biography: Comprising the Lives of Eminent Deceased Physicians and Surgeons from 1610 to 1910*, Vol. 2, 36, W.B. Saunders Company, 1912. Accessed March 20, 2024. https://books.google.com.

[497] "Nitre and Mining Bureau," *Wikipedia.* Accessed March 26, 2024. https://en.wikipedia.org/wiki/Nitre_and_Mining_Bureau.

[498] Liebig was a German chemist who made significant contributions to the analysis of organic compounds, the application of chemistry to biology and agriculture, as well as the organization of laboratory-based chemistry education. "Justis, baron von Liebig," *Britannica.* Accessed March 26, 2024. https://www.britannica.com/biography/Justus-Freiherr-von-Liebig.

[499] James received a degree from the medical school at Medizinische Fakultaet der Ludwig Maximilian Universitaet, Muenchen, Bayern, in 1861, *Directory of Deceased American Physicians,* 1804-1929, *Ancestry.com.* Accessed April 18, 2024. https://www.ancestry.com.

[500] Necrology, James, *Transactions of the American Microscopical Society,* Vol. 28, 207-209.

[501] David Sesser, "Fourth Military District," *CALS Encyclopedia of Arkansas.* Accessed March 10, 2020. https://encyclopediaofarkansas.net/entries/fourth-military-district-9123/.

[502] Ibid.

[503] "Register of Legal Voters, Arkansas," 1867-1868, Arkansas Register of Legal Voters Arkansas Digital Archives, *Arkansas State Archives,* Little Rock, Arkansas. MS.000628, Box 3, Folder 2, Mississippi County. Accessed February 14, 2020. https://digitalheritage.arkansas.gov/voters-1867-1868/55/.

[504] "Register of Legal Voters, Arkansas," 1867-1868, Update to the Register of Legal Voters, Mississippi County, MS.000628, Box 5, Folder 43, Arkansas Register of Legal Voters, Arkansas Digital Archives, *Arkansas State Archives,* Little Rock, Arkansas. Accessed February 14, 2020. https://digitalheritage.arkansas.gov/voters-1867-1868/.

[505] Records of the Field Offices for the State of Arkansas, Bureau of Refugees, Freedmen, and Abandoned Lands, 1865 -1872, 42. Internet Archive, downloaded PDF. Accessed August 13, 2022. https://openlibrary.org/books/OL24353223M/Records_of_the_field_offices_for_the_state_of_Arkansas_Bureau_of_Refugees_Freedmen_and_Abandoned_Lan.

[506] Retained Copy of Report Relative to Treatment of Freedmen, November 24, 1866, Little Rock, Arkansas, Records of the Assistant Commissioner for the State of Arkansas, Bureau of Refugees, Freedmen and Abandoned Lands, 1865-1869, National Archives Microfilm Publication, M979 Roll 52, "Miscellaneous Records 1865-1868," *The Freedmen's Bureau Online: Records of the Bureau of Refugees, Freedmen, and Abandoned Lands.* Accessed March 2, 2020. http://freedmensbureau.com/arkansas/arkreport.htm.

[507] DeBlack, "Civil War through Reconstruction, 1861 through 1874," *CALS Encyclopedia of Arkansas.*

[508] David Sesser, "Militia Wars of 1868-1869," *CALS Encyclopedia of Arkansas.* Accessed August 13, 2022. https://encyclopediaofarkansas.net/entries/militia-wars-of-1868-1869-7904/.

[509] Ruth C. Hale, "Black Hawk War of 1872," *CALS Encyclopedia of Arkansas.* Accessed August 13, 2022. https://encyclopediaofarkansas.net/entries/black-hawk-war-of-1872-5282/.

[510] Lucien Coatsworth Gause, Papers in the Case of L.C. Gause Vs Asa Hodges: First Congressional District of Arkansas, U.S. Government Printing Office, January 1873, 236. Accessed August 13, 2022. https://play.google.com/store/books/details?id=oZ0mAQAAMAAJ&rdid=book-oZ0mAQAAMAAJ&rdot=1.

[511] Hale, "Black Hawk War of 1872," *CALS Encyclopedia of Arkansas.*

[512] "Captain Bowen Tells of Early Days in Mississippi County," 4-13.

[513] Hale, "Black Hawk War of 1872," *CALS Encyclopedia of Arkansas.*

[514] *The Osceola Times,* Osceola, Arkansas, July 13, 1878, 5, *Newspapers.com by Ancestry.* Accessed January 2, 2023. https://www.newspapers.com.

[515] *The Osceola Times*, Osceola, Arkansas, July 31, 1880, 1, *Newspapers.com by Ancestry*. Accessed January 2, 2023. https://www.newspapers.com.

[516] *The Osceola Times*, Osceola, Arkansas, April 7, 1888, 4; "Judges and Clerks," June 30, 1888, 4. *Newspapers.com by Ancestry*. Accessed December 29, 2022. https://www.newspapers.com.

[517] "Mississippi, Arkansas, United States Records," County Court Records, Mississippi County, Arkansas, Court Records 1865-1879, 392, *FamilySearch*, image 67 of 325. Accessed April 17, 2024. https://www.familysearch.org.

[518] Reilly, Robert F., "Medical and Surgical Care During the American Civil War, 1861-1865." Baylor University Medical Center Proceedings, Vol. 29, Issue 2, 2016, 138-142. Accessed January 10, 2025. https://doi.org/10.1080/08998280.2016.11929390.

[519] William Hector, "Missouri U.S., Wills and Probate Records," 1766-1988, Record of Administrators Bonds, Letters, Vol. 1, 1872-1904, 45, Probate Court, Dunklin County, Missouri, *Ancestry*.com. Missouri, U.S., Wills and Probate Records, 1766-1988, Lehi, Utah, USA: *Ancestry.com* Operations, Inc., 2015. Accessed January 10, 2025. https://www.ancestry.com.

[520] "Mississippi, Arkansas, United States records," Hector, Melisa Ann, Sam W. Bunch, April 19, 1874, married by H.T. Blythe, Methodist minister. Marriage Records, Mississippi County Courthouse, Blytheville, Arkansas. *FamilySearch*, "Arkansas, County Marriages, 1837-1957," 29, *FamilySearch*. Accessed March 9, 2021. https://www.familysearch.org.

[521] Arkansas Probate Records, 1817-1979. Administration and Guardian Bonds and letters 1863-1921, Vol. A-B, Images 6, 15, 26, 37, and Probate Record 1857-1887, Vol. A-B, Images 34, 47, 60, 90. Both records are in Wittsburg, Cross County, Arkansas, *FamilySearch*. Accessed July 22, 2021. https://www.familysearch.org. These records are not probate records but are store records of purchases in 1857 from an unknown store in Wittsburg, Cross County, Arkansas.

[522] *The Osceola Times*, Osceola, Arkansas, "Local Column," August 9, 1873, 3. *Newspapers.com by Ancestry*. Accessed December 29, 2022. https://www.newspapers.com.

[523] "Colt M1861 Navy," *Wikipedia*, Wikimedia Foundation Inc. Accessed March 10, 2020. https://en.wikipedia.org/wiki/Colt_M1861_Navy.

[524] Arkansas Confederate Pensions, 1901-1929, Hector, J.A., *FamilySearch*, Mississippi County, Arkansas. Accessed September 12, 2022. http://FamilySearch.org.

[525] William P. Hale, Affidavit, August 1908, says William Hector died in 1865. John William Perry, Eastern Cherokee application 34708.

[526] Martha's death certificate would cite _____ Hector as her father. Martha Ann Goodwin, Arkansas, Death Certificates, 1914-1969, Arkansas Department of Vital Records; Little Rock, Year: 1940; Roll: 5, *Ancestry.com*. Lehi, Utah, USA: Ancestry.com Operations, Inc., 2019. Accessed September 7, 2022. https://www.ancestry.com.

Endnotes, Chapter 9

[527] Also known as Chuck-a-lee, *Biographical and Historical Memoirs of Northeast Arkansas*, 452; Chekeli in the 1822 treaty. "Documents relating to the negotiation of an unratified treaty of August 9, 1822, between the Cherokee and Osage Indians," *National Archives*, August 9, 1822, 1-6. *University of Wisconsin Digital Collections* (UWDC), The History Collection. Accessed April 2, 2022. http://digital.library.wisc.edu/1711.dl/History.Unrat1822no4; Chickalah in Yell County, Arkansas. Meridith Martin-Moats, "Chickalah (Yell County)," *CALS Encyclopedia of Arkansas*; Chih-kil-leh in Washburn's account. Washburn, *Reminiscences of the Indians*, 185; Chikilly in 1813 complaint, Huddleston, "Some Indian Incidents Along White River," Vol. 15, No. 4, 37-38; Chickelley in 1814 bond. Chisholm, May 23, 1814, Records of the Cherokee Indian Agency in Tennessee, 1801-1835, 120-122; Che.kil.lee in 1819 letter from Meigs to Arkansas Cherokee Chiefs, Records of the Cherokee Indian Agency in Tennessee; Chookalee in Lesieur, *Early History*, Article III, 10; Chickalee is the name that this author's grandmother Hettie Jane Hector Appleba said was the family Indian name.

[528] It was a common discussion during that time on whether the mounds were created by ancestors of modern Indians or a different race. James believed the latter, as he noted in his memoir to the Mississippi River Commission. James, "Appendix Q, A Memoir to accompany the map of Mississippi County, Arkansas," 234.

[529] Smithsonian Institution, 1880, *Annual Report of the U.S. Bureau of Ethnology to the Secretary of the Smithsonian Institution*, Vol. 12, Washington Government Printing Office, 1894, 207-212, Biodiversity Heritage Library. Accessed April 20, 2024. https://www.biodiversitylibrary.org/item/88468#page/279/mode/1up.

[530] The Miller Mounds were in Section 10, Township 10 North, Range 6 East, on the banks of the St. Francis River. Smithsonian Institution, 1880, *Annual Report*, 207.

[531] Necrology, James, *Transactions of the American Microscopical Society*, Vol. 28, 207-209.

[532] Thomas McAdory Owen, L.L.D., "James, Frank Lowber," *History of Alabama and Dictionary of Alabama Biography*, Volume III, The S.J. Clarke Publishing Company, Chicago, Illinois, 1921, 895. Accessed April 19, 2022. https://play.google.com/books/reader?id=nkoUAAAAYAAJ&pg=GBS.PP10&hl=en

[533] Necrology, James, *Transactions of the American Microscopical Society*, Vol. 28, 207-209.

[534] One Article sent to the *Memphis Appeal*, Memphis, Tennessee, in 1875, about the murder of Frank Williams, was also published in *The Osceola Times*, Osceola, Arkansas, on July 31, 1875, page 2. *Newspapers.com* by Ancestry. https://www.newspapers.com. The person who murdered Williams was lynched.

[535] Baird, *Years of Discontent*, xiv.

[536] Edrington, *History of Mississippi County, Arkansas,* 175.

[537] Baird, *Years of Discontent*, 6, *footnote* 23.

[538] Ibid, 7.

[539] Likely Samuel Semmes, who practiced law and was later elected as County Judge in 1882 for one term. *Biographical and Historical Memoirs of Northeast Arkansas*, 554.

[540] Baird, *Years of Discontent,* 29.

[541] Isaac Edward Daugherty, Application Number 27074; Eastern Cherokee Applications, 8/29/1906-5/26/1909, Record Group 123: Records of the U.S. Court of

Claims, 1835-1984; M1104. *National Archives* at College Park, College Park, Maryland. Accessed March 20, 2022. www.archives.gov.

[542] Baird, *Years of Discontent*, 44-45.

[543] James, "Role of Superstition in Therapeutics," 13.

[544] Baird, *Years of Discontent,* 44.

[545] James, "Role of Superstition in Therapeutics," 13.

[546] James, "Appendix Q, A Memoir to accompany the map of Mississippi County, Arkansas," 234.

[547] Baird, *Years of Discontent,* 48, *footnote* 169.

[548] Accession numbers for some of the items James donated include 006829, 006268, 008048, and 008063. Smithsonian, Collections. Accessed March 19, 2024. https://www.si.edu.

[549] "Report of Professor Baird, Secretary of the Smithsonian Institution, for 1878," *Annual Report of the Board of Regents of the Smithsonian Institution Showing Operations, Expenditures and Conditions of the Institution For The Year 1878*, 47, Government Printing Office, Washington, D.C., 1879. Accessed April 13, 2022. https://books.google.com.

[550] "Anthropology," *The American Naturalist,* Vol. 13, 528, Press of McCalla & Stavely, Philadelphia, Pennsylvania, 1879. Accessed April 13, 2022. https://books.google.com.

[551] Morse and Morse, *Archaeology for the Central Mississippi Valley*, 19.

[552] Smithsonian Institution, 1880, *Annual Report*, 207-212.

[553] Smithsonian, Collections.

[554] Smithsonian Institution, 1880, *Annual Report*, 207-212.

[555] Baird, *Years of Discontent*, 8.

[556] Ibid, xvii.

[557] Necrology, James, *Transactions of the American Microscopical Society*, Vol. 28, 207-209; Owen, *History of Alabama*, Vol. III, 895.

[558] Jeter, Marvin D., editor, *Edward Palmer's Arkansaw Mounds*, The University of Alabama Press, 1990, 127.

[559] Ibid, 125.

[560] Ibid, 121, 129.

[561] See Chapter 8.

[562] Jeter, *Edward Palmer's Arkansaw Mounds*, 129.

[563] Ibid, 126.

[564] John Peterson, 1880, "1880 United States Federal Census," Big Lake, Mississippi, Arkansas, Roll 51, 227B, Enumeration District 201, Lehi, Utah. Accessed March 21, 2022. https://www.ancestry.com.

[565] Jeter, *Edward Palmer's Arkansaw Mounds*, 126 and 129-130.

[566] Childs, H. Terry, and Charles H. McNutt, "Chickasawba," *The Arkansas Archaeologist*, Bulletin of the Arkansas Archaeological Society, Vol. 48, 30, for 2008, Published in 2009.

[567] Jeter, *Edward Palmer's Arkansaw Mounds*, 126 and 129-130; A footnote on the vessel says it was a bottle of the Nodena red and white type, which dated to the late Mississippian and Protohistoric periods, Jeter, *Edward Palmer's Arkansaw Mounds*, 374.

[568] Childs, and McNutt, "Chickasawba," 15, 51.

[569] Chickasawba was probably a Chickasaw Indian. McCall, Sheila, "Mississippi County history extends from Mastodon bones to jets," Focus on Government and

Business, 1996 Progress Edition, Section C, 3, *Blytheville Courier News*, October 27, 1996.

[570] *Biographical and Historical Memoirs of Northeast Arkansas,* 452, 504.

[571] Childs and McNutt, "Chickasawba," 33.

[572] Ibid, 33. Letter found with accession 6268 artifact, dated November 22, 1877; This is the same accession number as one of the artifacts James sent to the Smithsonian. (Endnote 545).

[573] James saying that Sam was half Shawnee may indicate that he had some Shawnee heritage in addition to Cherokee. Sam and his father were identified as Cherokee in the family's Guion Miller applications. Sam visited with McGavock for help to establish his Cherokee membership. (Chapter 10, 113).

[574] James, "Role of Superstition in Therapeutics," 13.

[575] *The Osceola Times*, Osceola. Arkansas, June 22, 1876, 3. *Newspapers.com by Ancestry*. https://www.newspapers.com.

[576] This author walked in the fields in the late 1990s with Marion Haynes, a local historian, and picked up small pottery shards. Haynes was later an assistant at the Blytheville Research Station of the Arkansas Archaeological Survey.

[577] Jeter, *Edward Palmer's Arkansaw Mounds*, 121, 158, 165.

[578] Ibid, 163.

[579] Ibid, 161, 163.

[580] Ibid, 158-159.

[581] Ibid, 165, 396, 398.

[582] "Arkansas Mounds," Publications of the Arkansas Historical Association, Vol. 4, 390-448, *Arkansas Historical Association*, Little Rock, Arkansas, 1917, 396, 398.

[583] A balmoral at this time may have referred to a petticoat, popular during the Civil War era. The petticoat was meant to show below the hem of a drawn-up skirt.

[584] "Arkansas Mounds," *Arkansas Historical Association*, Vol. 4, 408-409.

[585] Edrington, *History of Mississippi County, Arkansas*, 115-116; *Biographical and Historical Memoirs of Northeast Arkansas*, 115.

[586] McGavock, F.G., Provost Marshal General's Bureau, Images 1-7.

[587] Edrington, *History of Mississippi County, Arkansas*, 115-116; *Biographical and Historical Memoirs of Northeast Arkansas*, 530.

[588] "Arkansas Mounds," *Arkansas Historical Association*, 409.

[589] Toney Butler Schlesinger, "Goodspeed Histories," *CALS Encyclopedia of Arkansas*. Accessed August 23, 2022. https://encyclopediaofarkansas.net/entries/goodspeed-histories-6283/.

[590] *Biographical and Historical Memoirs of Northeast Arkansas*, 445.

[591] Hempstead, *A Pictorial History of Arkansas,* 91.

[592] Monette was John Wesley Monette, who wrote *History of the Discovery and Settlement of the Mississippi, by the Three Great European Powers, Spain, France, and Great Britain, and the Subsequent Occupation, Settlement, and Extension of Civil Government by the United States, Until the Year 1846*, Vol. 1, 290.

[593] Herndon, Dallas Tabor, *Centennial History of Arkansas*, Vol. 1, 97, S.J. Clark Publishing Company, 1922.

[594] Ibid, 993.

[595] *Biographical and Historical Memoirs of Northeast Arkansas*, 452.

[596] Ibid, 452-453.

[597] Ibid, 448.

[598] Mitchem, Jeffrey M., "Casqui (1491?-?)," *CALS Encyclopedia of Arkansas.* Accessed August 29, 2022. https://encyclopediaofarkansas.net/entries/casqui-1614/.

[599] *Biographical and Historical Memoirs of Northeast Arkansas*, 446-449; Edrington, *History of Mississippi County, Arkansas*, 24. Edrington went on to say that the remains of a cross were found at Sam's home. "Sam Hector was a living witness to this ditch on his Big Lake farm and the remains of a cross, erected by de Soto was unearthed hereabouts."

[600] Mitchem, Jeffrey M., PhD, "The Expedition of Hernando de Soto in Sixteenth-Century Arkansas," *Arkansas Archeological Survey*, Fayetteville, Arkansas, PDF. Accessed June 5, 2020. http://archeology.uark.edu/wp-content/uploads/2015/06/Expedition-of-Hernando-de-Soto.pdf. www.arkansasarcheology.org.

[601] Jeffrey Mitchem, Parkin Research Station, 50 Moments in Survey History, No. 33, "Investigating the Possible Base of the Cross Raised at Casqui by Hernando de Soto in 1541," *Arkansas Archaeological Survey*, University of Arkansas System. Accessed August 31, 2021. https://archeology.uark.edu/who-we-are/50moments/parkincross/. www.arkansasarcheology.org.

[602] Childs, H. Terry, and Charles H. McNutt, "Hernando De Soto's Route From Chicaca Through Northeast Arkansas: A Suggestion," *Southeastern Archaeology*, Vol. 28, No. 2, 2009, 165-183. Accessed, downloaded August 31, 2021. *Academia* at https://www.academia.edu/13811566/Hernando_De_Sotos_Route_from_Chicaca_th rough_Northeast_Arkansas_a_Suggestion.

[603] Marlon Mowdy, "Nodena Site," *CALS Encyclopedia of Arkansas.* Accessed August 29, 2022. https://encyclopediaofarkansas.net/entries/nodena-site-7925/.

[604] Hector, Samuel, "1870 United States Federal Census," Big Lake, Mississippi, Arkansas; Roll M593 58, 527B, *Ancestry*, Ancestry.com Operations, Inc., 2009. Accessed March 21, 2022. https://www.ancestry.com.

[605] Baird, *Years of Discontent,* 7.

[606] Hector, Sam, "1880 United States Federal Census," Big Lake, Mississippi, Arkansas, Roll 51, Enumeration District 201, Lehi, Utah, 227A. *Ancestry.* Accessed March 21, 2022. https://www.ancestry.com; Ibid, Bunch, Sam, 225A.

[607] Ibid, Perry, John, 227B.

[608] William Hector, "Missouri U.S., Wills and Probate Records," 1766-1988, Record of Administrators Bonds, Letters, Vol. 1, 1872-1904, 45, Probate Court, Dunklin County, Missouri, *Ancestry.com.* Missouri, U.S., Wills and Probate Records, 1766-1988, Lehi, Utah, USA: Ancestry.com Operations, Inc., 2015. Accessed January 10, 2025. https://www.ancestry.com.

[609] Heckter, [sic] Alfred, "1880 United States Federal Census," Clay, Dunklin, Missouri; Roll: 685, 653C; Enumeration District: 047, *Ancestry.com*, Lehi, Utah, USA: Ancestry.com Operations Inc, 2010. Accessed August 22, 2022. https://www.ancestry.com.

Endnotes, Chapter 10

[610] Wayne Capooth, M.D., *Red Letter Days,* Gateway Press, Inc., Baltimore, Maryland, 1995, 121-137. While the story is mostly fiction, it is partly based on facts. The information concerning Sam is partly based upon a newspaper article in the *Memphis Evening Scimitar* on November 20, 1895, per Capooth in a telephone conversation on December 20, 2022. Information used in this chapter about Sam Hector was garnered from the news article, shared by Capooth with this author in an email on December 17, 2022.

[611] *The Osceola Times,* Osceola, Arkansas, October 12, 1895. *Newspapers.com by Ancestry.* Accessed December 29, 2022. https://www.newspapers.com.

[612] *The Osceola Times,* Osceola, Arkansas, "Local Happenings," October 27, 1900, 7. *Newspapers.com by Ancestry.* Accessed December 29, 2022. https://www.newspapers.com.

[613] Edrington, *History of Mississippi County, Arkansas,* 162-164.

[614] Capooth, *Red Letter Days, Memphis Evening Scimitar.*

[615] Frank Lowber James, *Directory of Deceased American Physicians, 1804-1929, Ancestry.com.* Accessed April 18, 2024. https://www.ancestry.com.

[616] Dr. Joseph J. Kinyoun, Father of the NIH, "Kinyoun's Early Years," *National Institute of Allergy and Infectious Diseases.* Accessed April 19, 2024. https://pubweb-prod.niaid.nih.gov/about/joseph-kinyoun-indispensable-man-early-years#:~:text=The%20St.,Medical%20College%20later%20that%20year.

[617] "Necrology, Frank L. James," *Transactions of the American Microscopical Society,* Vol. 28, 207-209, American Microscopical Society, United States, 1908. https://books.google.com.

[618] Owen, *History of Alabama,* Vol. III, 895.

[619] "Death of Dr. Frank L. James," *The National Druggist,* Vol. 37, 189-191, June 1907, St. Louis, Missouri, Henry R. Strong, Publisher. Accessed April 19, 2024. https://books.google.com. This eulogy offers a glimpse into James' personality. A lot more could be written about James.

[620] *The Osceola Times,* Osceola, Arkansas, "For Sale," December 15, 1900, 6. *Newspapers.com by Ancestry.* Accessed December 29, 2022. https://www.newspapers.com.

[621] *The Osceola Times,* Osceola, Arkansas, "The Fire Fiend," February 20, 1892, 4. *Newspapers.com by Ancestry.* Accessed December 30, 2022. https://www.newspapers.com.

[622] "Mississippi Flyway," *Wikipedia,* Wikimedia Foundation, Inc. Accessed November 1, 2020 https://en.wikipedia.org/wiki/Mississippi_Flyway.

[623] Capooth, *Red Letter Days; Memphis Evening Scimitar.*

[624] Wells Woodbridge Cooke, *Distribution & Migration of Warblers, Ducks & Geese, Herons, Shore-Birds, Rails,* United States, U.S. Government Printing Office, 1904, 23. Accessed December 28, 2022. https://books.google.com.

[625] Ted R. Worley, "Early Days in Osceola." *The Arkansas Historical Quarterly,* Vol. 24, No. 2, 120–126, Summer 1965. Arkansas Historical Association. Accessed August 4, 2022. *JSTOR,* https://doi.org/10.2307/40027594.

[626] Capooth, *Red Letter Days; Memphis Evening Scimitar.*

[627] Hector, William, Arkansas Tax Records, Mississippi County, 1852, 9, 10. "Mississippi, Arkansas, United States Records," images, Arkansas Tax Records, Mississippi County 1834-1869, *FamilySearch.* Accessed January 17, 2023. https://www.familysearch.org/en/united-states/.

[628] Samuel Hector, "1870 United States Federal Census," Big Lake, Mississippi, Arkansas; Roll M593 58, 527B *Ancestry*, Ancestry.com Operations, Inc., 2009. Accessed March 21, 2022. https://www.ancestry.com; Samuel Hector, "1880 United States Federal Census," Big Lake, Mississippi, Arkansas, Roll 51, 227A; Enumeration District 201, Lehi, Utah. Accessed March 21, 2022. https://www.newspapers.com. Samuel Hector, "1850 United States Federal Census," Big Lake, Mississippi, Arkansas, Roll: 28, 353b. *Ancestry.* Ancestry.com Operations, Inc., 2009, Lehi, Utah. Accessed March 21, 2022. https://www.newspapers.com; James A. Hector, "1870 United States Federal Census," Big Lake, Mississippi, Arkansas; Roll M593 58, 525A. *Ancestry.* Ancestry.com Operations, Inc., 2009. Accessed March 21, 2022. https://www.newspapers.com; Alfred Heckter, "1880 United States Federal Census," Big Lake, Mississippi, Arkansas; Roll 685, 653C, Enumeration District 047, *Ancestry*, Ancestry.com Operations, Inc., 2009. Accessed March 21, 2022. https://www.newspapers.com.

[629] *The Osceola Times*, Osceola, Arkansas, "Osceola Rain Drops," October 12. 1895, 4. This was a Saturday. *Newspapers.com by Ancestry*. Accessed December 29, 2022. https://www.newspapers.com.

[630] Bear meat. *The Osceola Times*, Osceola, Arkansas, "Osceola Rain Drops," October 23, 1886, 4. *Newspapers.com by Ancestry*. Accessed December 29, 2022. https://www.newspapers.com.

[631] Ted R. Worley, "Days in Osceola." *The Arkansas Historical Quarterly*, Vol. 24, No. 2, Arkansas Historical Association, 1965, 120-26. Accessed August 34, 2022. https://doi.org/10.2307/40027594.

[632] This could be James East (James Alfred East Hector), as he also went by that name. *The Osceola Times*, Osceola, Arkansas, "Chickasawba Items," November 30, 1889, 4. *Newspapers.com by Ancestry*. Accessed December 30, 2022. https://www.newspapers.com.

[633] Leonidas Polk Sandels, Joseph Morrison Hill, *A Digest of the Statutes of Arkansas Embracing All Laws of a General Nature in Force at the Close of the Session of the General Assembly of One Thousand Eight Hundred and Ninety-three,* United States, Press of E.W. Stephens, 1994, 1605. Accessed September 25, 2022. https://books.google.com.

[634] Hector, Sam, "Mississippi, Arkansas, United States Records," "In the matter of wild cat and wolf scalps," (Mississippi County, Arkansas) County Court records, Court Records, Vol. 3, 1885-1890, 616. Accessed September 25, 2022. https://www.familysearch.org.

[635] This could be James, Sam's son, or James Alfred East Hector.

[636] Sam Hector and James Hector, "Mississippi, Arkansas, United States Records, "In the matter of wild cat & w scalps," (Mississippi County, Arkansas) County Court records, Court records, Vol. 4, 1895-1895, 228. Accessed September 25, 2022. https://www.familysearch.org.

[637] Annalea K. Bowers, Leah D. Lucio, David W. Clark, Susan P. Rakow, and Gary A. Heidt, (2001) "Early History of the Wolf, Black Bear, and Mountain Lion in Arkansas," *Journal of the Arkansas Academy of Science:* Vol. 55, Article 4, 22-27. Accessed November 8, 2022. Downloaded PDF. https://scholarworks.uark.edu/jaas/vol55/iss1.

[638] McCall, "Mississippi County history extends from Mastodon bones to jets," Section C, 3.

[639] *Biographical and Historical Memoirs of Northeast Arkansas*, 454.

[640] Jeannie Whayne, *Delta Empire, Lee Wilson and the Transformation of Agriculture in the New South,* 1, Louisiana State University Press, Baton Rouge, Louisiana, 2011.

[641] *Biographical and Historical Memoirs of Northeast Arkansas,* 568-569.

[642] Deanna Snowden, Editor, *Mississippi County, Arkansas: Appreciating the Past, Anticipating the Future,* compiled and edited by Deanna Snowden. Copyright 1986, Mississippi County Community College Foundation, August House, Little Rock, Arkansas, 1986. Robert E. Lee Wilson, III, interview, 47.

[643] Fox, *The Garden Spot of the Mississippi Valley*, 18.

[644] Ibid, 18-20.

[645] Ibid, 58.

[646] Douglass, *History of Southeast Missouri,* Vol. I, 508.

[647] Fox, *The Garden Spot of the Mississippi Valley*, 45.

[648] Dew, Lee A. "The J.L.C. and E.R.R. and the Opening of the 'Sunk Lands' of Northeast Arkansas." *The Arkansas Historical Quarterly*, Vol. 27, No. 1, 22-39, Arkansas Historical Association, 1968. Accessed August 4, 2022. https://doi.org/10.2307/40018324.

[649] Ibid.

[650] Ibid.

[651] Ibid.

[652] "Map of Mississippi County, Arkansas," Bardstown, Arkansas, James Anthony, C.E., 1898, Library of Congress Geography and Map Division, Washington, D.C., 20540-4650 USA dcu, G4003.M5G46 1898.A5, Library of Congress website. Accessed December 13, 2024. www.loc.gov/item/2011590024/.

[653] Fox, *The Garden Spot of the Mississippi Valley,* 45.

[654] Illegal saloons.

[655] Dew, "The J.L.C. and E.R.R.," *The Arkansas Historical Quarterly*, Vol. 27, No. 1, 22-39.

[656] Arkansas: Miller-Monroe; Record Group 28: Records of the Post Office Department, 1773-1971, Reports of Site Locations, 1837-1950; Images 527-533, *National Archives* at College Park, College Park, Maryland, online version available through the Archival Research Catalog, ARC identifier 68211197. Accessed March 16, 2022. www.archives.gov.

[657] Postmaster Appointments for Mississippi County, Arkansas, Image 9.

[658] Arkansas: Miller-Monroe, Post Office Department, National Archives, Images 398-414.

[659] Postmaster Appointments for Mississippi County, Arkansas, Image 8.

[660] Arkansas: Miller-Monroe, Post Office Department, National Archives, Images 398-414.

[661] "Widner-Magers Farm Historic District," Dell, Mississippi County, Arkansas, Site MSO301, Registration Form, *Arkansas Heritage*, National Register of Historical Places, Arkansas Historic Preservation Program, Little Rock, Arkansas. PDF. Accessed August 4, 2022. https://www.arkansasheritage.com.

[662] Steven Teske, "Dell (Mississippi County)," *CALS Encyclopedia of Arkansas*. Accessed August 4, 2022. https://encyclopediaofarkansas.net/entries/dell-mississippi-county-7124/.

[663] Plat map of Mississippi County, Arkansas, 1903. When photocopied by the author, the map was in the possession of the now-defunct Blytheville Research Station of the Arkansas Archaeological Survey.

[664] Arkansas: Miller-Monroe, Post Office Department, *National Archives*, Images 398-414.

[665] Arkansas Railroad Commission, *Annual Report of the Railroad Commission of the State of Arkansas,* United States, Thompson Lithograph and Print. Company, 1904, 200. Google Books. Accessed March 19, 2022. https://books.google.com.

[666] Widner-Magers Farm Historic District, *Arkansas Heritage*. MSO301.

[667] *The Osceola Times*, Osceola, Arkansas, "Dell Locals," September 2, 1905, 1, *Newspapers.com by Ancestry*. Accessed January 2, 2023. https://www.newspapers.com.

[668] Arkansas: Miller-Monroe, Post Office Department, *National Archives*, Images 365-373.

[669] Fox, *The Garden Spot of the Mississippi Valley,* 44.

[670] *The Courier News*, Blytheville, Arkansas, May 25, 1954.

[671] Postmaster Appointments for Mississippi County, Arkansas, Images 6, 7.

[672] Arkansas: Miller-Monroe, Post Office Department, *National Archives*, Images 605.

[673] Donna Brewer Jackson, "Manila (Mississippi County)," *CALS Encyclopedia of Arkansas.* Accessed March 23, 2022. https://encyclopediaofarkansas.net/entries/manila-mississippi-county-20/.

[674] Fox, *The Garden Spot of the Mississippi Valley,* 42-45.

[675] McCall, Sheila, "Blytheville's history spans two centuries," Focus on Government and Business, 1996 Progress Edition, Section C, 5, *Blytheville Courier News*, October 27, 1996.

[676] *The Osceola Times*, Osceola, Arkansas, October 21. 1893, 4. *Newspapers.com by Ancestry*. Accessed December 30, 2022. https://www.newspapers.com.

[677] Fox, *The Garden Spot of the Mississippi Valley,* 29-31.

[678] Ted R. Worley, "Early Days in Osceola." *The Arkansas Historical Quarterly*, Vol. 24, No. 2, 120-126, Arkansas Historical Association, Summer, 1965. Accessed August 4, 2022. https://doi.org/10.2307/40027594.

[679] Fox, *The Garden Spot of the Mississippi Valley,* 60-61.

[680] Ibid, 64.

[681] Ibid, 68.

[682] "Post route map of the state of Arkansas and of Indian and Oklahoma territories showing post offices with the intermediate distances on mail routes in operation on the 1st of December, 1897." United States. Post Office Dept. Map. Washington, D.C., The Dept., 1897. *Norman B. Leventhal Map & Education Center*. Accessed March 13, 2022. https://collections.leventhalmap.org/search/commonwealth:cj82kk753.

[683] Arkansas: Miller-Monroe, Post Office Department, National Archives, Images 376-378.

[684] Arkansas: Miller-Monroe, Post Office Department, *National Archives*, Images 376-378, Images 221-224, and 237-238.

[685] Postmaster Appointments for Mississippi County, Arkansas, Images 7, 9, 4.

[686] Postmaster Appointments for Mississippi County, Arkansas, Images 7, 9.

[687] A doorless, four-wheeled carriage used in the U.S. in the late 19th and early 20th centuries. "Surrey (carriage)," *Wikipedia*, Wikimedia Foundation, Inc. Accessed September 15, 2021. https://en.wikipedia.org/wiki/Surrey_(carriage).

[688] Deanna Snowden, Compiler and Editor, Alice Marie Ross, interview, 51, 54, *Mississippi County, Arkansas: Appreciating the Past, Anticipating the Future,*

Mississippi County Community College Foundation, August House, Little Rock, Arkansas, 1986.

[689] W.P. Hale is pictured in the following book with a group of pioneers, including Charles Bowen. Fox, *The Garden Spot of the Mississippi Valley,* 5.

[690] Edrington, *History of Mississippi County, Arkansas,* 128.

[691] Simonson, "Origin of Drainage Projects in Mississippi County," Vol. 5, No. 3, 263-273.

[692] Ibid.

[693] Dew, "The J.L.C. and E.R.R.," *The Arkansas Historical Quarterly*, Vol. 27, No. 1, 22-39.

[694] Deanna Snowden, Compiler and Editor, Robert E. Lee Wilson, III, interview, 68, *Mississippi County, Arkansas: Appreciating the Past, Anticipating the Future,* 1986, Mississippi County Community College Foundation, August House, Little Rock, Arkansas.

[695] *The Osceola Times,* Osceola, Arkansas, "Personal and Local," December 3, 1904, 5, *Newspapers.com by Ancestry.* Accessed January 2, 2023. https://www.newspapers.com. The report says Sam was about 90. He was 80. It was reported that he was born in Mississippi County, however, he was born in the New Madrid area. Thomas J. Daughtery's affidavit, in the Guion Miller application of John W. Perry, half-brother, says he always understood Sam was born in New Madrid, Missouri. John William Perry, Eastern Cherokee application 34708; S. W. Bunch affidavit in Bertie Holsclaw, Eastern Cherokee application stated Sam lived in New Madrid in 1834-1835. Bertie Holsclaw, Application Number 33256, Eastern Cherokee Applications, 8/29/1906-5/26/1909, Record Group 123: Records of the U.S. Court of Claims, 1835-1984; M1104. National Archives at College Park, College Park, Maryland. Accessed March 20, 2022. www.archives.gov.

[696] *The Osceola Times,* Osceola, Arkansas*,* "Personal and Local," September 30, 1905, 3, *Newspapers.com by Ancestry.* Accessed January 2, 2023. https://www.newspapers.com. "Mrs. Sam Bunch of Big Lake, died last Monday, at the residence of her daughter near Dell, and was buried last Tuesday."

[697] James A. East (James Alfred East Hector), Guion Miller application said she died "about" 1899. James A. East, Eastern Cherokee application 40265.

[698] Thomas J. Daugherty affidavit, John W. Perry's Guion Miller Eastern Cherokee application says she died September 9. John William Perry, Eastern Cherokee application 34708.

[699] Eastern Cherokee Applications of Samuel, 34102, Don, 34103, and William Thomas Hector, 32322; William Thomas Hector, Application Number 32322, Eastern Cherokee Applications, 8/29/1906-5/26/1909, Record Group 123: Records of the U.S. Court of Claims, 1835-1984; M1104. National Archives at College Park, College Park, Maryland. Accessed March 20, 2022. www.archives.gov; Samuel Hector, Application Number 34102; Eastern Cherokee Applications, 8/29/1906-5/26/1909, Record Group 123: Records of the U.S. Court of Claims, 1835-1984; M1104. National Archives at College Park, College Park, Maryland. Accessed March 20, 2022. www.archives.gov; Don Hector, Application Number 34103, Eastern Cherokee Applications, 8/29/1906-5/26/1909, Record Group 123: Records of the U.S. Court of Claims, 1835-1984; M1104. National Archives at College Park, College Park, Maryland. Accessed March 20, 2022. www.archives.gov.

[700] *The Osceola Times*, April 2, 1892, 4, *The Osceola Times, Osceola, Arkansas, 1873-1900, Death Notices, Suicides and Murdered, Including Notice of Persons*

Reported as Not Expected to Survive, Dangerously Ill, or lying Low, Extracted from Microfilm by Joyce Hambleton Whitten, Genealogy Society of Craighead County, Arkansas, 2015.

[701] *The Osceola Times*, Osceola, Arkansas, May 7, 1892, 1, *Newspapers.com* by *Ancestry.* https://www.newspapers.com.

[702] *The Osceola Times,* Osceola, Arkansas, December 10, 1892, and May 6, 1893. *Newspapers.com* by *Ancestry.* https://www.newspapers.com.

[703] James A. Hector and Parlee Gardner, August 30, 1896, Marriage Bond, Marriage Records, Book 9, 35, Mississippi County Court House, Blytheville, Arkansas.

[704] *The Osceola Times*, Osceola, Arkansas, "A Chance," March 26, 1898, 4. *Newspapers.com by Ancestry.* Accessed December 30, 2022. https://www.newspapers.com.

[705] Don Hector said his father died on November 1, 1901, and James H. was born in March 1902, in his Guion Miller application. Don Hector, Application Number 34103; Eastern Cherokee Applications, 8/29/1906-5/26/1909, Record Group 123: Records of the U.S. Court of Claims, 1835-1984; M1104. National Archives at College Park, College Park, Maryland. Accessed March 20, 2022. www.archives.gov.

[706] *The Osceola Times*, Osceola, Arkansas, "Osceola Rain Drops," July 22, 1893, 4. *Newspapers.com by Ancestry.* Accessed December 29, 2022. https://www.newspapers.com.

[707] John William Perry, Eastern Cherokee application 34708.

[708] *Biographical and Historical Memoirs of Northeast Arkansas,* 470-472.

[709] Chickalee was the Hector Indian name. William Thomas Hector, Eastern Cherokee application 32322; Samuel Hector, Eastern Cherokee application 34102; Don Hector, Eastern Cherokee application 34103.

[710] "My great-grandfather was William Hector - Indian name Chickalee, said John W. Perry. John William Perry, Eastern Cherokee application 34708; Samuel Perry, Application Number 40269; Charles H. L. Perry, Application Number 40270; Eastern Cherokee Applications, 8/29/1906-5/26/1909, Record Group 123: Records of the U.S. Court of Claims, 1835-1984; M1104. National Archives at College Park, College Park, Maryland. Accessed March 20, 2022. www.archives.gov.

[711] Thomas J. Daugherty, Application Number 32978; Eastern Cherokee Applications, 8/29/1906-5/26/1909, Record Group 123: Records of the U.S. Court of Claims, 1835-1984; M1104. National Archives at College Park, College Park, Maryland. Accessed March 20, 2022. www.archives.gov. Thomas may have based his knowledge on the first affidavit of Isaac Daugherty (June 1907), since Thomas' application is dated July 7, 1907. Later, Isaac would recant that claim in John W. Perry's application, dated August 25, 1908.

[712] Jane Bunch Merriman, Eastern Cherokee application 36059; Bertie Holsclaw, Eastern Cherokee application 33256; Nervie Bunch, Eastern Cherokee application 36058; Sallie Bunch, Application Number 36060, Eastern Cherokee Applications, 8/29/1906-5/26/1909, Record Group 123: Records of the U.S. Court of Claims, 1835-1984; M1104. National Archives at College Park, College Park, Maryland. Accessed March 20, 2022. www.archives.gov.

[713] Nervie Bunch, Eastern Cherokee application 36058.

[714] Pinkie Bunch, Application Number 36062; Eastern Cherokee Applications, 8/29/1906-5/26/1909, Record Group 123: Records of the U.S. Court of Claims, 1835-1984; M1104. National Archives at College Park, College Park, Maryland. Accessed March 19, 2022. www.archives.gov.

[715] James A. East, Eastern Cherokee application 40265.

[716] John William Perry, Application Number 34708; Eastern Cherokee Applications, 8/29/1906-5/26/1909, Record Group 123: Records of the U.S. Court of Claims, 1835-1984; M1104. National Archives at College Park, College Park, Maryland. Accessed March 20, 2022. www.archives.gov.

[717] Isaac Edward Daugherty, Eastern Cherokee application 27074.

[718] John William Perry, Eastern Cherokee application 34708. Daugherty would also say that his mother's father, Joe Johnson, was half Cherokee.

[719] Ibid.

[720] James A. East. "1870 United States Federal Census," Big Lake, Mississippi, Arkansas; Roll: M593 58; 525A, Ancestry.com Operations, Inc., Provo, Utah, 2009. *Ancestry.* Accessed March 21, 2022. https://www.ancestry.com.

[721] James A. East, Eastern Cherokee application 40265.

[722] Temperance Neel. "1910 United States Federal Census," Neal, Mississippi, Arkansas, Roll T624_58, 9A, Enumeration District: 0081, *Ancestry.* Accessed March 21, 2022. https://www.ancestry.com.

[723] Josiah W. East, Eastern Cherokee application 40267; John William Perry, Eastern Cherokee application 34708.

[724] James A. East, Eastern Cherokee application 40265.

[725] John William Perry, Eastern Cherokee application 34708.

[726] *Biographical and Historical Memoirs of Northeast Arkansas*, 452.

[727] John William Perry, Eastern Cherokee application, 34708.

[728] Edrington, *History of Mississippi County, Arkansas*, 286.

[729] Thomas J. Daugherty affidavit in John W. Perry Eastern Cherokee application. John William Perry, Eastern Cherokee application 34708.

[730] Bertie Holsclaw, Eastern Cherokee application, 33256.

[731] Julia F. Jolliff, Application Number 40266; Eastern Cherokee Applications, 8/29/1906-5/26/1909, Record Group 123: Records of the U.S. Court of Claims, 1835-1984; M1104. National Archives at College Park, College Park, Maryland. Accessed March 20, 2022. www.archives.gov.

[732] Montie J. East Pack. Pack, Marrtie [sic] J., Application Number 40268; Eastern Cherokee Applications, 8/29/1906-5/26/1909, Record Group 123: Records of the U.S. Court of Claims, 1835-1984; M1104. National Archives at College Park, College Park, Maryland. Accessed March 20, 2022. www.archives.gov.

[733] John Perry, Application Number 40271; Eastern Cherokee Applications, 8/29/1906-5/26/1909, Record Group 123: Records of the U.S. Court of Claims, 1835-1984; M1104. National Archives at College Park, College Park, Maryland. Accessed March 20, 2022. www.archives.gov.

[734] *Arkansas Democrat*, Little Rock, Arkansas, "Jonesboro Plans to Preserve Rich Lore of East Arkansas," May 14, 1922, 2. *Newspapers.com by Ancestry.* Accessed December 29, 2022. https://www.newspapers.com.

[735] Simonson, "High Waters on the Mississippi River," 419-429.

[736] Smyth-Davis, *History of Dunklin County, Mo.,* 19.

[737] *Arkansas Township Digest, Minor Civil Divisions, 1820-1990,* compiled by Desmond Walls Allen, Arkansas Research, Conway, Arkansas, 1994.

[738] *The Osceola Times*, Osceola, Arkansas, "Road Tax Fund Apportioned," July 20, 1901, 1, *Newspapers.com by Ancestry.* Accessed January 3, 2023. https://www.newspapers.com.

[739] Fox, *The Garden Spot of the Mississippi Valley,* 35.

[740] *Biographical and Historical Memoirs of Northeast Arkansas*, 489-490; *Blytheville Courier News*, January 26, 1937, "Death Claims John B. Driver, County Pioneer."

[741] William Hector certificate 1926, Sam Hector, certificate 1892. Historical Documents, Maps and More, Swamp Lands (1850), Entry Books, Book 1, North-East, 428-429, State of Arkansas, Commissioner of State Lands, History and Archives. Accessed August 23, 2022. https://www.cosl.org.

[742] William Hector and July Ann Hector to Samuel Hector, Deed, July 15, 1857, filed and recorded May 15, 1885, Record Book 13, 402-403, Mississippi County Osceola District, Osceola, Arkansas. Deed Records 1884, Deed Records 1886-1888, Deed Records 1884-1886, *Family Search*. Accessed January 11, 2023. https://www.familysearch.org. This land was the south half of the southwest quarter of Section 12, Township 14 North, Range 9 East.

[743] Proof of Loss deeds were issued for swamp land certificates 2857, 2027, 1927, 1926, 1885, 1886, and 1887 (Chapter 7, Endnote 410). The reissued deeds are listed as forfeited. William Hector, Arkansas State Land Records, *Arkansas State Archives*, Little Rock, Arkansas.

[744] Proof of Loss certificate 2857, William Hector, Arkansas State Land Records, *Arkansas State Archives*, Little Rock, Arkansas.

[745] *The Osceola Times,* Osceola, Arkansas, "Personal and Local," October 10, 1903, 1. *Newspapers.com by Ancestry.* Accessed December 29, 2022. https://www.newspapers.com.

[746] W. I. Wells signed as a witness to a deed (see Endnote 748) between his mother, Sam, and W.B. Flanigan, October 1903. Irvin was listed as the son of Dora Wells (Dosha or Docia) in the 1900 New Madrid census. "1900 United States Federal Census," New Madrid, Missouri; Roll: 877, 9; Enumeration District: 0075; *Ancestry.com,* Ancestry.com Operations Inc., 2004. Accessed September 13, 2022. https://www.ancestry.com.

[747] Docia Mager, District 62, New Madrid, Missouri; Roll: 408; 274b, *Ancestry.com.* "1850 United States Federal Census," Ancestry.com Operations, Inc., 2009, Lehi, Utah, Images reproduced by *FamilySearch*, Original data: Seventh Census of the United States, 1850; (National Archives Microfilm Publication M432, 1009 rolls); Records of the Bureau of the Census, Record Group 29; National Archives, Washington, D.C. Accessed September 13, 2022. https://www.ancestry.com.

[748] Docia Wells and Sam Hector to W.B. Flanigan, Quit claim deed, Chancery Court Records, Mississippi County, Arkansas, 1865-1941, Vol. 2, Deed Record, Vol. 27, 463, Mississippi County, Osceola District, *FamilySearch.* Accessed September 12, 2022. https://www.familysearch.org. The sale was for $5,000 in hand.

[749] W. B. Flanigan was the father of Mabel Edrington, author of the *History of Mississippi County, Arkansas.* He moved to the county in 1903. He became a title lawyer and gave his time to real estate transactions and the clearing of land titles. Edrington, *History of Mississippi County*, 281.

[750] Samuel Hector to W.B. Flanigan, Quit Claim Deed, Recorded July 9, 1903, Record Book 27, 413, *FamilySearch.* Accessed September 12, 2022. https://www.familysearch.org. Lands were the south half and the west half of the northwest quarter of Section 14, Township 12 North, Range 8 East; the West half of Section 22, Township 12 North, Range 8 East; and the East half of Section One, Township 14 North, Range 9 East.

[751] Hector, Samuel to W.J. Lamb, Deed, Recorded April 9, 1903, Record Book 27, 344, *FamilySearch.* Accessed September 12, 2022. https://www.familysearch.org.

The land was the Northwest quarter of the Northwest quarter of Section 14, Township 13 North, Range 9 East.

[752] Mosby, Joe, "Big Lake Wars," *CALS Encyclopedia of Arkansas*. Accessed September 15, 2022. https://encyclopediaofarkansas.net/entries/big-lake-wars-7591/.

[753] "Big Lake National Wildlife Refuge," About Us, U.S. Fish and Wildlife Service. Accessed August 4, 2922. https://www.fws.gov/refuge/big-lake/about-us.

[754] "Big Lake Wilderness," Wilderness Connect website. Accessed March 17, 2022. https://wilderness.net.

[755] "Big Lake National Wildlife Refuge," State of Arkansas Parks. Accessed March 17, 2022. https://stateparks.com/big_lake_national_wildlife_refuge_in_arkansas.html

Bibliography

Abstracts of Cape Girardeau County Deeds, Books A/B-F, 1796-1826, Cape Girardeau County Genealogical Society, Jackson, Missouri, 2000, 152, Abstracted by Bill Eddleman and Jane Randol Jackson.

Allsopp, Fred W., *Folklore of Romantic Arkansas*, Vol. 1, The Grolier Society, 1931.

American State Papers, House of Representatives, 24th Congress, First Session, Public Lands: Vol. 8, 303.

"Anthropology," *The American Naturalist,* Vol. 13, Press of McCalla & Stavely, Philadelphia, Pennsylvania, 1879. Accessed April 13, 2022. https://books.google.com.

"Appendix Q, A Memoir to accompany the map of Mississippi County, Arkansas," 229-235, Compiled by Frank L. James, MD, PhD, for the Mississippi River Commission, 1881, *Letter from the Secretary of War: Transmitting, in Compliance with the Requirements of the River and Harbor Act of August, 1882, a Report of the Mississippi River Commission with Accompanying Papers and Maps*, United States. Mississippi River Commission, U.S. Government Printing Office, January 1883. https://books.google.com.

Arkansas Confederate Pensions, 1901-1929, Hector, J.A., *FamilySearch*, Mississippi County, Arkansas. Accessed September 12, 2022. http://FamilySearch.org.

Arkansas, Death Certificates, 1914-1969, Arkansas Department of Vital Records; Little Rock: 1940; Roll: 5, *Ancestry.com*. Lehi, Utah, USA: Ancestry.com Operations, Inc., 2019. Accessed September 7, 2022. https://www.ancestry.com.

Arkansas Democrat, Little Rock, Arkansas, "Jonesboro Plans to Preserve Rich Lore of East Arkansas," May 14, 1922, 2. *Newspapers.com by Ancestry.* Accessed December 29, 2022. https://www.newspapers.com.

"Arkansas Mounds," *Publications of the Arkansas Historical Association*, Vol. 4, 390-448, Arkansas Historical Association, Little Rock, Arkansas, 1917.

Arkansas: Miller-Monroe; Record Group 28: Records of the Post Office Department, 1773-1971, Reports of Site Locations, 1837-1950; *National Archives* at College Park, College Park, Maryland, online version available through the Archival Research Catalog, ARC identifier 68211197. Accessed March 16, 2022. www.archives.gov.

Arkansas Probate Records, 1817-1979. Administration and Guardian Bonds and letters 1863-1921, Vol. A-B, Images 6, 15, 26, 37, and Probate Record 1857-1887, Vol. A-B, Images 34, 47, 60, 90, Wittsburg, Cross County, Arkansas, *FamilySearch*. Accessed July 22, 2021. http://FamilySearch.org.

Arkansas Railroad Commission, *Annual Report of the Railroad Commission of the State of Arkansas,* United States, Thompson Lithograph and Print. Company, 1904, 200. Google Books. Accessed March 19, 2022. https://books.google.com.

Arkansas Township Digest, Minor Civil Divisions, 1820-1990, compiled by Desmond Walls Allen, Arkansas Research, Conway, Arkansas, 1994.

"A Treaty of Amity and Friendship," United States Office of Indian Affairs, Central Superintendency, St. Louis, Missouri, Miscellaneous letters and documents,

1813-1825, Vol. 2, 93-95. *Kansas Historical Society*, Kansas Memory. Accessed April 2, 2022. www.kansasmemory.org.

Atkinson, J. H., and Elliott Fletcher. "A Civil War Letter of Captain Elliott Fletcher Jr.," *The Arkansas Historical Quarterly*, Vol. 22, No. 1, 49-54, 1963.

Baird, David W., Editor, *Years of Discontent: Doctor Frank L. James in Arkansas, 1877-1878*, Memphis State University Press, Memphis, Tennessee, 1977.

"Batesville, Arkansas," *Wikipedia,* Wikimedia Foundation, Inc. Accessed April 4, 2022. https://en.wikipedia.org/wiki/Batesville,_Arkansas.

"Big Lake, National Wildlife Refuge," U.S. Fish & Wildlife Service. Accessed March 28, 2022. https://www.fws.gov/refuge/big-lake.

"Big Lake National Wildlife Refuge," About Us, U.S. Fish and Wildlife Service. Accessed August 4, 2922. https://www.fws.gov/refuge/big-lake/about-us.

"Big Lake Wilderness," *Wilderness Connect* website. Accessed March 17, 2022. https://wilderness.net.

Biographical and Historical Memoirs of Northeast Arkansas: Comprising a Condensed History of the State, a Number of Biographies of Distinguished Citizens of the Same, a Brief Descriptive History of Each of the Counties Named Herein, and Numerous Biographical Sketches of the Prominent Citizens of Such Counties. The Goodspeed Publishing Company, 1889.

Biographical and Historical Memoirs of Western Arkansas: Comprising a Condensed History of the State, a Number of Biographies of Distinguished Citizens of the Same, a Brief Descriptive History of Each of the Counties Mentioned, and Numerous Biographical Sketches of the Citizens of Such Counties, 118, A Southern Publishing Company (Chicago, Illinois), 1891, Southern Historical Press. https://books.google.com.

"Boyer, Francis and Charley, James Jr. by McGee, M.W. v. Dively, Michael admin of will of Gillis, William (Deceased) and Donnelly, Bernard and Black, F.M., executor of the will of Troost, Mary A. (Deceased," Missouri Supreme Court Historical Database, 58 MO 510, Box 1112, Folder 4, *Missouri Digital Heritage.* Accessed January 13, 2025. https://www.sos.mo.gov/mdh/.

Bowen, Charles - Age [Blank], Year: 1865 - Miscellaneous, Arkansas, A-I, 7, Compiled Service Records of Confederate Soldiers Who Served in Organizations from the State of Arkansas. National Archives and Records Administration, Washington, D.C. Accessed February 8, 2020. https://catalog.archives.gov.

Bowers, Annalea K., Leah D. Lucio, David W. Clark, Susan P. Rakow, and Gary A. Heidt, (2001) "Early History of the Wolf, Black Bear, and Mountain Lion in Arkansas," *Journal of the Arkansas Academy of Science:* Vol. 55, Article 4, 22-27. Accessed November 8, 2022. Downloaded PDF. https://scholarworks.uark.edu/jaas/vol55/iss1.

Buffaloe, W.T., "'Uncle France' Varner," *Arkansas Historical Quarterly*, Vol. 20, No. 2, 161-163. Summer 1961.

Buffaloe, W.T., "'Uncle France' Varner," *The Craighead County Historical Quarterly*, Vol. 2, No. 2, 4-14, Spring 1964.

Bunch, James, Record Group 109: War Department Collection of Confederate Records, 1825 - 1927 Series: Carded Records Showing Military Service of Soldiers Who Fought in Confederate Organizations, 1903 - 1927. Missouri, Bunch, James, Age 30, Year: 1862, Seventh Cavalry, A-D. Images 1-10. ARC

Identifier 31973585, Fold3 2016. Accessed August 12, 2022. https://catalog.archives.gov.

Burr, David H, and John Arrowsmith. *Map of Mississippi, Louisiana & Arkansas exhibiting the post offices, post roads, canals, rail roads, &c.* [London: J. Arrowsmith, 1839] Map. Accessed July 31, 2022. Library of Congress. https://www.loc.gov/resource/g3935.rr001340/?r=0.572,0.028,0.178,0.085,0.

Butrick, Daniel S., *The Journal of Rev. Daniel S. Butrick, May 19, 1838, to April 1, 1839*, Cherokee Removal, The Trail of Tears Association, Oklahoma Chapter, The Association for Core Texts and Courses, Saint Mary's College of California. Accessed April 6, 2022. PDF. https://www.coretexts.org/old/cherokeelessons/unit5/downloads/Butrick%20Journal%20cherokee_removal_1.pdf.

Caldwell, Norman W. "Fort Massac: Since 1805." *Journal of the Illinois State Historical Society (1908-1984)*, Vol. 44, No. 1, 47-60. University of Illinois Press, 1951. http://www.jstor.org/stable/40189112.

"Cape Girardeau, Missouri, United States Records," images, Court Records V, A-D, 1815-1824, *FamilySearch*. Accessed December 5, 2024. https://www.familysearch.org/en/united-states/.

Capooth, Wayne, MD, *Red Letter Days*, Gateway Press, Inc., Baltimore, Maryland, 1995, 121-137.

"Captain Bowen Tells of Early Days in Mississippi County." *Delta Historical Review*, Fall 1996, 4-13.

Carter, Clarence Edwin, ed., "Cherokee Council to Reuben Lewis and William Bradford," February 10, 1820, The Territorial papers of the United States, Vol. 19, 1819-1825, 151-152, *Hathi Trust Digital Library*. Accessed April 4, 2022. https://www.hathitrust.org.

Carter, Clarence Edwin, editor, "William Lovely to the Cherokee," The Territorial papers of the United States, Vol. 14, 1806-1814, 721, *Hathi Trust Digital Library*. Accessed April 4, 2022. https://www.hathitrust.org.

Carter, Clarence Edwin, ed., "William Russel to Delegate Hempstead," The Territorial papers of the United States, V.14, 1806-14, 720. Accessed April 4, 2022. *Hathi Trust Digital Library*. https://www.hathitrust.org.

Chicago Tribune, Chicago, Illinois, April 19, 1862, 1, *Newspapers.com by Ancestry*. Accessed April 11, 2024. https://www.newspapers.com.

"Chickamauga Cherokee," *Wikipedia*, Wikimedia Foundation, Inc. Accessed January 5, 2021. http://en.wikipedia.org/wiki/Chickamauga_Cherokee.

Childs, H. Terry, and Charles H. McNutt, "Chickasawba," *The Arkansas Archaeologist*, Bulletin of the Arkansas Archaeological Society, Vol. 48 for 2008, Published in 2009.

Childs, H. Terry, and Charles H. McNutt, "Hernando de Soto's Route From Chicaca Through Northeast Arkansas: A Suggestion," *Southeastern Archaeology*, Vol. 28, No. 2, 2009, 165-183. Accessed, downloaded August 31, 2021. *Academia*, https://www.academia.edu/13811566/Hernando_De_Sotos_Route_from_Chicaca_through_Northeast_Arkansas_a_Suggestion.

Chilitica, Indian Chief to John Miller, Governor of the state of Missouri, Memorial, October 1831, William Clark Papers, *Kansas State Historical Society*, Vol. 6, 314-316.

Chisholm, John D., Cherokee Village on the River Arkansas, the 23d May, 1814, May 23, 1814, Correspondence and Miscellaneous Records, Records of the

Cherokee Indian Agency in Tennessee, 1801-1835, M208, 120-122. Accessed November 5, 2018. https://www.fold3.com.

Chouteau, P., Jr. to Godfrey Lesieur and his son G.A. Lesieur, Point Pleasant, Missouri, Letters, LS, October 14, 1850 to January 29, 1851, Lesieur Collection, Godfrey Lesieur Papers, *Missouri History Museum Archives*, St. Louis, Missouri.

Chouteau, P., Jr. & Co., St. Louis, Mo. to Mr. Godfrey Lesieur, Point Pleasant, Mo., Letter, February 6, 1849, Lesieur Collection, Godfrey Lesieur Papers, *Missouri History Museum Archives*, St. Louis, Missouri.

Chouteau, P., Jr. & Co., St. Louis, Mo., to Mr. Godfrey Lesieur, Point Pleasant, Mo., Letter, March 9, 1849, Lesieur Collection, Godfrey Lesieur Papers, *Missouri History Museum Archives*, St. Louis, Missouri.

Chouteau, P., Jr. & Co., St. Louis, Mo. to Godfrey Lesieur, Point Pleasant, Mo., Letter, December 31, 1849, Lesieur Collection, Godfrey Lesieur Papers, *Missouri History Museum Archives*, St. Louis, Missouri.

Clark, William, Diary, Kansas State Historical Society, United States Office of Indian Affairs, Central Superintendency, St. Louis, Missouri, Vol. 31, 123-124. *Kansas Memory*. Accessed March 26, 2022. https://www.kansasmemory.org.

Clark, Wm., Superintendency of Indian Affairs, St. Louis, Mo., to Gen. Geo Gibson, Commissary Genl. Of Substinence, Washington, D.C., Letter, August 5, 1835. *The Foreman Transcripts*, Commissioner of Indian Affairs, Seven Volumes, Vol. 1, 59, Western Superintendency, Miscellaneous and schools. Accessed July 28, 2022. https://www.okhistory.org/research/foremantranscripts.

Clark, Governor William, St. Louis, Missouri, to Governor James Miller, Osage Indian Affairs, Transcript, November 10, 1820, L.C. Gulley collection, *Arkansas State Archives,* Little Rock, Arkansas. Accessed April 4, 2024.

Clay, Floyd M., PhD, *A Century on the Mississippi, A History of the Memphis District U.S. Army Corps of Engineers 1876-1976*, U.S. Army Corps of Engineers, Memphis District, January 1976.

Clements, Derek Allen, "Wittsburg (Cross County)," *CALS Encyclopedia of Arkansas*. Accessed August 24, 2022. https://encyclopediaofarkansas.net/entries/wittsburg-cross-county-6202/.

Christ, Mark K., "Engagement at Plum Point Bend," *CALS Encyclopedia of Arkansas*. Accessed April 11, 2024. https://encyclopediaofarkansas.net/entries/engagement-at-plum-point-bend-15748/.

"Colt M1861 Navy," *Wikipedia*, Wikimedia Foundation Inc. Accessed March 10, 2020. https://en.wikipedia.org/wiki/Colt_M1861_Navy.

Combined Personal Tax Assessment Lists of Greene County, Arkansas, 1834-1840, 3-8, compiled by James Logan Morgan, Arkansas Records Association, Newport, Arkansas, 1972.

Cooke, Wells Woodbridge, *Distribution & Migration of Warblers, Ducks & Geese, Herons, Shore-Birds, Rails*, United States, U.S. Government Printing Office, 1904. https://books.google.com.

"Copies of Accounts, Receipts And Disbursements, 1801-20," Records of the Cherokee Indian Agency in Tennessee, 1801-1835, 114. Accessed November 30, 2020. https://www.fold3.com.

"Correspondence on the Subject of the Emigration of Indians, between the 30th November, 1831, and 27th December, 1833, with Abstracts of Expenditures

By Disbursing Agents," GovInfo, Congressional Serial Set, 23rd Congress, No. 248, Senate Document No. 512. Accessed December 7, 2024. Downloaded PDF. https://www.govinfo.gov/app/collection/serialset.

"Correspondence and Miscellaneous Records, 1813," Records of the Cherokee Indian Agency in Tennessee, 1801-1835, 120. Accessed January 2, 2021. https://www.fold3.com.

Crowley, H.B., "History of Greene County, as written in 1906 by H.B. Crowley," Fourth Installment. *The Greene County Historical Quarterly*, Vols. 1-3, 1965-1967, Winter 1967, Vol. 3, No. 1, 19-24, *The Greene County Historical Society*, Paragould, Arkansas.

Crowley, *H.B., History of Greene County*, as written in 1906, Ninth Edition. Transcribed by Sandy Hardin. Accessed April 26, 2022. http://www.argenweb.net/greene/AUTHORSSHOWCASE/greenecohbhcrh.htm.

Crowley, Hon. Benjamin, "Reprint of a Historical Writing on Greene County," Spring, 1966, Vol. 2, No. 2, 12-16, *The Greene County Historical Quarterly*, Vols. 1-3, 1965-1967, Paragould, Arkansas.

"Crowley's Ridge," *Wikipedia*, Wikipedia Foundation. Last modified January 25, 2022. Accessed August 1, 2022. https://en.wikipedia.org/w/index.php?title=Crowley%27s_Ridge&oldid=1067926854.

Correspondence relative to St. Francis Indians and licenses to trade, Sample Invoice to be filled out in applying for license to trade with the Indians, 1826. Richard Graham Papers, Missouri History Museum, *Missouri Historical Society*, St. Louis, Missouri.

"Death of Dr. Frank L. James," *The National Druggist*, Vol. 37, 189-191, June 1907, St. Louis, Missouri, Henry R. Strong, Publisher. Accessed April 19, 2024. https://books.google.com.

DeBlack, Thomas A., "Civil War through Reconstruction, 1861 through 1874," *CALS Encyclopedia of Arkansas*. Accessed March 6, 2020. https://encyclopediaofarkansas.net/entries/civil-war-through-reconstruction-1861-through-1874-388/.

Dew, Lee A. "The J.L.C. and E.R.R. and the Opening of the 'Sunk Lands' of Northeast Arkansas." *The Arkansas Historical Quarterly*, Vol. 27, No. 1, 22-39, Arkansas Historical Association, 1968. Accessed August 4, 2022. https://doi.org/10.2307/40018324.

"Documents relating to the negotiation of an unratified treaty of August 9, 1822, between the Cherokee and Osage Indians," National Archives, August 9, 1822, 1-6. *University of Wisconsin Digital Collections* (UWDC), The History Collection. Accessed April 2, 2022. http://digital.library.wisc.edu/1711.dl/History.Unrat1822no4.

Dooley, J.E., Record Group 109: War Department Collection of Confederate Records, 1825-1927 Series: Carded Records Showing Military Service of Soldiers Who Fought in Confederate Organizations, 1903-1927 File Unit: [Missouri] Dooley, J E – Age [Blank], Year: 1861 - State Guard, Cu-E, Images 1-3. ARC Identifier 32143364, Fold3, National Archives Catalog. Accessed December 7, 2019. https://catalog.archives.gov.

Dougan, Michael B., *Arkansas Odyssey, The Saga of Arkansas from Prehistoric Times to present*, Rose Publishing Company, Inc., Little Rock, Arkansas, 1994.

Douglass, Robert Sidney, AB, LLB, *History of Southeast Missouri, A Narrative Account of its Historical Progress, Its People and its Principal Interests*. The Lewis Publishing Company, Chicago, Illinois, 1912.

"Dragging Canoe," *Wikipedia*, Wikimedia Foundation, Inc. Accessed April 3, 2022. https://en.wikipedia.org/wiki/Dragging_Canoe.

Draper, Lyman Copeland, Draper Manuscripts, Draper Mss., 1-5YY129, (microfilm edition) *State Historical Society of Wisconsin.*

"Eaker Site," *Wikipedia*, Wikimedia Foundation, Inc. Accessed March 28, 2022. http://en.wikipedia.org/wiki/Eaker_Site.

"Early Lutheranism in Missouri," *Theological Quarterly*, Volume 3, 319-353. Concordia Publishing House, St. Louis, Missouri, 1899. Google Books. https://books.google.com.

Eastern Cherokee Applications, 8/29/1906-5/26/1909, Record Group 123: Records of the U.S. Court of Claims, 1835-1984; M1104. National Archives at College Park, College Park, Maryland. Accessed March 19-20, 2022, April 3, 2024. www.archives.gov.

East, John, Confederate Soldier from the State of Mississippi, Twenty-fifth Infantry. Record Group 109, War Department Collection of Confederate Records, 1825-1927, Roll 319, Carded Records Showing Military Service of Soldiers who fought in Confederate Organizations, 1903-1927. ARC Identifier 145379110, Fold3 2019. Accessed August 14, 2022. https://catalog.archives.gov.

East, John, Ninth Infantry, D-G, Record Group 109, War Department Collection of Confederate Records, 1825-1927, Roll 319, Carded Records Showing Military Service of Soldiers who fought in Confederate Organizations, 1903-1927. ARC Identifier 30357535, Fold3. Accessed August 14, 2022. https://catalog.archives.gov.

Early, Ann M., "Treaty of Council Oaks," *CALS Encyclopedia of Arkansas*. Accessed April 4, 2022. https://encyclopediaofarkansas.net/entries/treaty-of-council-oaks-4833/.

Eaves, Erica, "Richard Searcy (1794-1832)," *CALS Encyclopedia of Arkansas*. Accessed April 1, 2024. https://encyclopediaofarkansas.net.

Eddlemon, Sherida K., New Madrid County, Missouri, Delinquent Tax List, 1833, Capitol Fire Documents, Box 16, Folder 1062. *Missouri Genealogical Records and Abstracts, Vol. 2: 1752-1839*, Heritage Books, Inc., Bowie, Maryland, 1990.

Edrington, Mable F., *History of Mississippi County, Arkansas*, Ocala Star-Banner, Ocala, Florida, 1962.

"1830 United States Federal Census," *Ancestry.com*. New Madrid, Missouri, Series: M19; Roll: 73; Family History Library Film: 0014854, Provo, Utah, USA: Ancestry.com Operations, Inc., 2010. Images reproduced by FamilySearch. Original data: Fifth Census of the United States, 1830. (NARA microfilm publication M19, 201 rolls). Records of the Bureau of the Census, Record Group 29. National Archives, Washington, D.C. Accessed January 3, 2025. https://www.ancestry.com.

"1830 United States Federal Census," Cape Girardeau, Missouri, Provo, Utah, U.S.A., *Ancestry*, Ancestry.com Operations, Inc., 2010. Images reproduced by FamilySearch. Original data: Fifth Census of the United States, 1830. (NARA microfilm publication M19, 201 rolls). Records of the Bureau of the Census,

Record Group 29. National Archives, Washington, D.C. Accessed August 2, 2022. https://www.ancestry.com.

"1850 United States Federal Census," Big Lake, Mississippi, Arkansas, Roll: 28, *Ancestry*. Ancestry.com Operations, Inc., 2009, Lehi, Utah. https://www.ancestry.com.

"1850 United States Federal Census," Ancestry.com Operations, Inc., 2009, Lehi, Utah, Images reproduced by *FamilySearch*, Original data: Seventh Census of the United States, 1850; (National Archives Microfilm Publication M432, 1009 rolls); Records of the Bureau of the Census, Record Group 29; National Archives, Washington, D.C. Accessed September 13, 2022. https://www.ancestry.com.

"1860 United States Federal Census," Big Lake, Mississippi, Arkansas; Roll: M653_46, *Ancestry*, Ancestry.com Operations, Inc., Provo, Utah, 2009. Accessed April 14, 2022. https://www.ancestry.com.

"1860 United States Federal Census," Little River, Mississippi, Arkansas; Roll: M653_46; 740. *Ancestry*, Ancestry.com Operations, Inc., Provo, Utah, 2009. Accessed April 14, 2022. https://www.ancestry.com.

1860 United States Federal Census, Mitchel, Poinsett, Arkansas; Roll: M653_48, 566; Family History Library Film: 803048, *Ancestry.com*. 1860 United States Federal Census, Provo, Utah, USA: Ancestry.com Operations, Inc., 2009. Accessed April 14, 2022. https://www.ancestry.com.

"1860 U.S. Federal Census - Slave Schedules," Thomas S. James, Mobile Ward 7, Mobile, Alabama, The National Archives in Washington, D.C.; Washington, D.C., USA; Eighth Census of the United States 1860; Series Number: M653; Record Group: Records of the Bureau of the Census; Record Group Number: 29. *Ancestry.com*. Lehi, Utah, USA: Ancestry.com Operations Inc., 2010. Accessed January 10, 2025. https://www.ancestry.com.

"1870 United States Federal Census," Big Lake, Mississippi, Arkansas; Roll M593 58, *Ancestry*, Ancestry.com Operations, Inc., 2009. Accessed March 21, 2022. https://www.ancestry.com.

"1880 United States Federal Census," Big Lake, Mississippi, Arkansas, Roll 51, Enumeration District 201, Lehi, Utah. Accessed March 21, 2022. https://www.ancestry.com.

"1880 United States Federal Census," Big Lake, Mississippi, Arkansas; Roll 685, Enumeration District 47, *Ancestry,* Ancestry.com Operations, Inc., 2009. Accessed March 21, 2022. https://www.ancestry.com.

"1880 United States Federal Census," Clay, Dunklin, Missouri; Roll: 685; Enumeration District: 047, *Ancestry.com*, Lehi, Utah, USA: Ancestry.com Operations Inc., 2010. Accessed August 22, 2022. https://www.ancestry.com.

"Felix Valle, State Historic Site." Accessed April 2, 2022. https://www.visitstegen.com/felix-valle-state-historic-site/.

"15th Arkansas Infantry Regiment (Josey's)," *Wikipedia*, The Free Encyclopedia, Wikimedia Foundation, Inc. Accessed March 2, 2020. https://en.wikipedia.org/wiki/15thArkansas_Infantry_Regiment_(Josey%27s).

Fletcher, James, letter to the *Pittsburgh Gazette* (1812), February 14, 1812, Eyewitness Accounts, New Madrid Compendium, The University of Memphis, *Center for Earthquake Research and Information*. Memphis, Tennessee. Accessed September 25, 2013. https://www.memphis.edu/ceri/compendium/.

Flora, S.D., "The Great Flood of 1844 Along the Kansas and Marais Des Cygnes Rivers," *The Kansas Historical Quarterly*, Vol. XX, No. 2, May 1951, 73-81, Published by *Kansas State Historical Society*, Topeka, Kansas. https://www.kansasmemory.org.

Ford, Clyde, "Poinsett County," *CALS Encyclopedia of Arkansas*. Accessed April 5, 2022. https://encyclopediaofarkansas.net/entries/poinsett-county-799/.

Foreman, Carolyn Thomas, "Dutch, the Cherokee," *The Chronicles of Oklahoma*, Vol. 27, No. 3, 252-255, Autumn 1949; Oklahoma City, Oklahoma, The Gateway to Oklahoma History. https://gateway.okhistory.org.

Foreman, Grant, *Indians and Pioneers, The Story of the American Southwest Before 1830*, Yale University Press, 1930.

Fox, J.A., *The Garden Spot of the Mississippi Valley in the St. Francis Basin of Arkansas*, (Edited and published by J.A. Fox, assistant engineer, St. Francis Levee Board, Osceola, Arkansas), 1902.

Gause, Lucien Coatsworth, Papers in the Case of L.C. Gause Vs Asa Hodges: First Congressional District of Arkansas, U.S. Government Printing Office, January 1873, 236. Accessed August 13, 2022. https://play.google.com/store/books/details?id=oZ0mAQAAMAAJ&rdid=book-oZ0mAQAAMAAJ&rdot=1.

"General Abstract of All Disbursements or Expenditures made by Pierre Menard, Indian Sub-Agent at Kaskaskia from the first October 1831 to the 30th September, 1832, both dates inclusive," *House Documents, Otherwise Publ. as Executive Documents:* 13th Congress, 2d Session-49th Congress, 1st Session. United States: n.p., 1832, No. 33, 135, H.R. Doc. No. 137, 22nd Cong., 2nd Sess. Accessed December 7, 2024. https://books.google.com.

Gerstäcker, Friedrich. *Wild Sports in the Far West*. 365-366, United States, Crosby, Nichols, 1859, 365-366. Accessed April 4, 2022. https://books.google.com.

Glenn, Robert A., "The Osage War," *Missouri Historical Review*, Vol. 14, No. 2, 201-210, January 1920, State Historical Society of Missouri. Accessed January 1, 2025. https://digital.shsmo.org/digital/collection/mhr.

Goodspeed, Weston Arthur, editor, *The Province and the States: A History of the Province of Louisiana under France and Spain, and of the Territories and States of the United States Formed Therefrom,* Vol. 1, Western Historical Association, Louisiana, 1904.

Graham, R., ALS, to Col. P. Menard, Letter, June 28, 1825, Kaskaskia, Illinois, Richard Graham Papers, Missouri Historical Society, *Missouri History Museum*, St. Louis, Missouri.

Graham, R., DS, U.S. Indian Agent, to Francois Lesieur and son, License to trade for one year with the Shawnees and Delawares on St. Francis River, November 17, 1824, Godfrey Lesieur Papers, *Missouri History Museum Archive*, St. Louis, Missouri.

Graham, R. to Adam Rittenhouse, Letter, April 9, 1825, Richard Graham Papers, *Missouri History Museum*, Missouri Historical Society, St. Louis, Missouri.

Graham, R. U.S. Indian Agent, to Francois Lesieur and son, License to trade for one year with the Shawnees and Delawares on St. Francis River, November 17, 1824, Godfrey Lesieur Papers, *Missouri History Museum Archive*, St. Louis, Missouri.

Graham, R., St. Louis, to Capt. Samuel G. Hopkins, New Madrid, Mo., A.L.S. Letter, February 16, 1826, Richard Graham Papers, Missouri History Museum, *Missouri Historical Society*, St. Louis, Missouri.

Graham, R. to Col. P. Menard, Kaskaskia, Ill., A.L.S. Letter, June 28, 1825, Richard Graham Papers, Missouri History Museum, *Missouri Historical Society*, St. Louis, Missouri.

Gray, Robert, *The McGavock Family: A Genealogical History of James McGavock and His Descendants from 1760 to 1903.* United States: W. E. Jones, 1903. Accessed December 6, 2024. https://books.google.com.

"Great Comet of 1811," *Wikipedia,* Wikimedia Foundation, Inc. Accessed April 1, 2022. https://en.m.wikipedia.org/wiki/Great_Comet_of_1811.

"Great Flood of 1844," *Wikipedia*, Wikimedia Foundation, Inc. Last edited, February 20, 2022. Accessed August 12, 2022. https://en.wikipedia.org/wiki/Great_Flood_of_1844.

Griffith, Nancy, "Oil Trough, (Independence County)," *CALS Encyclopedia of Arkansas.* Accessed July 28, 2022. https://encyclopediaofarkansas.net/entries/oil-trough-independence-county-5603/.

Grisham, Cindy, "Tyronza River," *CALS Encyclopedia of Arkansas.* Accessed July 29, 2022. https://encyclopediaofarkansas.net/entries/tyronza-river-7456/.

Guion, W. Bowling, U.S. Civil Engineer, "A report of the survey of the St. Francis River as called for by a resolution of the Senate of the 28th of Feb. 1837," Public Documents Printed By Order Of The Senate Of The United States, Second Session Of The Twenty-Fourth Congress Begun And Held At The City Of Washington In Three Volumes, Volume III, 1837. Accessed August 2, 2022. https://books.google.com.

Hale, Ruth C., "Black Hawk War of 1872," *CALS Encyclopedia of Arkansas.* Accessed August 13, 2022. https://encyclopediaofarkansas.net/entries/black-hawk-war-of-1872-5282/.

Hamblen, Mack, "Greene County," *CALS Encyclopedia of Arkansas.* Accessed August 12, 2022. https://encyclopediaofarkansas.net/entries/greene-county-772/.

Harmon, Margaret Cline, "Gen. N.W. Watkins – Missouri Statesman And a Lawyer of 60 Years active practice. Accessed October 22, 2020. http://www.rootsweb.ancestry.com/~moscott/articles-cem/page-001.htm.

Harrison, Robert W., and Walter M. Kollmorgen. "Land Reclamation in Arkansas under the Swamp Land Grant of 1850." *The Arkansas Historical Quarterly*, Vol. 6, No. 4, 1947, 369-418. Accessed August 29, 2022. *JSTOR.* https://doi.org/10.2307/40027472.

Haveman, Christopher D., "The Removal of the Creek Indians from the Southeast, 1828-1838," dissertation, 2009, Auburn University's database of Master's theses and PhD Dissertations, Auburn University, Alabama. Accessed April 6, 2022. Downloaded PDF. https://etd.auburn.edu/handle/10415/2184.

Hecter, [sic] William A., Record Group 109: War Department Collection of Confederate Records, 1825-1927 Series: Carded Records Showing Military Service of Soldiers Who Fought in Confederate Organizations, 1903-1927 File Unit: [Missouri] Hecter, William A - Age [Blank], Year: [BLANK] - State Guard, H-Hi, *National Archives* Catalog, Images 1, 2. Fold3 2016, ARC Identifier 32147063. Accessed December 7, 2019. https://catalog.archives.gov.

Hector, Gilbert, Byrd Township, Territorial Taxes in the county of Cape Girardeau, C3677, Cape Girardeau County, Missouri, Tax Lists, 1812, 1814, *Missouri Historical Society*, St. Louis, Missouri.

Hector, James A., and Parlee Gardner, August 30, 1896, Marriage Bond, Marriage Records, Book 9, 35, Mississippi County Court House, Blytheville, Arkansas.

Hector, Joseph A., Record Group 109, War Department Collection of Confederate Records, 1825-1927 Series: Carded Records Showing Military Service of Soldiers Who Fought in Confederate Organizations, 1903-1927 File Unit: [Missouri] Hector, Joseph Alford - Age 28, Year: 1862 - Seventh Cavalry, E-K. ARC Identifier 31975210, Fold3. Accessed August 12, 2022. https://catalog.archives.gov.

Hector, Melisa Ann, Sam W. Bunch, April 19, 1874, married by H.T. Blythe, Methodist minister. Marriage Records, Mississippi County Courthouse, Blytheville, Arkansas. *FamilySearch*, Arkansas, County Marriages, 1837-1957, 29. Accessed March 9, 2021. https://www.familysearch.org.

Hector, Samuel to W.J. Lamb, Deed, Recorded April 9, 1903, Record Book 27, 344, *FamilySearch*. Accessed September 12, 2022. https://www.familysearch.org.

Hector, Samuel to W.B. Flanigan, Quit Claim Deed, Recorded July 9, 1903, Record Book 27, 413, *FamilySearch*. Accessed September 12, 2022. https://www.familysearch.org.

Hector, William, and July Ann Hector to Samuel Hector, Deed, July 15, 1857, filed and recorded May 15, 1885, Record Book 13, 402-403, Mississippi County, Osceola District, Osceola, Arkansas. Deed Records 1884, Deed Records 1886-1888, Deed Records 1884-1886, *Family Search*. Accessed January 11, 2023. https://www.familysearch.org.

Hector, William, Arkansas State Land Records, *Arkansas State Archives*, Little Rock, Arkansas.

Hector, William, "Missouri U.S., Wills and Probate Records," 1766-1988, Record of Administrators Bonds, Letters, Vol. 1, 1872-1904, 45, Probate Court, Dunklin County, Missouri, *Ancestry.com*. Missouri, U.S., Wills and Probate Records, 1766-1988, Lehi, Utah, USA: Ancestry.com Operations, Inc., 2015. Accessed January 10, 2025. https://www.ancestry.com.

Heinritz, Susan Martinez, "Takatoka (1755?-1824)," *CALS Encyclopedia of Arkansas*. Accessed April 2, 2022. https://encyclopediaofarkansas.net/entries/takatoka-4288/.

Hempstead, Fay, *A Pictorial History of Arkansas, from Earliest Times to the Year 1890*, 91, *footnote*, N.D. Thompson Publishing Company, 1890, St. Louis and New York. Downloaded, Google Books. https://books.google.com/.

Hendricks, Nancy, "The 1927 Flood," *CALS Encyclopedia of Arkansas*. Accessed August 23, 2022. https://encyclopediaofarkansas.net/entries/flood-of-1927-2202/.

Herndon, Dallas Tabor, *Centennial History of Arkansas*, Vol. 1, 520-521, The S.J. Clarke Publishing Company, 1922. Accessed August 8, 2022. https://books.google.com.

Hildebrand, Samuel S., *Autobiography of Samuel S. Hildebrand, the Renowned Missouri 'Bushwacker' and Unconquerable Rob Roy of America, Being his Complete Confession*, Compiled by James W. Evans and A. Wendell Keith, MD, of St. Francois County, Missouri. State Times Book and Job Printing

House, Jefferson City, Missouri, 1870. Ebook, Project Gutenberg. https://www.gutenberg.org.

Historical Documents, Maps and More, Swamp Lands (1850), Entry Books, State of Arkansas, Commissioner of State Lands, History and Archives. Accessed April 14, 2022. https://www.cosl.org.

History of Boone County, Missouri: Written and Comp. from the Most Authentic Official and Private Sources; Including a History of Its Townships, Towns, and Villages. Together with a Condensed History of Missouri; the City of St. Louis... Biographical Sketches and Portraits of Prominent Citizens ..., 345-347, Western Historical Company, St. Louis, Missouri, 1882. https://books.google.com.

History of Southeast Missouri: embracing an historical account of the counties of Ste. Genevieve, St. Francois, Perry, Cape Girardeau, Bollinger, Madison, New Madrid, Pemiscot, Dunklin, Scott, Mississippi, Stoddard, Butler, Wayne and Iron, and including a department devoted to the preservation of personal, professional and private records, Goodspeed Publishing Company, 1888.

History of the Organization and Operations of the Board of Directors St. Francis Levee District of Arkansas 1893-1945, West Memphis, Arkansas. *Hathi Trust*. https://babel.hathitrust.org.

Hoig, Stan, *Jesse Chisholm: Ambassador of the Plains*, University of Oklahoma Press, Norman, Oklahoma, 2005.

Holcomb, Henry, Record Spotlight, *SEMO Record*, Dunklin County, Missouri Genealogical Society, Vol. 1-3, 1983-1985, Vol. 3, No. 1, January 1985.

Hopkins, Samuel Goode, New Madrid, Mo. to Major Richard Graham, Indian Agent at St. Louis, Mo., Letter, January 29, 1826, Richard Graham Papers, Missouri History Museum, *Missouri. Historical Society*, St. Louis, Missouri.

Hopkins, S.G., Point Pleasant, Mo. to Major Richard Graham, Agent for Indian Affairs, St. Louis, A.L.S. Letter, August 6, 1825, Richard Graham Papers, Missouri History Museum, *Missouri Historical Society*, St. Louis, Missouri.

Hopkins, S.G., New Madrid, Mo. to Genl. Wm. Clark, S.I.A., St. Louis, Mo., Letter, August 12, 1831, William Clark Papers, *Kansas State Historical Society*, Topeka, Kansas, Vol. 6, 273-279.

Hopkins, S.G., Point Pleasant, New Madrid County, Mo. to Richard Graham, Letter, February 4, 1826, Richard Graham Papers, Missouri History Museum, *Missouri Historical Society*, St. Louis, Missouri.

Houck, Louis, *A History of Missouri from its Earliest Explorations and Settlements Until the Admission of the State into the Union*, Volumes 1, II, R.R. Donnelley & Sons Company, Chicago, Illinois, 1908.

Houck, Louis, *The Spanish Regime in Missouri: A Collection of Papers and Documents Relating to Upper Louisiana Principally Within the Present Limits of Missouri During the Dominion of Spain, from the Archives of the Indies at Seville, Etc., Translated from the Original Spanish Into English, and Including Also Some Papers Concerning the Supposed Grant to Col. George Morgan at the Mouth of the Ohio*, 407 and 413. The Congressional Library. (1909). United States: R. R. Donnelley & sons Company. Accessed August 1, 2022. https://books.google.com.

Huddleston, Duane, "Some Indian Incidents Along White River 1813-1814," Vol. XV, No. 4, 37-38, *Independence County Chronicles,* July 1974.

Huddleston, Duane, Pat Wood, and Sammie Rose. *Steamboats and Ferries on the White River: A Heritage Revisited*, New ed., Fayetteville: University of Arkansas Press, 1998.

"Invoice of merchandise forwarded to that part of the Cherokee Nation removed to the river Arkansas in charge of John Ross, 1812 Nov. 30," MS2033, Penelope Johnson Allen, Special Collections Library, The University of Tennessee, Knoxville, Tennessee, presented in the *Digital Library of Georgia.* https://dlg.usg.edu.

"Itinerary of the District of Saint Louis," Report No. 1, commanded by Brig. Gen. Thomas Ewing Jr., U.S. Army, and "Reports of John T. Burris, Tenth Kansas Infantry," Report No. 2, July 18-August 6, 1864 – Operations in Southeast Missouri and Northeastern Arkansas, with skirmishes at Scatterville, Ark. (July 28), at Osceola, Ark. (August 2), and at Elk Chute, Mo. (August 4) The War of the Rebellion: A compilation of the Official Records of the Union and the Confederate Armies, Series 1, Vol. 41, Part 1, 77-81. Accessed August 13, 2022. *HathiTrust.* https://babel.hathitrust.org/cgi/mb?a=listis&c=1930843488.

Jackson, Donna Brewer. "Manila (Mississippi County)," *CALS Encyclopedia of Arkansas.* Accessed March 23, 2022.
https://encyclopediaofarkansas.net/entries/manila-mississippi-county-20/.

James, Edwin, *Account of an expedition from Pittsburgh to the Rocky Mountains*, Vol. 3, 146. Botanist and geologist to the expedition of U.S. Army explorer Stephen Harriman Long. https://books.google.com.

James, Frank Lowber, Directory of *Deceased American Physicians, 1804-1929, Ancestry.com.* Accessed April 18, 2024. https://www.ancestry.com.

James, Frank L., PhD, MD, "Role of Superstition in Therapeutics," *St. Louis Medical and Surgical Journa*l. United States, n.p, 1895, 68, No. 1, 9-19.

"Jean-Pierre Chouteau," *Wikipedia*, Wikimedia Foundation. Accessed April 15, 2022. https://en.wikipedia.org/wiki/Jean-Pierre_Chouteau.

Jeter, Marvin D., editor, *Edward Palmer's Arkansaw Mounds*, The University of Alabama Press, 1990.

"John and James Pettigrew & Heirs of," *Reports of Committees, 16th Congress, 1st Session – 49th Congress*, Vol. 3, Report No. 406, 1-4, March 22, 1832. Accessed April 2, 2022. https://books.google.com.

Jones, W.R., "Marion County, Arkansas, Some Marion County History Articles from the *Mt. Echo* newspaper," 1929, transcribed by Gladys Horn Brown. Accessed April 1, 2022. www.argenweb.net/marion/stories/marion-co-ar-wr-jones.html.

"Journal of Edward Deas – Creek Removal, 1837," *Sequoyah National Research Center,* Trail of Tears, Eyewitness Accounts, University of Arkansas at Little Rock. Accessed April 6, 2022.
http://ualrexhibits.org/trailoftears/eyewitness-accounts/journal-of-edward-deas-creek-removal-1837/.

"Justis, baron von Liebig," *Britannica.* Accessed March 26, 2024. https://www.britannica.com/biography/Justus-Freiherr-von-Liebig.

Kelly, Howard Atwood, *A Cyclopedia of American Medical Biography: Comprising the Lives of Eminent Deceased Physicians and Surgeons from 1610 to 1910*, Vol. 2, W.B. Saunders Company, 1912. https://books.google.com.

Key, Joseph Patrick, "Indians and Ecological Conflict in Territorial Arkansas," 135. *Arkansas Historical Quarterly*, Vol. LIX, No. 2, Summer, 2000.

Key, Joseph Patrick, "European Exploration and Settlement, 1541 through 1802," *CALS Encyclopedia of Arkansas.* Accessed July 29, 2022. https://encyclopediaofarkansas.net/entries/european-exploration-and-settlement-1541-through-1802-2916/.

Kinyoun, Dr. Joseph J., Father of the NIH, "Kinyoun's Early Years," *National Institute of Allergy and Infectious Diseases.* Accessed April 19, 2024. https://pubweb-prod.niaid.nih.gov/about/joseph-kinyoun-indispensable-man-early-years#:~:text=The%20St.,Medical%20College%20later%20that%20year.

Lankford, George E., "Losing the Past: Draper and the Ruddell Indian Captivity," *The Arkansas Historical Quarterly*, Vol. 49, No. 3, 214-239, Arkansas Historical Association, 1990. https://doi.org/10.2307/40030798.

Lesieur, Godfrey, New Madrid, Mo. to Gov. John Miller, Letter, October 6, 1831, Vol. 6, 311-312, William Clark Papers, *Kansas State Historical Society,* Topeka, Kansas.

Lesieur. Francois, and Son, Point Pleasant, Mo. to Col. Pierre Menard, Kaskaskia, Ill., A.L.S. Letter, August 4, 1825, Richard Graham Papers, Missouri History Museum, *Missouri Historical Society*, St. Louis, Missouri.

Lesieur, Francis and Son, New Madrid, Mo. to Richard Graham, U.S. Indian Agent, St. Louis, Mo., Letter, September 24, 1825, Richard Graham Papers, Missouri History Museum, *Missouri Historical Society*, St. Louis, Missouri.

Lesieur, Francis Valle, Early History: Biographical Sketches of the First Settlers of New Madrid – Their Descendents and Historical Events, with excerpts by Godfrey Lesieur, *Missouri Historical Society,* St. Louis, Missouri.

Lewis, J.M., Commissioner of Immigration, Gainesville, Greene County, Arkansas, August 26, 1868, State of Arkansas, Commissioner of State Lands, History and Archives, 1868 Report. Accessed April 5, 2022. https://history.cosl.org.

Lingbeck Jody M., Corliss A. O'Bryan, Elizabeth M. Martin, Joshua P. Adams, Phillip G. Crandall. "Sweetgum: An Ancient Source of Beneficial Compounds with Modern Benefits." *Pharmacognosy Reviews*, Vol. 9, Issue 17, Jan.-June, 2015. Accessed January 3, 2025. Downloaded PDF. https://www.phcogrev.com/content/pharmacognosy-reviews-vol-9-issue-17-jan-jun-2015.

Logan, Charles Russell, *The Promised Land: The Cherokee, Arkansas and Removal, 1794-1839, Arkansas Historic Preservation Program.* PDF downloaded November 15, 2024. https://www.arkansasheritage.com.

Lovely, William L. to Col. Return Meigs, April 10, 1813, Correspondence and Miscellaneous Records, 1813," Records of the Cherokee Indian Agency in Tennessee, 1801-1835, 158, M208. Accessed November 14, 2020. https://www.fold3.com.

Lyell, Sir Charles. *A Second Visit to North America*, Vol. 2. Accessed March 28, 2022. Google Books. https://books.google.com.

Magers, Elizabeth, Estate, 1859, New Madrid County Probate Court, Box 0011, Folder 0120, Missouri Judicial Records Historical Database, Collections, *Missouri Digital Heritage*, John R. Ashcroft, Missouri Secretary of State. Accessed August 24, 2022. https://www.sos.mo.gov/mdh/.

Martin-Moats, Meridith, "Chickalah (Yell County)," *CALS Encyclopedia of Arkansas.* Accessed April 4, 2022. https://encyclopediaofarkansas.net/entries/chickalah-yell-county-7006/.

"Map of the Mississippi River, from Cairo to the Gulf of Mexico, Showing the Positions of the Rebel Fortifications at the Mouth of the River, Those Already Taken and Those Remaining to be Captured, Etc," *Frank Leslie's Illustrated Newspaper*, May 10, 1862, Murray Hudson Antique Maps, Globes, Books & Prints, Halls, Tennessee.

"Map of Mississippi County, Arkansas," Bardstown, Arkansas, James Anthony, C.E., 1898, Library of Congress Geography and Map Division, Washington, D.C. 20540-4650 USA dcu, G4003.M5G46 1898. A5, Library of Congress website. Accessed December 13, 2024. www.loc.gov/item/2011590024/.

McCall, Sheila. "Beneath the Delta – Local man discovers rich history," *Blytheville Courier News*, October 6, 1996, Blytheville, Arkansas.

McCall, Sheila, "Mississippi County history extends from Mastodon bones to jets," Focus on Government and Business, 1996 Progress Edition, Section C, 3, *Blytheville Courier News*, October 27, 1996, Blytheville, Arkansas.

McCall, Sheila, "Blytheville's history spans two centuries," Focus on Government and Business, 1996 Progress Edition, Section C, 5, *Blytheville Courier* News, October 27, 1996, Blytheville, Arkansas.

McDermott, John Francis, *A Glossary of Mississippi Valley French 1673-1850*, 56, Washington University, St. Louis, Missouri, 1941, downloaded PDF. https://archive.org.

McGavock, F.G., Louisiana, 1864, 3/3/1863-8/28/1866, Papers relating to citizens, War Department. The Adjutant General's Office. 1821-4/28/1904; War Department. Provost Marshal General's Bureau. Record Group 109, War Department Collection of Confederate Records, 1825-1927, ARC Identifier 28066782, Fold3 2014, Images 1-7. National Archives Catalog. Accessed August 12, 2022. https://catalog.archives.gov.

Meek, Seth Eugene, PhD, *A List of Fishes and Mollusks Collected in Arkansas and Indian Territory in 1894*, Vol. 15, 344-349 of the Fishery bulletin, Government Printing Office, 1896. Google Books. https://books.google.com.

Meigs, Return J. to the Arkansas Cherokee Chiefs, Letter, June 14, 1819, Correspondence and Miscellaneous Records, Records of the Cherokee Indian Agency in Tennessee, 1801-1835, 126-128, M208. Accessed January 1, 2022. https://www.fold3.com.

Melton, Senator Emory, "Delaware Town and the Swan Trading Post, 1822-1831," *White River Valley Historical Quarterly*, Vol. 6, No. 3, 1-11. Spring 1977. Accessed October 22, 2020.
http://thelibrary.org/lochist/periodicals/wrv/V6/N3/Sp77d.htm.

"Memphis to Little Rock Road - Henard Cemetery Road Segment" Properties, National Register of Historic Places, Arkansas Heritage, *Arkansas Historic Preservation Program.* Accessed April 6, 2022. PDF.
http://www.arkansaspreservation.com.

Memo, description of strip of land between swamps on west Little River and Castor swamps in Missouri and the swamps in Arkansas, Chouteau, P. Jr. to Godfrey Lesieur and his son G.A. Lesieur, Point Pleasant, Mo., LS Letters, October 14, 1850 to January 29, 1851, Lesieur Collection, Godfrey Lesieur Papers, *Missouri History Museum Archives*, St. Louis, Missouri.

Menard, Pierre, Kaskaskia, to Gen. William Clark, Supt. Of Indian Affairs, St. Louis, Letter, November 2, 1830, William Clark Papers, *Kansas State Historical Society*, Vol. 6, 65-66. www.kansasmemory.org.

Menard, Col. Pierre, U.S. Ind. Sub Agt., Kaskaskia, Ill. to Wm. Miers, letter July 18, 1831, William Clark Papers, *Kansas State Historical Society*, Topeka, Kansas, Vol. 6, 280.

Miller, Adam, "Jacksonport (Jackson County)," *CALS Encyclopedia of Arkansas*. Accessed August 26, 2022. https://encyclopediaofarkansas.net/entries/jacksonport-jackson-county-2804/.

Miller, John, Missouri Governor, City of Jefferson, Mo. to William Clark, S.IA., St. Louis, Mo., Letter, June 24, 1831, Vol. 6, 265-266, William Clark Papers, *Kansas State Historical Society*, Topeka, Kansas.

Miller, John, Missouri Governor, City of Jefferson, Mo. to William Clark, S.IA., St. Louis, Mo., Letter, October 25, 1831, Vol. 6, 307-316, William Clark Papers, *Kansas State Historical Society*, Topeka, Kansas.

"Mississippi, Arkansas, United States Records," Arkansas Tax Records, Mississippi County 1834-1869, *FamilySearch*. Accessed April 26, 2024, January 17, 2023. https://www.familysearch.org/en/united-states/.

"Mississippi, Arkansas, United States Records," County Court Records, Mississippi County, Arkansas, Court Records 1865-1879, 392, *FamilySearch*. Accessed April 17, 2024. https://www.familysearch.org/ark:/61903/3:1:3Q9M-C9BW-6Y5M.

"Mississippi, Arkansas, United States Records," "In the matter of wild cat and wolf scalps," County Court records (Mississippi County, Arkansas), Court Records, Vol. 3, 1885-1890, 616, *FamilySearch*. Accessed September 25, 2022. https://www.familysearch.org.

"Mississippi, Arkansas, United States Records, "In the matter of wild cat & w scalps," County Court records (Mississippi County, Arkansas), Court records, Vol. 4, 1895-1895, 228. *FamilySearch*. Accessed September 25, 2022. https://www.familysearch.org.

"Mississippi Flyway," *Wikipedia*, Wikimedia Foundation, Inc. Accessed November 1, 2020 https://en.wikipedia.org/wiki/Mississippi_Flyway.

"Mississippi River floods." *Wikipedia*, Wikipedia Foundation, Last modified September 15, 2018. Accessed January 30, 2021. https://en.wikipedia.org/w/index.php?title=Mississippi_River_floods&oldid=859630702.

"Missouri County Marriage, Naturalization, and Court Records, 1800-1991 *FamilySearch*. Accessed January 11, 2025. https://www.familysearch.org/en/united-states/.

"Missouri Probate Records, 1750-1998," New Madrid Probate Packets, Drawer 4, No. 94-109, *FamilySearch. Missouri State Archives*, Jefferson City, Missouri. Accessed March 30, 2022. https://www.familysearch.org/en/united-states/.

"Missouri Probate Records, 1750-1998," New Madrid Probate Packets, images, Drawer 6, No. 155-159, *FamilySearch, Missouri State Archives*, Jefferson City, Missouri. Accessed March 30, 2022. https://www.familysearch.org/en/united-states/.

Missouri Probate Records, 1750-1998," images, Cape Girardeau, Letters testamentary, wills, 1807-1867, Vol. A-C, Missouri State Archives, Jefferson City, *FamilySearch*. Accessed September 22, 2014. https://www.familysearch.org/en/united-states/.

Mitchem, Jeffrey M., "Casqui (1491?-?)," *CALS Encyclopedia of Arkansas*. Accessed August 29, 2022. https://encyclopediaofarkansas.net/entries/casqui-1614/.

Mitchem, Jeffrey M., Phd, "The Expedition of Hernando de Soto in Sixteenth-Century Arkansas," *Arkansas Archeological Survey*, Fayetteville, Arkansas, PDF. Accessed June 5, 2020. www.arkansasarcheology.org., http://archeology.uark.edu/wp-content/uploads/2015/06/Expedition-of-Hernando-de-Soto.pdf.

Mitchem, Jeffrey, Parkin Research Station, 50 Moments in Survey History, No. 33, "Investigating the Possible Base of the Cross Raised at Casqui by Hernando de Soto in 1541," *Arkansas Archaeological Survey*, University of Arkansas System. Accessed August 31, 2021. https://archeology.uark.edu/who-we-are/50moments/parkincross/. www.arkansasarcheology.org.

Mosby, Joe, "Big Lake Wars," *CALS Encyclopedia of Arkansas*. Accessed September 15, 2022. https://encyclopediaofarkansas.net/entries/big-lake-wars-7591/.

Moseley, Thomas Jr., New Madrid, Mo., to Gen. Wm. Clark, S. Int. Indian Affairs, St. Louis, Mo., Letter, July 4, 1835. *The Foreman Transcripts, Commissioner of Indian Affairs*, Seven Volumes, Vol. 1, 53-55, Western Superintendency, Miscellaneous and schools. https://www.okhistory.org/research/foremantranscripts.

Monette, John Wesley, *History of the Discovery and Settlement of the Mississippi, by the Three Great European Powers, Spain, France, and Great Britain, and the Subsequent Occupation, Settlement, and Extension of Civil Government by the United States, Until the Year 1846*, Vol. 1. https://books.google.com.

Morse, Dan F., Phyllis A. Morse, *Archaeology of the Central Mississippi Valley*, 32, Academic Press, Inc., San Diego, California, 1983.

Morse, Phyllis A., "History of the Buffalo Island Area," Chapter 4, 23-31, *An Archaeological Survey Initial Site Testing and Geomorphic Study of Ditches 7, 13, and Lower Buffalo Creek*, April 1988. https://apps.dtic.mil/sti/tr/pdf/ADA263200.pdf.

Moulton, Gary E., *John Ross, Cherokee Chief*, 10, University of Georgia Press, 1978. Accessed December 5, 2024. https://books.google.com.

Mowdy, Marlon, "Nodena Site," *CALS Encyclopedia of Arkansas*. Accessed August 29, 2022. https://encyclopediaofarkansas.net/entries/nodena-site-7925/.

Myers, Robert A., "Cherokee Pioneers in Arkansas: The St. Francis Years, 1785-1813," *The Arkansas Historical Quarterly*, Vol. LVI, Summer 1997.

Myers, Robert. "Nick Trammell: The Making of an Old Southwest Legend." *The Arkansas Historical Quarterly*, Vol. 74, No. 4, 352-378, Arkansas Historical Association, 2015. http://www.jstor.org/stable/26281833.

Myers, William to Col. Pierre Menard, U.S. Ind. Sub Agt., Kaskaskia, Illinois, Letter, August 7, 1831, William Clark Papers, Vol. 6, 280, *Kansas State Historical Society*, Topeka, Kansas.

"Native American Removal Routes in Arkansas, (Cherokee, Chickasaw, Choctaw, Creek, and Seminole)," Staff, Arkansas Historic Preservation Program, The Cherokee, *Arkansas Heritage, Arkansas Historic Preservation Program*, Publications, Trail of Tears Native American Removal Routes in Arkansas. Accessed April 6, 2022. Downloaded PDF. http://www.arkansaspreservation.com.

"Necrology, Frank L. James, PhD., MD," *Transactions of the American Microscopical Society*, Vol. 28, 207-209, 1908. Accessed March 19, 2024. Google Books, https://books.google.com.

"New Madrid, Missouri, United States Records," images, Missouri. County Court (New Madrid County). Image group 007630841, *FamilySearch.* Accessed September 22, 2022. https://www.familysearch.org/en/united-states/.

"1900 United States Federal Census," New Madrid, Missouri; Roll: 877, 9; Enumeration District: 0075; *Ancestry.com*, Ancestry.com Operations Inc., 2004. Accessed September 13, 2022. https://www.ancestry.com.

"1910 United States Federal Census," Neal, Mississippi, Arkansas, Roll T624_58, 9A, Enumeration District: 0081, *Ancestry.* Accessed March 21, 2022. https://www.ancestry.com.

"Ninth Arkansas Infantry Regiment," *Wikipedia*, Wikimedia Foundation, Inc. Accessed April 14, 2022. https://en.wikipedia.org/wiki/9th_Arkansas_Infantry_Regiment.

"Nitre and Mining Bureau," *Wikipedia.* Accessed March 26, 2024. https://en.wikipedia.org/wiki/Nitre_and_Mining_Bureau.

Owen, Thomas McAdory, LLD, "James, Frank Lowber," *History of Alabama and Dictionary of Alabama Biography*, Volume III, The S.J. Clarke Publishing Company, Chicago, Illinois, 1921, 895. Accessed April 19, 2024. https://play.google.com/books/reader?id=nkoUAAAAYAAJ&pg=GBS.PP10&hl=en.

"Papers of Original Claimants (1777-1851) submitted before the First Board of Land Commissioners to determine the validity of the French and Spanish land grants made before the Louisiana Purchase." Missouri Secretary of State Office, *Missouri Digital Heritage* Web Pages, RG 951 U.S. Recorder of Land Titles, RG951.01 First Board Papers of Original Claimants, 1777-1851. Accessed March 29, 2022. https://www.sos.mo.gov.

Parkman, Francis, *Prairie and Rocky Mountain Life; Or, The California and Oregon Trail*, United States. George P. Putnam, 1852. https://books.google.com.

"Peoria people," *Wikipedia*, Wikimedia Foundation, Inc. Accessed March 29, 2022. http://en.wikipedia.org/wiki/Peoria_tribe.

Pike, Zebulon M., Fort Pickering, Chickasaw Bluff to David Henley, Knoxville, Letter, June 3, 1800, *Papers of the War Department, 1784-1800*, Roy Rosenzweig Center for History and New Media, Fred Manning Collection of Documents from Various Series, RG217. Accessed April 2, 2022. https://wardepartmentpapers.org/s/home/item/76187.

Pinkerton, Gary L., *Trammel's Trace, The First Road to Texas From the North*, Texas A&M University Press, College Station, Texas, 2016.

Plat of Section 6, Township 13 North, Range 7 East," Original Survey Plat, Craighead County, Arkansas, April 21, 1848, *General Land Office Records*, Bureau of Land Management, U.S. Department of the Interior. Accessed August 4, 2022. https://glorecords.blm.gov.

Plat map of Mississippi County, Arkansas, 1903. When photocopied by the author, the map was in the possession of the now-defunct Blytheville Research Station of the Arkansas Archeological Survey.

Plat of Township 15 North, Range 9 East, U.S. Department of the Interior, Bureau of Land Management, *General Land Office Records*, Survey Plats and Field Notes, Arkansas. Accessed April 14, 2022. https://glorecords.blm.gov.

"Plat of Township 18 North, Range 9 East," 1848, April 3, 1848, Missouri Department of Agriculture, Land Survey Program, Land Survey Index, GLO (General Land Office). Downloaded PDF February 3, 2016.

https://agriculture.mo.gov/weights/landsurvey/.

"Plat of Township 16 North, Range 4 East," 1825, Greene County, Arkansas, U.S. Department of the Interior, Bureau of Land Management, *General Land Office Records*. Accessed April 5, 2022. https://glorecords.blm.gov.

"Plat of Township 16 North, Range 5 East," Greene County, Arkansas Survey Plat, 1825, U.S. Department of the Interior, Bureau of Land Management, *General Land Office Records*. Accessed April 5, 2022. https://glorecords.blm.gov.

Polston, Mike, "Greensboro (Craighead County)," *CALS Encyclopedia of Arkansas*. Accessed August 4, 2022. https://encyclopediaofarkansas.net/entries/greensboro-craighead-county-7919/.

Polston, Mike, "Bolivar (Poinsett County)," *CALS Encyclopedia of Arkansas*. Last updated December 7, 2021. Accessed August 29, 2022. https://encyclopediaofarkansas.net/entries/bolivar-poinsett-county-7386/.

Polston, Mike, "Davidsonville (Randolph County)," *CALS Encyclopedia of Arkansas*. Accessed August 26, 2022. https://encyclopediaofarkansas.net/entries/davidsonville-randolph-county-6090/.

Poole, Fred R., Major, Commanding Expedition to Col. [J.B.] Rogers, Commanding Cape Girardeau, Mo., Letter, Sept. 7-30, 1863, "Report of Maj. Frederick R. Poole, Second Missouri State Militia Cavalry, Sept. 7-30, 1863, Expedition to Big Lake, Mississippi County, Ark., Headquarters, Camp Lowry, October 1, 1863, *The War of the Rebellion: a compilation of the official records of the Union and Confederate armies*, Series 01, Vol. 22, Part 01, 616. Accessed August 13, 2022. *HathiTrust*. https://babel.hathitrust.org/cgi/mb?a=listis&c=1930843488.

"Post route map of the state of Arkansas and of Indian and Oklahoma territories showing post offices with the intermediate distances on mail routes in operation on the 1st of December, 1897." United States. Post Office Dept. Map. Washington, D.C., The Dept., 1897. *Norman B. Leventhal Map & Education Center*. Accessed March 13, 2022. https://collections.leventhalmap.org/search/commonwealth:cj82kk753.

Postmaster Appointments for Dunklin County, Missouri; Record Group 28: Records of the Post Office Department, 1773 - 1971, Records of Appointment of Postmasters and the Establishment of Post Offices, 7/1/1931 - 10/31/1971; *National Archives* at College Park, College Park, Maryland, [online version available through the Archival Research Catalog (ARC identifier 78753540) Ancestry 2018. Accessed February 24, 2022. www.archives.gov.

Postmaster Appointments for Greene County, Arkansas Territory, Record Group 28: Records of the Post Office Department, 1773 - 1971, Records of Appointment of Postmasters and the Establishment of Post Offices, 7/1/1931 - 10/31/1971; National Archives at College Park, College Park, Maryland, [online version available through the Archival Research Catalog (ARC identifier 7872653) at www.archives.gov; Ancestry 2018. Accessed August 12, 2022. www.archives.gov.

Postmaster Appointments for Mississippi County, Arkansas, Record Group 28: Records of the Post Office Department, 1773 - 1971, Records of Appointment of Postmasters and the Establishment of Post Offices, 7/1/1931 - 10/31/1971; *National Archives* at College Park, College Park, Maryland, [online version available through the Archival Research Catalog (ARC identifier 78726975); Ancestry 2018. Accessed February 22, 2022. www.archives.gov.

Postmaster Appointments for St. Francis County, Arkansas; Record Group 28: Records of the Post Office Department, 1773 - 1971, Records of Appointment of Postmasters and the Establishment of Post Offices, 7/1/1931 - 10/31/1971; *National Archives* at College Park, College Park, Maryland [online version available through the Archival Research Catalog (ARC identifier 78727324) at www.archives.gov; HMS/MLR Entry Number, A1 322; Ancestry 2018. Accessed July 27, 2022. www.archives.gov.

"Post Route," The Congressional Globe, Senate, 31st Congress, First Session, Part 2, 1559. *A Century of Lawmaking for a New Nation: U.S. Congressional Documents and Debates, 1774-1875.* Accessed February 23, 2022. Downloaded PDF. https://memory.loc.gov/ammem/amlaw/.

Prior, N., Cantonment Gibson to Gen. Wm. Clark, United States Office of Indian Affairs, Central Superintendency, St. Louis, Missouri. Letter, January 22, 1831, Vol. 6, 104, *Kansas State Historical Society*, Kansas Memory, Correspondence. Accessed March 26, 2022. https://www.kansasmemory.org.

Purdy, Jonathan, New York, Revolutionary War Pension and Bounty Land Warrant Application File S. 5, 996, Record Group 15: Records of the Department of Veteran's Affairs, 1773-2007, Case Files of Pension and Bounty-Land Warrant Applications Based on Revolutionary War Services, ca. 1800-ca.1812, Fold3, M804, Roll 1985, ARC Identifier 144211314, *National Archives*, Washington, D.C. Accessed August 24, 2022. https://catalog.archives.gov.

"Ramsay Place Names File, 1928-1945 (C2366)," Columbia Manuscript Collections, *The State Historical Society of Missouri.* https://collections.shsmo.org/manuscripts/columbia/C2366.

Ramsay, Andrew, Will, Missouri Probate Records, 1750-1998, images, *FamilySearch.* https://www.familysearch.org/en/home/portal/.

Records of the Field Offices for the State of Arkansas, Bureau of Refugees, Freedmen, and Abandoned Lands, 1865 -1872, 42. Internet Archive, downloaded PDF. Accessed August 13, 2022. https://openlibrary.org/books/OL24353223M/Records_of_the_field_offices_f or_the_state_of_Arkansas_Bureau_of_Refugees_Freedmen_and_Abandoned _Lan.

"Register of Legal Voters, Arkansas," 1867-1868, Arkansas Register of Legal Voters, Arkansas Digital Archives, *Arkansas State Archives,* Little Rock, Arkansas. MS.000628, Box 3, Folder 2, Mississippi County. Accessed February 14, 2020. https://digitalheritage.arkansas.gov/voters-1867-1868/55/.

"Register of Legal Voters, Arkansas," 1867-1868, Update to the Register of Legal Voters, Mississippi County, MS.000628, Box 5, Folder 43, Arkansas Register of Legal Voters, Arkansas Digital Archives, *Arkansas State Archives*, Little Rock, Arkansas. Accessed February 14, 2020. https://digitalheritage.arkansas.gov/voters-1867-1868/.

Reilly, Robert F., "Medical and Surgical Care During the American Civil War, 1861-1865." Baylor University Medical Center Proceedings, Vol. 29, Issue 2, 2016,138–142. Accessed January 10, 2025. https://doi.org/10.1080/08998280.2016.11929390.

"Reports of Brig. Gen. M. Jeff Thompson, Missouri State Guard, of the advance from Piketon and skirmishes at Big River Bridge and Blackwell Station," HDQRS

First Military District, Mo. S.G., Camp Spring Hill, Mo., October 11, 1861, *The War of the Rebellion: A compilation of the Official Records of the Union and the Confederate Armies,* Vol. III, 223-225, 1881, Chapter X - Operations in Missouri and Arkansas, Kansas and Indian Territory, May 10-Nov. 19, 1861, (Vol. 3, Chapter 19). Accessed August 13, 2022. *Hathi Trust.* https://babel.hathitrust.org/cgi/mb?a=listis&c=1930843488.

"Report of Professor Baird, Secretary of the Smithsonian Institution, for 1878," *Annual Report of the Board of Regents of the Smithsonian Institution Showing Operations, Expenditures and Conditions of the Institution For The Year 1878,* Government Printing Office, Washington, D.C., 1879. https://books.google.com.

"Research Sheds New Light on Pierre Menard," Press Release, August 12, 2004, *Illinois.Gov.* Accessed April 15, 2022. https://www.illinois.gov/news/press-release.3272.html.

Retained Copy of Report Relative to Treatment of Freedmen, November 24, 1866, Little Rock, Arkansas, Records of the Assistant Commissioner for the State of Arkansas, Bureau of Refugees, Freedmen and Abandoned Lands, 1865-1869, National Archives Microfilm Publication, M979 Roll 52, "Miscellaneous Records 1865-1868."

"Report of Maj. John W. Rabb, Second Missouri Light Artillery," Report No. 1, Headquarters Post, New Madrid, Mo., April 10, 1864, and "Report of Capt. Valentine Pruiett, First Military Cavalry," Report No. 2, April 5-9, 1864 – Expedition from New Madrid, Mo. and skirmishes in the swamps of Little River, near Osceola, and on Pemiscot Bayou, Ark., Series I, Vol. 34, Pt. 1, 872-875, *The War of the Rebellion: A compilation of the Official Records of the Union and the Confederate Armies.* Accessed August 13, 2022. *HathiTrust.* https://babel.hathitrust.org/cgi/mb?a=listis&c=1930843488.

Rice, Paschal, Confederate Soldier from the State of Mississippi, Twenty-fifth Infantry. Record Group 109, War Department Collection of Confederate Records, 1825-1927, Roll 319, Carded Records Showing Military Service of Soldiers who fought in Confederate Organizations, 1903-1927. ARC Identifier 143380267, Fold3 2019. Accessed August 14, 2022. https://catalog.archives.gov.

Robinson, Dell, Mrs. of Corning, Arkansas to the *Piggott Times*, *SEMO Record*, Dunklin County, Missouri Genealogical Society, Vol. 1-3, 1983-1985, Vol. III, No. I, January 1985.

Rozier, Firmin A., *Rozier's History of the Early Settlement of the Mississippi Valley*, G.A. Pierrot & Son, Printers, St. Louis, Missouri, Publisher, 1890.

Sandels, Leonidas Polk, Joseph Morrison Hill, *A Digest of the Statutes of Arkansas Embracing All Laws of a General Nature in Force at the Close of the Session of the General Assembly of One Thousand Eight Hundred and Ninety-three*, 1605, United States, Press of E.W. Stephens, 1994. Accessed September 25, 2022. https://books.google.com.

Sanford, Henry Vs. Hector, William, Reel C11873, Justice of the Peace Case Files, Cape Girardeau, *Missouri State Archives,* Jefferson City, Missouri.

Scharf, John Thomas, *History of Saint Louis City and County: From the Earliest Periods to the Present Day: Including Biographical Sketches of Representative Men*, Vol. 1, 287-288. Accessed July 29, 2022. https://books.google.com/books.

Schlesinger, Toney Butler, "Goodspeed Histories," *CALS Encyclopedia of Arkansas*. Accessed August 23, 2022. https://encyclopediaofarkansas.net/entries/goodspeed-histories-6283/.

Searcy, Richard, White River, Arkansas, to Governor James Miller, Cherokee Indian Affairs, Transcript, November 21, 1820, L.C. Gulley collection, *Arkansas State Archives*, Little Rock, Arkansas. Accessed April 4, 2024. https://www.arkansasheritage.com/arkansasstatearchives/home.

Selma Dollar Times, Selma, Alabama, *Newspapers.com by Ancestry.* https://www.newspapers.com.

Sesser, David, "Conscription," *CALS Encyclopedia of Arkansas*. Accessed February 5, 2020. https://encyclopediaofarkansas.net/entries/conscription-5013/.

Sesser, David, "Fourth Military District," *CALS Encyclopedia of Arkansas*. Accessed March 10, 2020. https://encyclopediaofarkansas.net/entries/fourth-military-district-9123/.

Sesser, David, "Militia Wars of 1868-1869," *CALS Encyclopedia of Arkansas*. Accessed August 13, 2022. https://encyclopediaofarkansas.net/entries/militia-wars-of-1868-1869-7904/.

Sherif, Yousery E., Nasser M. Hosny, Ahmad H. Alghadir, and Rayan Alansari, "Phytochemicals of Rhus spp. As Potential Inhibitors of SARS-CoV-2 Main Protease: Molecular Docking and Drug Likeness Study," *Evidence-Based Complementary and Alternative Medicine, Hindawi.* https://www.hindawi.com/journals/ecam/2021/8814890/.

Simonson, S. E. "The St. Francis Levee and High Waters on the Mississippi River." *The Arkansas Historical Quarterly*, Vol. 6, No. 4, 419-429, Arkansas Historical Association, 1947.

Simonson, S. E. "Origin of Drainage Projects in Mississippi County." Vol. 5, No. 3, 263-273, *The Arkansas Historical Quarterly*, Arkansas Historical Association, 1946.

Sloan, Kitty, "Trail of Tears," *CALS Encyclopedia of Arkansas*. Accessed April 5, 2022. http://www.encyclopediaofarkansas.net/encyclopedia/entry-detail.aspx?entryID=2294.

Smithsonian Institution, 1880, *Annual Report of the U.S. Bureau of Ethnology to the Secretary of the Smithsonian Institution*, Vol. 12, Washington Government Printing Office, 1894, 207-212, Biodiversity Heritage Library. Accessed April 20, 2024. https://www.biodiversitylibrary.org/item/88468#page/279/mode/1up.

Smyth-Davis, Mary F., *History of Dunklin County, Mo., 1845-1895. Embracing an Historical Account of the Towns and Post-Villages of Clarkton, Cotton Plant, Cardwell, Caruth, Gibson, Halcomb, Hornersville, Kennett, Lulu, Malden, Nesbit, Senath, Valley Ridge, Vincent, White Oak, and Wrightsville. Including a Department Devoted to the Description of the Early Appearance, Settlement, Development, Resources, and Present Appearance of the County. With an Album of its People and Homes Profusely Illustrated*, Nixon-Jones Printing Co., St. Louis, Missouri, 1896.

Snowden, Deanna, Compiler and Editor, *Mississippi County, Arkansas: Appreciating the Past, Anticipating the Future*, Mississippi County Community College Foundation, August House, Little Rock, Arkansas, 1986.

Spurgeon, John, "Flood of 1937," *CALS Encyclopedia of Arkansas*. Accessed August 23, 2022. https://encyclopediaofarkansas.net/entries/flood-of-1937-4878/.

State Vs Hector, William, Reel C21015, Circuit Court Case File, Cape Girardeau County, *Missouri State Archives*, Jefferson City, Missouri.

State of Missouri versus Samuel Jones, on Indictment for Larceny, August 15, 1823, "Cape Girardeau, Missouri, United States Records," images, *FamilySearch*. https://www.familysearch.org/en/home/portal/.

State of Missouri Vs Hector, William, Reel C21015, Circuit Court Case File, Cape Girardeau County, *Missouri State Archives*, Jefferson City, Missouri.

Stevens, Walter Barlow, *Missouri: the Center State*, Volume II, 567-570, S.J. Clarke Publishing Company, Chicago, Illinois, 1920. https://books.google.com.

"St. Francis Sunken Lands Natural Area," *Arkansas Heritage*, Arkansas Natural Heritage Commission, Little Rock, Arkansas. Accessed April 12, 2024. https://www.arkansasheritage.com/arkansas-natural-heritage/naturalareas/find-a-natural-area/st-francis-sunken-lands-natural-area.

"Stoddard, Missouri, United States Records," Stoddard County Circuit Court, October 1837, images, *FamilySearch*. Accessed September 18, 2022. https://www.familysearch.org/en/united-states/.

Stoddard County, Missouri Circuit Court, October 1837, Court Records 1836–1844, Book A, 25, 26, *FamilySearch*. Accessed September 18, 2022. https://www.familysearch.org/en/united-states/.

"Stoddert [sic] County," *American State Papers*, House of Representatives, 24th Congress, First Session, Public Lands, Vol. 8, 302-303. Accessed April 6, 2022. https://memory.loc.gov/ammem/amlaw/lwsp.html.

Stone, Thomas Ashley, *Recollections of Early Life in Poinsett County*, 7-8, Poinsett County, Arkansas, 1927.

Strange, L. R. (2016). *The Civil War and Reconstruction in Mississippi County: The Story of Sans Souci Plantation*. Graduate Theses and Dissertations. Accessed at https://scholarworks.uark.edu/etd/1694.

Street, Ron, John D. Kiefer, and Jerry L. Raisor, "Assessing the Felt Reports of the 1811-12 New Madrid Earthquakes in the Central United States" (2008). Kentucky Geological Survey Report of Investigations. Accessed April 1, 2022. Downloaded PDF. https://uknowledge.uky.edu/kgs_ri/22.

Stuck, Charles A., *The Story of Craighead County, A Narrative of People and Events in Northeast Arkansas*, 111, Charles A. Stuck, publisher, 1960.

Stuck, Charles A., "The Creation of Craighead County," *Craighead County Historical Quarterly*, Vol. XIII, No. 2, 12-17, Spring, April 1, 1975, Jonesboro, Arkansas.

Stuck, Charles A., "W.W. Nisbett and Minnie Nisbett Armour," Vol. 2, No. 4, 13-15, *Craighead County Historical Society*, Autumn 1964.

Sullivan, John to Gov. Clark, Letter, July 9, 1816, United States Office of Indian Affairs, Central Superintendency, St. Louis, Missouri, Vol. 3, 44-45, Miscellaneous letters and documents, 1815-1817. *Kansas Historical Society*. Accessed April 3, 2022. Kansas Memory. www.kansasmemory.org.

"Surrey (carriage)," *Wikipedia*, Wikimedia Foundation, Inc. Accessed September 15, 2021. https://en.wikipedia.org/wiki/Surrey_(carriage).

Suter, Mary C., "Swamp Land Act of 1850," *CALS Encyclopedia of Arkansas*. Accessed July 20, 2021. http://www.encyclopediaofarkansas.net/encyclopedia/entry-detail.aspx?entryID=7402.

"Swamp Lands in Missouri and Arkansas," February 28, 1849, Second Session, Thirtieth Congress, House of Representatives, *Reports of Committees: 16th*

Congress, 1st Session - 49th Congress, 1st Session, United States, 1848, Vol. I, Report No. 130, 1-16. Accessed January 4, 2025. http://books.google.com/.

Switzler, William Franklin, Switzler's Illustrated History of Missouri, From 1541 to 1877, C.R. Barns, Editor and Publisher, St. Louis, Missouri, 1879. https://books.google.com.

"Talks," Wabepelathy, American State Papers, Vol. 2, Senate, 14th Congress, 1st Session Indian Affairs, 11. Accessed December 9, 2024. https://www.hathitrust.org.

Teske, Steven, "Dell (Mississippi County)," CALS Encyclopedia of Arkansas. Accessed August 4, 2022. https://encyclopediaofarkansas.net/entries/dell-mississippi-county-7124/.

The American Journal of Science and Arts, Biodiversity Heritage Library, Carnegie-Mellon University. University Libraries, S. Converse, New Haven, 1821.

The Freedmen's Bureau Online: Records of the Bureau of Refugees, Freedmen, and Abandoned Lands. Accessed March 2, 2020.
http://freedmensbureau.com/arkansas/arkreport.htm.

The Morning Democrat, October 18, 1861, Davenport, Iowa. Newspapers.com by Ancestry. Accessed April 26, 2024. https://www.newspapers.com.

The Osceola Times, Osceola, Arkansas, Newspapers.com by Ancestry. https://www.newspapers.com.

The Osceola Times, Osceola Arkansas, 1873-1900, Death Notices, Suicides and Murdered, Including Notice of Persons Reported as Not Expected to Survive, Dangerously Ill, or lying Low, Extracted from Microfilm by Joyce Hambleton Whitten, The Osceola Times, April 2, 1892, 4, Genealogy Society of Craighead County, Arkansas, 2015.

"The Deep Snow," The Illinois Intelligencer, January 28, 1968, as part of the Illinois Sesquicentennial Celebration. Accessed October 22, 2020.
http://www.illinoishistory.com/deepsnow.htm.

The Weekly Globe, Containing Political Discussions, Documentary Proofs, Etc., Blair and Rives, editors, Washington, D.C., February 1843, Vol. 2, No. 9, 134. Accessed September 24, 2013. https://books.google.com.

Thwaites, Reuben Gold, Early Western Travels, 1748-1846: A Series of Annotated Reprints of Some of the Best and Rarest Contemporary Volumes of Travel, Descriptive of the Aborigines and Social and Economic Conditions in the Middle and Far West, During the Period of Early American Settlement. United States, A. H. Clark Company, 1906. https://books.google.com/.

"Title papers of the Clamorgan grant, of 536,904 arpens of alluvial lands in Missouri and Arkansas," New York, printed by T. Snowden, Internet Archive, Ebook and Texts Archive, Library of Congress.
http://archive.org/details/titlepapersofcla01clam.

Toluntiskee to Col. Return J. Meigs, Agent for the Cherokee, Letter from Arkansas, March 14, 1813, Correspondence and Miscellaneous Records, 1813, Records of the Cherokee Indian Agency in Tennessee, 1801-1835, 124-128, M208. Accessed January 2, 2021. https://www.fold3.com.

Tol-Lon-Tis-Kee, Head Chief of the Arkansas Cherokee to Jeremiah Evarts, Esq., The Panoplist, and missionary herald, Vol. 14, 391, 1818. Hathitrust. Accessed April 4, 2022. https://www.hathitrust.org.

Township 14 North, Range 9 East, Mississippi County, Arkansas, original survey plat, "road from Osceola, Ark. to Grand Prairie, Mo.," DM ID 5613, 3-17-1848,

General Land Office Records, U.S. Department of the Interior Bureau of Land Management. Accessed August 12, 2022. https://glorecords.blm.gov.

Turner, S.K. and S.A. Clark, *Twentieth Century History of Carroll County, Missouri*, Vol. I, 434-436. B.F. Bowen, Indianapolis, Indiana, 1911, Missouri Digital Heritage, Collections: Missouri County Histories. https://www.sos.mo.gov/mdh/.

Turner, Thomas, attorney in fact for Pierre Chouteau of St. Louis, Mo. to Sacoxy Anderson, of the Delaware Nation, August 12, 1831, permission to reside seven years on land granted to James Clarmorgan [sic] by the Spanish Government and conveyed to Chouteau on the "Grand Prairie," April 5, 1830, Vol. 6, 278, William Clark Papers, *Kansas State Historical Society*, Topeka, Kansas.

Tuttle, Martitia P., Eugene S. Schweig, John D. Sims, Robert H. Lafferty, Lorraine W. Wolf, and Marion L. Haynes, "The Earthquake Potential of the New Madrid Seismic Zone," *Bulletin of The Seismological Society of America*, Vol. 92, 2080-2089. 10.1785/0120010227, August 1, 2002. Downloaded PDF. https://www.researchgate.net/publication/241444348_The_Earthquake_Poten tial_of_the_New_Madrid_Seismic_Zone.

"U.S., Indexed Early Land Ownership and Township Plats, 1785-1898," Township 31 North, Range 13 East, 591, Township 32 North, Range 13 East, 597, Missouri, Fifth Principal Meridian, *Ancestry.com*. Provo, Utah, USA: Ancestry.com Operations, Inc., 2011. Accessed January 11, 2025. https://www.ancestry.com.

"U.S., Indexed Early Land Ownership and Township Plats, 1785-1898," Township 30 North, Range 13 East, 564, Missouri, Fifth Principal Meridian, *Ancestry.com*. Provo, Utah, USA: Ancestry.com Operations, Inc., 2011. Accessed January 11, 2025. https://www.ancestry.com.

"United States Census, 1840," William Huton [sic], Mississippi, Arkansas, United States, *FamilySearch*. Accessed June 10, 2022. https://www.familysearch.org/en/united-states/.

"United States Census, 1860," Entry for Thomas S. James and Laura James, Sixth Ward, City of Mobile, Mobile, Alabama, United States, *FamilySearch*. Accessed March 6, 2024. https://www.familysearch.org/en/united-states/.

U.S. Department of Veterans Affairs, National Cemetery Administration, grave locator. Accessed August 13. 2022. https://www.cem.va.gov/index.asp.

"U.S. Census Mortality Schedules, Arkansas, 1850-1880," Archive Roll Number: 1; Census Year: 1870; Monroe, Mississippi, Arkansas, *Ancestry*. Provo, Utah, Ancestry.com Operations, Inc., 2010. Accessed April 14, 2022. https://www.ancestry.com.

U.S. Serial Set, *The Library of Congress American Memory*, 23rd Congress, No. 248, Senate Document No. 512, 501. Accessed September 23, 2024. https://www.loc.gov/collections/united-states-congressional-serial-set/about-this-collection/.

Washburn, Cephas, and James Wilson Moore. *Reminiscences of the Indians*, 185. United States, Presbyterian committee of publication, 1869. Accessed April 2, 2022. https://books.google.com.

Watkins, N.W. to Gov. Miller, Letter, May 28, 1831, Vol. 6, 265-266, 273, William Clark Papers, *Kansas State Historical Society,* Topeka, Kansas.

Watkins, N. W., New Madrid Co. to Major Richard Graham, St. Louis, Mo. Letter, March 17, 1825, Richard Graham Papers, Missouri History Museum, *Missouri Historical Society*, St. Louis, Missouri.

Wells, Docia, and Sam Hector, to W.B. Flanigan, Quit claim deed, Chancery Court Records, Mississippi County, Arkansas, 1865-1941, Vol. 2, Deed Record, Vol 27, 463, Mississippi County, Osceola District, *FamilySearch*. Accessed September 12, 2022. https://www.familysearch.org.

Whayne, Jeannie, *Delta Empire, Lee Wilson and the Transformation of Agriculture in the New South*, 1, Louisiana State University Press, Baton Rouge, Louisiana, 2011.

"Widner-Magers Farm Historic District," Dell, Mississippi County, Arkansas, Site MSO301, Registration Form, *Arkansas Heritage*, National Register of Historical Places, Arkansas Historic Preservation Program, Little Rock, Arkansas. PDF. Accessed August 4, 2022. https://www.arkansasheritage.com.

Williams, Harry Lee, *The History of Craighead County, Arkansas*, Parke-Harper Co., Little Rock, Arkansas, 1930.

Williams, Harry Lee, "The Old Delaware Indian Trails," *Craighead County Historical Quarterly,* Vol. I, No. 4, 33-36, Autumn, 1963.

Williams, W. D., and Louis Bringier. "Louis Bringier and His Description of Arkansas in 1812." *The Arkansas Historical Quarterly*, Vol. 48, No. 2, 108-136, Arkansas Historical Association, 1989. *JSTOR*. https://www.jstor.org.

Wilson, Johnny H., Isaac A. Bratcher, Don Evans, and James O. Jeffers, *35 Degrees 24 Minutes North – 91 Degrees West: A Town Called Hickory Ridge*, 127, Trafford, Victoria, B.C., 2004.

Wood, Stephen E. "The Development of Arkansas Railroads Part 1," *The Arkansas Historical Quarterly*, Vol. 7, No. 2, 103-140. Summer 1948. Accessed December 10, 2024. *JSTOR*. https://doi.org/10.2307/40027484.

Worley, Ted R. "Early Days in Osceola." *The Arkansas Historical Quarterly*, Vol. 24, No. 2, 120-126, Summer 1965. Arkansas Historical Association. Accessed August 4, 2022. *JSTOR*. https://doi.org/10.2307/40027594**.**

Young, Gloria, Heritage Trail Partners Board of Directors, "The Benge Detachment of Cherokees on the Trail of Tears," *Northwest Arkansas Heritage Trail Partners*, Springdale, Arkansas. Accessed April 6, 2022. http://www.heritagetrailpartners.com/2015/06/benge-route/.

Zinn, Melba Pender, *Monongalia County, (West) Virginia: Records of the District, Superior, and County Courts,* Vol. 2, 193-194, 1800-1802, 1990.

Index

Bishop, Andrew J., 93
Blacks, 80, 83, 84, 85
Black Fork Bayou, 59
Black Fox, 37
Black Hawk War, 72, 84
Black Oak Ridge, Arkansas, 62
Black Oak, Arkansas, 108
Black River, 36
Blackwell Station, 73, 74
Blocker, John, 82
Bloomfield, Missouri, 17, 21, 22, 24, 42, 72
Blue Cane, 78
Blunt, Joe, 24
Blythe, Rev. Henry T., 110
Blytheville, Arkansas, 77, 93, 102, 105, 107, 108, 109, 110, 111, 117
Board of Swamp Land Commissioners, 65, 66
Boggs, Governor Lilbourn, 53
Bolin, Nate, 75
Bolivar, Arkansas, 45, 46
Bolivar, Old, Arkansas, 46, 48
Bono, Arkansas, 46, 47
Boone County, Missouri, 60
Bowen Township, 117
Bowen, Charles, 79, 80, 85, 94, 99, 113
Bowen, W. J., 113
Bowlin Island, 43
Bowlin, James B., 65
Boyce, John, 23
Bradford, William, 37
Brainerd Mission, 36
Brannum, Michael, 24, 25
Brannum's Point, 25
Brearley, David, 36
Bringier, Louis, 32
Broadway, Arkansas, 46
Brooklyn, Missouri, 60
Brooks, Joseph, 85
Brooks-Baxter War, 85
Brown, Jaley. *See* Hector, Jaley Brown Rice
Brown, John, a Seneca, 8, 43
Brown, Leonard, 115
Brownsville, Arkansas, 68
Buckeye, 40, 45, 64
Buffalo Creek, 40, 43, 69

Buffalo Island, 2, 8, 12, 13, 14, 40, 42, 43, 45, 46, 55, 56, 61, 103, 108
Buford Lake, 15
Bunch, Elizabeth, 99
Bunch, J.A. (James), 99
Bunch, James, 76, 82
Bunch, Jane, 114
Bunch, Lucinda "Cinda", 76, 85, 86, 109
Bunch, Melissa. *See* Hector, Melissa Bunch
Bunch, Nervie, 114
Bunch, Sallie, 114
Bunch, Sam, 86, 99, 110, 114, 116
Bunch, T.A. (Thomas), 99
Bunch, Willie, 114
Burns, Jane, murder, 23
Burris, Lt. Col. J.T., 79, 80
bushwhackers, 74, 79
Bussell, Luke, 78
Butcher knife. *See* Big Knife, John
Butrick, Daniel S., 53
Byrd Township, Cape Girardeau County, Missouri, 27
Cache River, 47, 59
Cairo, Illinois, 14, 62, 106
Camp Lowry, 74
Campbell, John, 33
Cape Girardeau, Missouri, 14, 17, 18, 21, 22, 24, 27, 28, 36, 60, 61, 79
Capooth, Wayne, v
Carnes, Joseph, 33
Carson Lake, 89, 94
Casqui, 16, 97, 98, 99
Castle Garden, New York, 95, 96
Castor River, 14, 17, 21, 22, 23, 56
Castor Township, Missouri, 27
Cavelier, Rene-Robert, Sieur de La Salle. See La Salle
Cerre, Gabriel, 56
Chalk Bluff, Arkansas, 39, 42, 44
Champagnolle, Arkansas, 66
Chapman, Rev. Epaphras, 37
Chataunga Mountain, 35
Cherokee, v, 18, 20, 21, 22, 23, 25, 29, 30, 31, 32, 33, 34, 35, 36, 37, 38, 44, 45, 50, 51, 52, 53, 54, 101, 113, 114, 115, 116
Cherokee complaint, 33